Power in Praise

Bringing Heaven into Hell

What's On Your Mind?

This omnibus edition first published 2001

ISBN 0 85476 928 5

Published by
KINGSWAY PUBLICATIONS
Lottbridge Drove, Eastbourne, BN23 6NT, England.
Email: books@kingsway.co.uk

Designed and produced for the publishers by
Bookprint Creative Services, P. O. Box 827, BN21 3YJ, England.
Printed in Great Britain.

Reproduced from the original typesetting
of the single-volume editions.

Power in Praise

MERLIN R. CAROTHERS

KINGSWAY PUBLICATIONS
EASTBOURNE

"If anyone could tell you the shortest, surest way to all happiness and perfection, he must tell you to make it a rule to yourself to thank and praise God for everything that happens to you. For it is certain that whatever seeming calamity happens to you, if you thank and praise God for it, you turn it into a blessing..."

> - William Law
> English clergyman, Eighteenth Century

"I thank God for my handicaps, for through them I have found myself, my work and my God."

> - Helen Keller

"Blessed is he who submits to the will of God; he can never be unhappy. Men may deal with him as they will...he is without care; he knows that all things work together for good to them that love God, to them who are called according to His purpose."

> - Martin Luther

"Cry for grace from God to be able to see God's hand in every trial, and then for grace...to submit at once to it. Not only to submit, but to acquiesce, and to rejoice in it...I think there is generally an end to troubles when we get to that."

> - Charles H. Spurgeon

CONTENTS

Chapter 1

The Power in Praise

Jim's father had been an alcoholic for thirty years. During all those years, Jim's mother, and later Jim and his young wife, had prayed that God would heal him, but with no apparent result. Jim's father refused to admit that he had a problem with alcohol, and stalked out in anger if anyone mentioned religion to him.

One day Jim heard me speak about the power that is released when we begin to praise God *for* everything in our lives instead of pleading with Him to change the circumstances that displease us.

Jim brought home a recording of my message and played it over and over again for his friends. Then one day it struck him; he had never tried praising God *for* his father's condition. Excitedly he shared the thought with his wife.

"Honey, let us thank God for Dad's alcoholism and praise the Lord that it is part of His wonderful plan for Dad's life!"

For the rest of that day they gave thanks and praised God for every aspect of the situation, and by evening they felt a new sense of excitement and expectation.

The next day the parents came over for the usual Sunday dinner visit. Always before, Jim's father had cut the visit as short as possible, leaving right after dinner. This time, over a cup of coffee, he suddenly asked a pointed question.

"What do you think about this Jesus Revolution?" He turned to Jim. "I saw something about it on the news last night. Is it just a fad, or is something happening to those kids who were hung up on drugs?"

1

The question led to a lengthy and open discussion about Christianity. The elder couple didn't leave till late in the evening.

Within weeks Jim's father came to admit his drinking problem, turned for help to Jesus Christ, and was completely healed. He now joins the rest of the family in telling others what praising God can do!

"Just think," Jim said to me. "For thirty years we prayed for God to change Dad. We spent only one day praising Him for the situation and look what happened!"

To praise God is to express our acceptance of something that God is permitting to happen. So to praise God *for* difficult situations, as sickness or disaster, means literally that we accept its happening, as part of God's plan to reveal His perfect love for us.

We can't really praise God without being thankful for the thing we are praising Him for. And we can't really be thankful unless we believe that an omnipotent, loving Father is working for our good. Praising, then, involves both gratitude and joy that God is keeping His Word to work good through *everything* if we love Him. (Romans 8:28)

The very fact that we praise *God* and not some unknown fate also means that we are accepting the fact that God is responsible for what is happening and will always make it work for our good. Otherwise it would make little sense thanking *Him* for it.

Always be joyful. Always keep on praying. No matter what happens, always be thankful, for this is God's will for you who belong to Christ Jesus (I Thessalonians 5:6-18).

I've met many people who are able to praise God for their circumstances, simply because they accept the word of the Bible that they are supposed to praise God in everything. Praising Him, they soon experience the results of an attitude of consistent thanksgiving and joy; and in turn, their faith is strengthened, and they can continue to live this way.

Others find it a little more difficult.

"I just don't understand," they say, "I try praising God, but it is so hard for me to believe that He really has a hand in all the horrible things that have happened to me lately."

We say we don't understand, and some of us get stuck right there; our understanding becomes a real stumbling block in our relationship with God. But God has a perfect plan for our understanding, and when we use it *His* way, it isn't a stumbling block, but a wonderful aid to our faith.

For God is the King of all the earth, said the psalmist. *Sing praises in a skillful psalm and with understanding* (Psalm 47:7 Amp).

We're not supposed to push our understanding out of the way, grit our teeth, and say, "It doesn't make sense to me, but I'll praise the Lord if it kills me, if that's the only way I can get out of this mess!"

That's not praising, that's manipulating. We've all tried to manipulate God, and it is wonderful to know that He loves us too much to let us get away with it! We are to praise God *with* our understanding, not in spite of it.

Our understanding gets us into trouble when we try to figure out *why* and *how* God brings certain circumstances into our lives. We can never understand *why* and *how* God does something, but He wants us to accept with our understanding *that* He does it. This is the basis of our praise. God wants us to understand that He loves us and that He has a plan for us.

And we know that all that happens to us is working for our good if we love God and are fitting into his plans (Romans 8:28).

Are you surrounded by difficult circumstances right now? Have you been struggling to understand *why* they have come to you? Then try to accept with your understanding that God does love you and has allowed those circumstances because *He knows that He can bring good out of this for you.* Praise Him for what He has brought into your life; do it deliberately and with your understanding.

One couple heard me speak on praising God for every-thing and went home quite disturbed. For months they had grieved over the condition of their daughter who had been committed to a mental institution and had been diagnosed hopelessly insane.

Prayer groups across the country had been asked to intercede for her, and daily the parents had pleaded with God on their knees to heal their daughter. Her condition remained unchanged.

Their initial response to the challenge that they praise God *for* the condition of their daughter had left them distraught and unhappy.

"It would be blasphemy," said the wife, "to thank God for something so obviously evil. If we thank Him, doesn't that mean we accuse Him of deliberately hurting our daughter? It just doesn't fit in with my idea of a loving God."

"It doesn't *seem* right," the husband agreed. "But what if Carothers *is* right?"

The wife looked helplessly at her husband.

"I just don't know," she said.

"We have nothing to lose, do we?" The husband looked thoughtful. "Why don't we try it?"

They knelt together.

"Dear God," the husband began, "we know that you love us and that you love our daughter even more than we do. We're going to trust that you're working out in her life what you know is best for her; so we thank you for her sickness, thank you that she's in the hospital, thank you for the doctors who haven't found a way to help her. We praise you God for your wisdom and love toward us . . . ."

The longer they prayed that day, the more they became convinced that God was indeed doing what was best.

The next morning the hospital psychiatrist called.

"Sir, there's been a remarkable change in your daughter," he said. "I suggest you come and see her."

Within two weeks she was released from the hospital. A year later a young man came up to me after a meeting.

He introduced himself as the girl's brother and told me that she was married, expecting a baby, and "is the happiest girl in the world!"

A mother came and wanted prayer for her daughter who was a go-go dancer in a nightclub. I told her I would be glad to pray with her and thank God for her daughter's situation. She looked at me in horror.

"Don't tell me I'm supposed to thank God that my daughter mocks common decency and laughs at religion. Surely I've got the devil to thank for her misery, not a loving God!"

This mother was faced with a difficult choice. All her life she had been conditioned to thank God for everything good and blame the devil for everything bad. Together we searched the pages of the Bible for verses stating that God is able to work all things for good for those who love and trust Him, and that he wants us to be thankful in everything, no matter how evil the situation appears.

"You can go on thinking that your daughter's situation is controlled by the devil - and by your lack of faith in God's supreme power make it difficult for Him to work out His perfect plan for her, or you can believe that God is at work, thank Him for everything and by your praise release His power to work in her life."

At last the mother agreed to try.

"I don't understand why it has to be this way," she said, "But I am going to trust that God knows what He's doing, and I'm going to thank Him for it."

We prayed together, and the mother went away with a new peace in her heart about the whole situation.

"For the first time, I'm not worried about my daughter," she beamed.

Later she told me what happened.

That same night her daughter was dancing nearly nude on her little platform when a young man came into the nightclub. He walked up to the girl, looked straight at her and said "Jesus really loves you!"

The go-go dancer was used to hearing all kinds of remarks from young men, but never anything like this. She came down from her platform, sat down with the young man at a table and asked, "Why do you say that?"

He explained that he was walking down the street when he felt God urge him to come into that particular nightclub and tell the go-go dancer that Jesus Christ was offering her the free gift of eternal life.

Stunned, the girl stared at him; then tears filled her eyes, and quietly she said, "I'd like to receive that gift."

And she did, right there at the table in the nightclub.

Praising God is not a magic formula for success. It is a way of life that is solidly backed up in God's Word. We praise God, not for the expected results, but for the situation just as it is.

As long as we praise God with an eye secretly looking for the expected results, we're only kidding ourselves, and we can be certain that nothing will happen to change us or our situation.

Praise is based on an acceptance of the present as part of God's loving, perfect will for us. Praise is not based on what we think or hope will happen in the future. This is an absolute "law," clearly observable in the practice of praise.

We praise God, not for what we expect will happen in or around us, but we praise Him for who He is and where and how we are *right now*.

It is, of course, a fact that when we honestly praise God, something *does* happen as a result. His power obviously flows into the situation, and we will soon notice a change in us or around us. The change may be that we come to experience a real joy and happiness in the midst of what once appeared to be a miserable situation, or the situation may change. But this is a *result* of praise, and must not be the motivation for praise.

Praise is not a bargaining position. We don't say, "I'll praise you so that you can bless me, Lord."

To praise God is to delight ourselves in Him. The psalmist wrote, *Be delighted with the Lord. Then he will give you all your heart's desires* (Psalm 37:4).

Notice the order of importance here. We don't list our heart's desires and then delight ourselves in the Lord in order to get them. We're first to be delighted, and once we've experienced being really delighted with God, we'll discover that everything else becomes secondary. Still, it is true that God does want to give us all our heart's desires. Nothing short of that is His wish and plan for us.

If we could only learn to be delighted with the Lord in everything first!

A Christian couple had two sons. One was their pride and joy; he lived at home and shared his parent's warm and happy Christian faith.

Once when I was having dinner with them, they confided in me that their older son was a rebel and gone from home. He had graduated from college with honors, but had turned his back on his parents and on established society. Now he roamed the country as a hippie, with no apparent objective in life.

The unhappy parents asked if I had any advice for them. I explained that I believed that God had given them this son and was answering their prayers for his salvation.

"If your prayers are sincere, then you can be sure that his present life will be used by God to work out what is best for him, and for you!" I said.

"I understand," said the father. "We want only what is best for our boy, and this must be God's way and will for all of us."

We joined hands around the dinner table and thanked God for working out His plan in the way He knew was best.

A short time later the family wrote me. Since our meeting, the parents had persisted in thanking God for their son's way of life, even if they found it hard to understand. Then one day their son had an accident on his bike and received a painful injury to his foot.

Temporarily crippled, he decided to come home for a while. He informed his parents that he'd left a trail of unpaid bills across the country. The parents prayed about it and decided that if God had really been at work in all the events in their son's life, He had also allowed the bills. So they thanked Him for every one of them and paid the debts in full!

Their son was amazed. He had expected to be reprimanded and told to take care of his own obligations. Instead, his parents were relaxed, loving, and appeared to accept his way-out style of dress and hair without cringing.

One evening some young Christians came to visit the younger son. The older brother was obviously irritated by the intrusion, but his painful foot kept him from leaving the house. Enthusiastically, the young Christians shared what Jesus Christ had done and was doing in their lives. At first the older brother offered scathing criticism of what he called their naive and unrealistic approach to life, but soon he was listening attentively and asking probing questions. Before the evening was over, he had turned his life over to Jesus Christ.

His parents joyfully wrote that there was an immediate and drastic change in their older son's life. He dedicated himself to follow Jesus and serve Him. Eagerly he studied the Bible, and within a few days he asked for and received the baptism in the Holy Spirit, the experience the followers of Jesus had received on the first Pentecost after Christ's death and resurrection. A few days later he met a Christian girl. Soon they were engaged to be married.

Months of anxious and concerned prayers had not brought a change in this young man. Only when the parents turned to God in joyful acceptance of the present condition of their son's life was the door opened for God to complete His perfect plan for all of them.

God does have a perfect plan for your life and for mine. We may look at the circumstances surrounding us and think we've been standing still forever in one painful spot. The more we pray and cry for God to help us, the more the circumstances seem to pile up. The turning point cannot come until we begin to praise God *for* our situation instead of crying for Him to take it all away.

A young woman wrote and told me how she had reached the end of her rope. Certain embarrassing personal circumstances had caused her to lose her self-respect, and she began to neglect her looks.

"Eating was my way out," she wrote, "and soon pounds began to pile up all over my body till I looked like a three-ring circus. My husband began looking at other women, and one day he moved out, asking for a divorce."

Bills began to accumulate, her nerves stretched to the breaking point, and the thought of suicide became more frequent.

"All this time I prayed continually," she wrote. "I read my Bible, went to church every time the doors were open, and asked everyone I knew to pray for me. My Christian friends kept telling me to keep the faith; don't let it get you down; things will be better tomorrow. But everything kept getting worse. Then someone gave me *Prison to Praise*, I read it, and at first I couldn't believe you were serious. No one in his right mind could expect me to be thankful for everything that was going on in my life right then! But the longer I read, the more I cried. Slowly it dawned on me that what you said was real. Those scripture verses about thanking God for everything -- I'd read them in my Bible countless times and never really understood what they meant."

She decided to try thanking God for everything. After all, what could she lose? She'd been gaining weight so rapidly that she knew she could suffer a serious heart attack any time. With a faint glimmer of hope she knelt in her living room to pray.

"God, I thank you that my life is just as it is. Every problem has been your gift to bring me to the place where I am right now. You wouldn't have permitted any of these things to happen if you hadn't known that it was best for me. God, you really *do* love me! I mean it God, I *know* you do love me . . . ."

At this point her prayer was interrupted by the dog barking loudly at the mailman. Every day the dog greeted every visitor to her house with intensive barking; that was one of many irritating little incidents that seemed to pile up to make her days miserable beyond endurance. As she got up and moved toward the door to silence the dog with the usual sharp command, she suddenly remembered, *I'm supposed to be thankful for everything.* "Okay, God. Thank You for my barking dog!"

The mailman brought a letter, and she stared at the familiar handwriting on the envelope. It couldn't be! She hadn't heard from her husband for months! God couldn't have moved *that* quickly. With trembling hands she opened the letter and read, "If you are still willing, there may be a way that we can work out our problems."

God's timing had been perfect. Joyfully, this young lady was now able to believe that God was indeed working in her life for good. She went on to lose weight like butter sliding off a hot plate. Her friends began to comment, "You look so good! What has happened to you? You don't look like the same person!"

The same person? Yes and no. She was the same physical being, but she now lived in a new dimension of faith, knowing that God was working in every detail of her life for good. Her husband returned and they were re-united. She wrote, "Some mornings I wake up hearing myself talking to God, saying things like, Oh God, thank you for a beautiful day. I love you!"

The turning point in her life came when she began to accept her present circumstances with thanksgiving. This is a perfect illustration of the spiritual principle at work.

God has a perfect plan for our lives, but he cannot move

us to the next step of His plan until we joyfully accept our present situation as part of that plan. What happens next is God's move, not ours.

Some people would like to deny that fact. They look at the transformation taking place in the lives of people who have learned to praise God for everything, and they insist that the explanation is a simple one.

"A changed attitude causes changed circumstances," they say. "It is simple psychology. When you stop complaining and start smiling, you feel different; others treat you differently, and your whole life can undergo a dramatic change for the better."

I will agree that the formula, "Smile and the world will smile with you; cry and you cry alone," is a sound piece of advice -- up to a point. But praising God is something more than a change in our own attitude.

The phrases "Praise the Lord!" or "Thank God!" are used so glibly by many of us that we tend to lose sight of their real meaning. There is power in our words of praise; there is power in our attitude of thankfulness and joy. But God is omnipotent and retains absolute control. We need to remind ourselves of that fact frequently. It is easy to fall into the trap of thinking that *we* have the power to manipulate or change a situation simply by reciting a certain form of prayer.

When we sincerely accept and thank God for a situation, believing that He has allowed it to come about, there is released into that situation a supernatural, divine force that causes changes beyond what can be explained as an unfolding of natural events.

While I was serving as a chaplain at Fort Benning, Georgia, a young soldier brought his wife to my office for help. She was suffering with horrible flashbacks from LSD, and the medical doctors had been unable to prescribe a cure. Fear and pain had etched deep lines into her pretty face.

"I can't sleep," she said. "I can't even close my eyes for a minute without seeing horrible animals rushing at me."

Her husband explained that whenever his wife fell

asleep from sheer exhaustion, she would begin to scream almost immediately.

"I try to shake her awake, but sometimes it takes ten minutes to bring her back to consciousness, and all that time she screams with an anguish that is driving me to despair as well," he said.

I listened to their tragic story and said, "I have only one suggestion. Please kneel with me, and let us thank God that you are like you are."

They stared at me as if they were sure I hadn't meant what I said. Carefully I explained how I had learned that God wants us to be thankful for all things.

"Everything that has happened in your life so far has served to bring you to this very point," I said. "I believe God loves you and is going to do something very wonderful for you. Now He wants you to thank Him for everything that has brought you to Him."

I leafed through my Bible and showed them the scriptures I had underlined.

Both accepted what they heard and knelt to thank God for everything in their lives, particularly for the flashbacks from drugs. I could feel the presence of God in the room.

"The Holy Spirit is making it clear that he is healing you right now," I said. I placed my hand on the girl's head and prayed, "Thank you, Lord, for healing this girl right now."

She opened her eyes and looked amazed.

"Something has happened to me. When I closed my eyes to pray I didn't see anything!"

"Jesus has healed you," I said. "Now He wants to come into your life as your Savior. Will you accept him?"

Both the girl and her husband eagerly said, "Yes!" Still on their knees, they asked Jesus to come into their lives. Then they walked out of my office rejoicing.

The girl's healing was permanent. Never again did the flashbacks return. The power of the drug over her mind had been broken by the power of God.

Medical authorities admit their helplessness in dealing with addicts who've spent years in slavery to drugs. Yet in recent years we've been hearing with increasing frequency of drug addicts who've been set free after years of dependency on drugs. They've been freed by the supernatural intervention of God in their lives.

This kind of change cannot be brought about by a new attitude or a determined effort of self-will. This is God's power at work in human lives.

Any form of sincere prayer opens the door for God's power to move into our lives. But the prayer of praise releases more of God's power than any other form of petition. The Bible gives examples which show this fact again and again.

But thou art holy, O thou that inhabitest the praises of Israel, we read in Psalm 22:3 KJV. No wonder God's power and presence is near when we praise Him. He actually dwells, inhabits, resides, in our praises!

A remarkable example of how God works while we praise Him is in II Chronicles 20.

Jehoshaphat was king of Judah, and one day he discovered that his little kingdom was surrounded by the powerful armies of his enemies - the Moabites, and the Ammonites. Jehoshaphat knew that little Judah didn't have a chance in its own might, and he cried out to God:

We have no might to stand against this great company that is coming against us. We do not know what to do, but our eyes are upon You (II Chronicles 20:12 Amp).

An important step in the act of praising God is to take our eyes off the threatening circumstances and look to God instead. Notice that Jehoshaphat wasn't just closing his eyes to the threat against his kingdom or pretending the enemies weren't there. He took careful stock of the situation, recognized his own helplessness, and turned to God for help.

We are not to be blind to the very real threats of evil in our lives. Seeing them for what they are only gives us greater cause to praise and thank God for working in them with perfect control and authority. But we are not to be pre-occupied with the appearance of evil around us. See it, admit our helplessness to cope with it in our own strength, then turn to God.

God said to Jehoshaphat, *Be not afraid or dismayed at this great multitude; for the battle is not yours, but God's* (II Chronicles 20:15 Amp).

Now that is a tremendous statement, I think. We don't have the power to deal with the circumstances of our lives, so obviously, the battle isn't ours, but God's!

You shall not need to fight in this battle; take your position, stand still, and see the deliverance of the Lord.... (II Chronicles 20:17).

What a promise! What did Jehoshaphat do while he was standing still and watching God at work?

The next morning Jehoshaphat gave the orders to his army. *He appointed singers to sing to the Lord and praise Him in their holy (priestly) garments, as they went out before the army, saying, Give thanks to the Lord, for His mercy and loving kindness endure for ever!* (II Chronicles 20:21 Amp).

This scene took place right in front of the massed ranks of the enemy armies ready to slaughter the men of Judah. Can you imagine the reaction of their captains as they saw the small band of singers coming out on the battlefield against them?

I was in the army for twenty years, and I've seen men prepare for many battles. But I've never seen a commanding general order his troops to stand still right in front of the enemy lines while a special band of singers went out ahead singing praises to God.

It sounds like a pretty farfetched idea, doesn't it? It is in this kind of situation that our understanding is most likely to balk.

"It's all well and good to praise the Lord when we're in a tough spot," we may say, "but let's not be ridiculous. God helps those who help themselves. The least we can do is go out there and fight as valiantly as we know how. Then we'll leave the rest to Him."

But what happened to Jehoshaphat and his men?

And when they began to sing and to praise, the Lord set ambushments against the men...who had come against Judah, and they were (self-) slaughtered (II Chronicles 20:22-23 Amp).

I think it is permissible to assume that if Jehoshaphat had decided that he had "better play it safe" and had ordered his men to fight, the outcome would have been very different.

Many of us are constantly defeated by the circumstances around us because we aren't ready to accept that the battle is God's, not ours. Even when we realize our own powerlessness to cope with the enemy, we are afraid to let go and trust ourselves to God's power. This is where we've allowed our own understanding to assume the wrong position in our lives. We say, "I don't understand; therefore I don't dare believe."

God's Word makes it clear that the only way out of *that* dilemma is a step of faith on our part. Believing that God's promises are true, accepting them, and daring to trust in them leads to understanding. The principle in the Bible is clear: Acceptance comes *before* understanding.

The reason for this is simple. Our human understanding is so limited that we can't possibly grasp the magnitude of God's plan and purpose for us. If our understanding had to come before our acceptance, we'd never be able to accept very much.

Jehoshaphat would never have dared follow God's plan for the battle if he had insisted on understanding it. God's promise undoubtedly staggered Jehoshaphat's understanding. But Jehoshaphat, we read in the account, was a man who *believed* and *trusted* God. As a result, he relied on and trusted in God.

Joshua was another leader who received battle orders from God that must have challenged his willingness to obey what probably seemed absurd to many who watched.

We've all sung, "Joshua fought the battle of Jericho -- and the walls came tumbling down."

The city of Jericho was a fortified stronghold, and the Israelites who had wandered for forty years in the wilderness didn't have the weapons or the power to take the city. But Joshua believed God when He promised to deliver the enemies of Israel into their hands.

God told Joshua to march around Jericho six days in a row. On the seventh day they were to blow their trumpets and shout. *And the wall of the enclosure shall fall down in its place, and the people shall go up (over it) every man straight before him* (Joshua 6:5 Amp).

Joshua trusted God, but I wonder what you or I would have thought if we'd been among his followers. Would we have grumbled and balked at his foolhardy orders? What did the inhabitants of Jericho think as they stood on the sturdy fortified walls of their city and watched the Israelites marching around, carrying the Ark of the Covenant with them.

I used to think that the story of Joshua and the battle of Jericho was a mixture of myth, exaggeration, and fairy tale. But archaeologists have located the ruins of old Jericho in recent years, and found ample evidence that the walls of the city did collapse at a time in history corresponding to the biblical record. The walls of Jericho *did* come tumbling down. The power of God *was* at work while His people showed their trust and confidence by praising Him with trumpets and shouts.

The examples of Jehoshaphat and Joshua clearly show that God wins victories by means and principles that look utterly foolish and contradictory to our human wisdom and strategies.

We are told to trust Him, praise Him, and watch Him work. This is essentially how Jesus Christ operated during His time of ministry in Israel. He openly admitted that of Himself He could do nothing; His part was to submit to His Father's will in perfect obedience, trust, and faith, so that

God's power could meet the needs of the people.

Look at a couple of Jesus' prayers concerning a difficult problem.

There was the time when over 5,000 had followed Him out of town to hear Him preach. They were hungry. The only food available was one little boy's lunch -- five loaves of bread and two fishes.

How did Jesus pray? Did He plead with God to perform a miracle?

He looked up to heaven, and praising God gave thanks, and broke the loaves, and kept on giving them to the disciples to set before the people; and He also divided the two fish among them all. And they all ate and were satisfied. And they took up twelve...baskets full of broken pieces from the loaves and of the fish (Mark 6:41-43 Amp).

Some of us may object here and say, "But that was Jesus; He *knew* what God could do. It wouldn't work for us!"

But Jesus told his followers, *In solemn truth I tell you, anyone believing in me shall do the same miracles I have done, and even greater ones, because I am going to be with the Father. You can ask him for anything, using my name, and I will do it, for this will bring praise to the Father...*(John 14:12-13).

Jesus said we could do *greater* things. Does that mean that God possibly has a plan concerning famines around the world and the projected food shortage that environmentalists and agricultural experts so solemnly predict?

Yes, I do believe it does. I know of several instances where people have taken God at His Word, thanked Him, praised Him for a limited food supply, and seen it stretch to feed many more than was originally expected.

When Jesus was confronted with the death of Lazarus, he again prayed a simple prayer of thanksgiving. When the stone was rolled away from the grave where Lazarus had been buried for four days, Jesus lifted His eyes and said, "*Father, thank you for hearing me*" (John 11:41). Then He

commanded Lazarus to come from the grave. The man who
had been dead four days walked out!

The Bible says that Jesus came to earth to make it
possible for us to praise God. Isaiah the prophet foretold
Jesus' coming and said that He would come *to preach the
Gospel of good tidings...to bind up and heal the brokenhearted, to proclaim liberty to the physical and spiritual
captives, and the opening of the prison and of the eyes to
those who are bound...to grant consolation and joy to those
who mourn...the oil of joy for mourning, the garment...of
praise instead of heavy, burdened and failing spirit* (Isaiah
61:1-3 Amp).

You may recognize your own condition on the list. Are
you brokenhearted? Bound by physical limitations,
sickness, spiritual limitations? In physical prison, or imprisoned by your own spiritual blindness? Are you mourning?
Unable to rejoice, be thankful, or praise God? Is your spirit
heavily burdened and failing?

Perhaps it is because you haven't fully accepted and
understood the Good News Jesus came to bring.

Praise is an active response to what we *know* God has
done and is doing for us - in our lives and in this world
through His Son Jesus Christ and the Holy Spirit.

If we doubt in our hearts what God has done and is
doing, we cannot wholeheartedly praise Him. Uncertainty
about the Good News will always be a barrier to praise. If
we want to be able to praise God for everything, we need to
be sure our foundation is solid and without cracks of doubt
and uncertainty.

Chapter 2

Hear the Good News

If I offer you ten cents as a free gift, you probably won't get very excited about it. You may wonder why I'm doing it, and you may even laugh at me. If I give you another dime and tell you again that it is free, you may shake your head, wondering some more and if I continue giving you dimes until I've given you twenty, your interest may be stimulated, but you will still be at a loss to figure out what I am trying to prove.

If, instead of a dime, I offer you a thousand-dollar bill, I'm sure you will get excited right away; and if I increase the gift to twenty thousand, you will stare at me in amazement as you begin to realize just how fortunate you are. You may cry for joy, and you probably will want to tell someone right away about the wonderful gift you've received. What great news to share with others! As long as you live, you'll want to talk about it.

"Say, did I ever tell you about the twenty thousand dollars I was given - for free?"

God has given us many wonderful gifts. They're free for the asking. But we may only know of them as ten-cent gifts. We don't get excited over ten cents. Our heart doesn't beat faster when we think of receiving a dime. Neither do we cry tears of gratitude and joy when we think of God's goodness. What's wrong? Is it God's gifts? No, we are living in a ten-cent world!

Many church-going people think of God's gift of eternal life as a ten-cent gift. They believe they have to struggle to live a good life to keep their "free gift." Trying hard to live a good life puts them under such a continual strain that they often wonder if trying hard to be a Christian is really worth it.

No wonder they aren't very enthusiastic about sharing the Good News with anyone else. To them it just means going to church on Sunday, staying away from things that might be a lot of fun, and giving their hard-earned cash in the offering plate.

If this is your "salvation," I understand why you spend all your free evenings watching TV. And why you never think of speaking to your neighbor or to a stranger on the street about God's wonderful love for us. As far as you know, God's gift to you is only equivalent to a dime, so why should you be interested in receiving any more? Dime gifts, you can do without.

But if you received a thousand-dollar gift, you'd be eager for more! And you would tell everyone where they could get theirs.

We all want thousand-dollar gifts. Americans spend billions of dollars every year hoping to win something for nothing. We have a built-in desire to get for ourselves anything of real value.

God's free gifts to us are worth more than millions of dollars. He doesn't give them just to those who meet some minimum standards of behavior. They are available to <u>all</u> who will accept them. Christ has already paid the price for every gift God wants to give to us.

God says, *I will destroy all human plans of salvation no matter how wise they seem to be, and ignore the best ideas of men, even the most brilliant of them* (I Corinthians 1:19).

Receiving forgiveness of sin and eternal life as a free gift doesn't fit into the normal pattern of life as we know it. We've been conditioned to believe that we only get what we deserve or are willing to pay for. God's plan of giving us a totally free gift seems so impossible to us that we try to attach something to His offer.

"I'll be good enough to receive His free gift if I do this or that or something else," we say.

It is from God alone that you have your life through Christ Jesus, wrote Paul. *He was the only one who made us acceptable to God; He made us pure and holy and gave Himself to purchase our salvation* (I Corinthians 1:30).

The major question for you to decide when you hear wonderful news like this is whether Christ has the authority and the power to give you eternal life without requiring that you do one thing to deserve it. If you think that He doesn't have the power and the authority, then you must do something to get yourself right with God. You will have to strive all your life to be sure you meet His standards. But God's Word declares that no matter how hard you try, you cannot be as good as He demands.

Through Christ, all the kindness of God has been poured out upon us undeserving sinners; and now he is sending us out around the world to tell all people everywhere the great things God has done for them (Romans 1:5).

Paul had received some of the "thousand-dollar bills," and he was excited! He was determined to let the whole world know.

This Good News tells us that God makes us ready for heaven - makes us right in God's sight - when we put our faith and trust in Christ to save us (Romans 1:17).

Paul said that *God makes us ready*. When God does it, can you depend on it being done right? Will there be any room for improvement? Are you ready to face Him at the end of this life if you are what **He** has made you?

We can't make ourselves good enough, no matter how hard we try.

No one can ever find God's favor by being good enough. *For the more we know of God's laws, the clearer it becomes that we aren't obeying them* (Romans 3:20).

The more you learn about what is right, the more you will be aware of how unrighteous you are. Only the proud of heart feel that they have made it to some state of personal goodness. Christ is the only unselfish, sinless force in the world. Only **His presence in you** makes you any better than the most sinful person who ever lived!

Then what can we boast about doing, to earn our salvation? Nothing at all. Why? Because our acquittal is not based on our good deeds; it is based on what Christ has done and our faith in him. So it is that we are saved by faith in Christ and not by the good things we do (Roman 3:27-28).

Paul emphasized that this doctrine of faith was nothing new. He pointed out that Abraham was never accepted by God because of his good deeds, but because of his faith.

In today's culture, we would not consider Abraham a good man. When he was going into an alien country, he knew that the people there might decide to rob him of some of his possessions, his cattle, or even his beautiful wife. So to make his journey safer, he decided to introduce his wife, Sarah, as his sister. This way, he reasoned, any dangerous male suitors would show him favors instead of trying to kill him. Sure enough, it happened as Abraham had expected. The king himself saw Sarah and wanted her for his wife. She was brought to his palace, and Abraham was bestowed with fine gifts.

Now what did Abraham do? Make plans to rescue his wife? Not at all. He simply enjoyed his good fortune. God Himself had to intervene and show the king that Abraham had been deceitful.

Would you accept Abraham as a member of your church? Consider the question carefully.

God accepted Abraham, not because he lived up to any moral standards, but because Abraham believed God. His faith was accepted as all the goodness he needed. Abraham may not be good in our eyes, but he was good in God's eyes, because he believed.

You may think more of your own goodness than you do of Abraham's or of some people you know, but in God's eyes, man's sinfulness is total and complete. Degrees of goodness and badness cannot determine our salvation or our usefulness in God's kingdom. Abraham didn't earn his way to heaven by being good.

Paul wrote, *For being saved is a gift; if a person could earn it by being good, then it wouldn't be free - but it is! It is given to those who do not work for it. For God declares sinners to be good in his sight if they have faith in Christ to save them from God's wrath* (Romans 4:5).

We are made *good in God's sight!*

If you really believed this, would you be excited about it? Would you want to tell others how simple it is to become a Christian? Just think of it: around you are millions of people who actually believe that to become a Christian they must be good enough. And they know only too well that they can never manage to become good enough. How desperate and bleak their future must look! How they need to hear the Good News!

God's gift is free! Paul wrote, *If it is by God's kindness* (we are saved), *then it is not by our being good enough. For in that case the free gift would no longer be free - it isn't free when it is earned* (Romans 11:6).

The Good News should be proclaimed everywhere, and yet most Christians are curiously tongue-tied when it comes to talking about it.

Have you ever gone up to a stranger and asked for directions to a bus station or to Joe's Pizza Parlor? Were you scared when you did it? Did your heart pound and your tongue feel dry and swollen? Of course not. Then why do you feel that way when you think of telling a stranger what Jesus Christ has done for him?

God wants us to share the Good News with everyone. Jesus told His disciples to go out and tell the whole world what He had done for us. So who do you think wants to keep it a secret?

Yes, there is an enemy prowling around, and his favorite trick is to make us fearful of sharing the wonderful news about God's free gifts. But if we are absolutely certain of what God has done for us, if we've accepted His free "thousand-dollar bills," then we are going to bubble over with the news.

Some people will still worry about how good God requires us to be once we've been forgiven of our sins and have received the free gift of eternal life. Paul wrote about that to the Romans.

Now then, the question: Is this blessing given only to those who have faith in Christ but also keep the Jewish laws, or is the blessing also given to those who do not keep the Jewish rules, but only trust in Christ? Well, what about Abraham? We say that he received these blessings through his faith. Was it by faith alone? Or because he also kept the Jewish rules? (Romans 4:9).

Paul draws an amazing conclusion: Abraham did not keep the law, because there was no law yet given!

It is clear, then, that God's promise to give the whole earth to Abraham and his descendants was not because Abraham obeyed God's laws but because he trusted God to keep his promise (Romans 4:13).

God has promised us an inheritance, too - not if we're good enough - but if we believe Him. You may not think that God's plan is a very good solution, but it is God's solution to our problem.

The Jews kept excusing themselves and insisted that they were not sinners. Many Christians misunderstand Jesus' answer to the Jews. He insisted that the law of God was far purer than they conceived it to be. They thought they were innocent, for example, of committing adultery. But Jesus explained that if they even looked at a woman and desired her, they had already committed adultery with her in their heart. Jesus knew the mind of man. Even if man doesn't want to sin, there is another part of him that wants to, and so we are always faced with this inward battle.

So what was Jesus trying to tell us? That we would have to work even harder to try to keep the law? No, He only wanted to show us how much we need Him. Nearly every parable and teaching of Jesus was meant to convince us of

our need for a Savior. Paul declared that faith in Christ was
the only way to keep the whole law.

If you try to whip your physical being into shape and
actually succeed in keeping some of His laws, what have you
accomplished? Nothing. Jesus made it clear that unless you
keep every law perfectly, you are guilty of breaking them all.

Christ wasn't trying to discourage you, but to *encourage*
you! He said He would provide the only deliverance from
the problem.

*Christ gives to those who trust in him everything they are
trying to get by keeping his laws!* (Romans 10:4).

When Christ enters your life, you'll still keep your
physical body. But there's a big difference: *When someone
becomes a Christian he becomes a brand new person inside.
He is not the same any more* (II Corinthians 5:17).

You may look much the same, but you *aren't* the same.
*Your body will die, because of sin; but your spirit will live,
for Christ has pardoned it* (Romans 8:10).

You've become a new spiritual being inside, because
Christ dwells there through the Holy Spirit. Your old
physical body will one day die, but you won't. You will live
forever, with Christ.

I have talked to thousands of church-going people and
asked them what they thought a man must do in order to get
to heaven. I've asked the question in some of the most
fundamental, Bible-believing churches in our country and
heard the same answers over and over.

Ninety-nine out of every hundred have told me about the
things we must do. Keep the commandments, go to church,
give your money, don't mistreat others, etc. - a never-ending
list of what *they* are trying to do.

Church-going people have heard and believed the lie
that salvation depends on what *we* do. No wonder the
spreading of the Good News has been slow. Who wants to
come to church, receive ten cents, and then go out to tell the
world about it?

Are you still convinced that God has offered you only ten-cent gifts? Have you thought that to receive God's blessing you have to have faith - plus something?

So if you still claim that God's blessings go to those who are "good enough", then you are saying that God's promises to those who have faith are meaningless, and faith is foolish (Romans 4:14).

Paul wrote, *But the fact of the matter is this: when we try to gain God's blessing and salvation by keeping his laws we always end up under his anger, for we always fail to keep them* (Romans 4:15).

Does that mean God gets angry with us for trying to be good and keep His law? Of course not. He gets angry because He knows *why* we're trying to keep His law. If we try to keep the law for fear that God will punish us if we don't, our efforts are worthless. If we try to keep it to deserve any of His blessings, we are striving in vain. So why should we even try to do anything good? Couldn't we just be as bad as we want, since salvation if free anyway?

Now that, of course, is utterly ridiculous. We should do good - because we love God and *want* to please Him. If we fully understand what His wonderful gifts to us are, we will respond to His love by loving Him. If you cling to the idea of trying to do good to deserve God's favor, you may *never* learn to love Him. You surely will never get excited about the "thousand-dollar bills."

Now God has shown us a different way to heaven - not by "being good enough" and trying to keep his laws, but by a new way (though not new, really, for the scriptures told about it long ago). Now God says He will accept and acquit us - declare us not guilty - if we trust Jesus Christ to take away our sins. And we all can be saved in this same way, by coming to Christ, no matter who we are or what we have been like (Romans 3:21-22).

The condition is, *"if we trust Jesus Christ."* To trust in yourself to be either "good enough" or "not too bad," is exactly the opposite.

What did Jesus Christ do for us?

God sent Christ Jesus to take the punishment for our sins and to end all God's anger against us. He used Christ's blood and our faith as the means of saving us from his wrath (Romans 3:25).

Both of these elements are essential. One without the other won't do the job. Christ did the doing, but that won't help us if we don't respond by believing. If we get tangled up in the "doing," we will never be free to do the believing.

He died for our sins and rose again to make us right with God, filling us with God's goodness (Romans 4:25). *Sin ruled over all men and brought them to death, but now God's kindness rules instead, giving us right standing with God and resulting in eternal life through Jesus Christ our Lord* (Romans 5:21).

Our choice is clearly between God's kindness or His just judgment. We are offered the free gift of eternal life, and the alternative is plainly death.

I remember an attractive young army nurse stationed at a hospital in Vietnam where I was chaplain. The nurse arrived full of life and vitality, but soon her happy smile faded away. She could not bear to see the young soldiers come back from the battlefront badly wounded and in pain. She often came to my office to speak about her feelings.

"How can you say that God loves these men when He lets them suffer so?" she asked me one day.

"It would be easier if you gave your worries and concern for your patients to God and trusted Him to help them," I suggested. "God loves these wounded soldiers far more than you and I are capable of."

The nurse shook her head.

"I can't, Chaplain," she said. "Maybe someday, but not now. It hurts too much to look at the suffering. I can't thank God for it now."

Her visits to the chaplain's office became less frequent. From the dull expression in her once bright eyes, I began to suspect that she was taking pills to fight her depression. She no longer seemed to respond to what was going on around her. She was transferred, and I lost track of her.

Just recently, I received a letter from a state reformatory for women in a midwestern state.

Dear Chaplain:

> I've traveled many miles in the wrong direction since I last saw you at the hospital in Vietnam. I seem to have lost the decent part of myself on the way. After Vietnam I couldn't find peace of mind, and I started to drift.

> It all began while I was watching the useless deaths and maiming of young bodies in the hospital. I blamed God for it all, and now I realize that by blaming Him I cut myself off from Him and destroyed myself. Now I am not able to respond to anything or anyone. I'm just existing in a gray, feelingless void.

> I know that God is the answer. I've fought it for many years, but now I know. I've wanted to write you for some time, but I've been ashamed. I remember how good it felt to be able to just talk with you in the chaplain's office. I didn't want to accept the answer then. I hope it isn't too late. Please pray for me....

The young nurse had turned away from the gift that God held out to her. Now she had come to recognize the consequences. But think of all the suffering she must have endured.

Receiving Christ's gift of eternal life is one of the easiest things you will ever do! There is nothing difficult about it. You don't have to be clever - even a little child can do it.

Paul wrote, *Salvation that comes from trusting Christ...is already within easy reach of each of us; in fact, it is as near as our own hearts and mouths. For if you tell others with your mouth that Jesus Christ is your Lord, and believe in your own heart that God has raised Him from the dead, you will be saved* (Romans 10:8-9).

So why do some people hesitate? What are they afraid of?

The young army nurse was afraid to trust herself to a God who could let young soldiers be killed and maimed in battle. She didn't trust God's love.

We need have no fear of someone who loves us perfectly, wrote John. *His perfect love for us eliminates all dread of what he might do to us. If we are afraid, it is for fear of what he might do to us, and shows that we are not fully convinced that he really loves us* (I John 4:18).

God *is* love. Everything He does is love in action. Our problem is we have such a limited picture of what love is all about. We've all been hurt and disappointed by human love, the kind that rewards us and accepts us when we're good and punishes and rejects us when we're bad. But that is not like God's love at all.

The Greek version of the New Testament uses two words that we translate simply as "love." One is *philio*, brotherly love; it means a deep, instinctive, personal affection. The other is *agape*, divine love. It is the kind Paul says that husbands and wives should have for each other, and *agape* is used to describe God's love for us. It means a reasoning, intentional, deliberate, spiritual devotion. It doesn't originate in feelings or emotions; it is a deliberate act of love, originating in the will. It never changes and can always be relied on, because it doesn't depend on how lovable or deserving the loved one is.

That is how God loves us. He loves us when we reject Him, when we disobey, and when we're mean. He loves us when we've made a mess of our lives, and He is always ready to accept and forgive us and to fill us with His joy and peace.

The free gift of God's love is eternal life in Christ Jesus, and it is as near to us as our mouth and our heart. We simply accept what Jesus has done for us, believe in our heart that

He lives, and tell others about it. It is so simple, yet some stop short even when they *know* what the gift is all about.

Nicodemus, a devoutly religious Jew, came to Jesus one night and asked Him how he could enter the kingdom of God. Nicodemus knew that Jesus was sent of God and had the answer.

Jesus told him, *With all the earnestness I possess I tell you this: Unless you are born again, you can never get into the Kingdom of God.*

Born again! exclaimed Nicodemus. What do you mean? How can an old man go back into his mother's womb and be born again?

Jesus replied, What I am telling you so earnestly is this: Unless one is born of water and the Spirit, he cannot enter the Kingdom of God. Men can only reproduce human life, but the Holy Spirit gives new life from heaven (John 3:3-6).

Nicodemus *knew* who Jesus was, but that wasn't enough. It is necessary also to act on what we know and to accept Jesus Christ as our personal Savior by inviting Him into our lives. When He comes in, by the Holy Spirit, we are spiritually born again. We can only communicate with God in our spirit, and so we must be born again in order to be equipped to know God. If we're not born again, we're still spiritually dead.

Paul wrote, *I have been crucified with Christ: and I myself no longer live, but Christ lives in me. And the real life I now have within this body is a result of my trusting in the Son of God, who loved me and gave himself for me* (Galations 2:20).

Paul told the Corinthians, *Check up on yourselves. Are you really Christians? Do you pass the test? Do you feel Christ's presence and power more and more within you? Or are you just pretending to be Christians when actually you aren't at all?* (II Corinthians 13:5).

Are you really a Christian? Have you been born again?

There are many like Nicodemus in our churches today. They spend time studying the scriptures and praying daily;

they attend Bible studies and prayer groups and teach Sunday School. Some are even preachers. They may have grown up in church, and call themselves "born" Methodist, Presbyterian, Lutheran, Catholic, Pentecostal, Baptist, or whatever denomination they happen to be in.

They know all *about* Christianity. They know that Jesus is the Son of God who died for their sins; they know He lives again; but they've never surrendered *their* lives to Him and invited Him to be Lord and Savior in *their* hearts. Thousands of people regularly attend worship services and go through all the outward forms of Christianity without ever having experienced Christ *in* their lives.

The gift of salvation and eternal life is absolutely free; you can do nothing to earn it or deserve it, but you *must* receive it before it can become yours. God reaches out, lovingly arranging circumstances to show us how much we need Him, to draw us to Himself.

Once a Christian sergeant brought a soldier from his platoon to my office. The soldier was facing a dishonorable discharge and a prison term for using and dealing in drugs. He'd been an addict since his early teens, and the time he spent in the army had only made matters worse. He had served in Vietnam where drugs were as easy to come by as chewing gum.

"I've made a mess of my life, and it's too late to change," he said. The look in his eyes was dark and desperate.

"What about God?" I asked. "He's got the power to change you."

The soldier shrugged.

"Why should He," he said. "I've never done anything for Him."

"He loves you," I said. "He sent Jesus to take the punishment for everything you've ever done. He can heal you, too."

The soldier looked glum.

"I've heard about Jesus," he said. "I'd like to ask Him to be my Savior, but I don't think it will do any good now. I can't stop using drugs no matter how hard I try. I've been a junkie too long."

"God can heal you," I said confidently. "Don't you think He is more powerful than drugs?"

The soldier looked doubtful.

"Are you willing to try Him?" I asked. The soldier nodded.

"I'll try anything," he said. "I want to get out of the hell I'm in now."

"Then thank God right now for what He's going to do for you in the next few minutes, and thank Him for everything that has happened in your life to bring you to this spot!"

"Now wait a minute!" The soldier looked upset. "You mean I'm supposed to thank God for everything in my life up to now, even that I'm an addict?"

"It's your addiction that brings you to Him, isn't it?" I said. "If God heals you, forgives you, and gives you a brand-new, eternal life with Jesus, don't you think you can thank Him for everything that made you see you needed Him?"

The dark look of doubt was still in the soldier's eyes.

"Will you let me pray for you?" I asked, and he nodded.

I placed my hands on his head. "Dear Heavenly Father," I prayed. "Thank you for loving this boy and drawing Him to you. Now send your Holy Spirit to help him believe that you've been working in every dark and lonely moment of his life to bring him to Christ."

When I finished there was a new light in the soldier's eyes. "It is very strange," he said, "but for some reason I really do believe that God has taken everything bad that ever happened to me and is working it for my good."

His eyes were moist and he bowed his head again, this time praying for himself, asking God to forgive him for his rebellion, and asking Jesus to come and take over his life.

What happened next, defies my ability to explain. I placed my hands on his head again, praying that God would heal him, cleanse his mind of all desire for drugs, and fill him instead with His love. I felt a force flow through to the young soldier. His face brightened like a child's and tears flowed down his cheeks.

"It has happened!" he shouted. "I don't need drugs anymore - Jesus lives in me!"

For the young soldier it was the moment of rebirth. He would never again be the same. He was born again, not because he *felt* the presence of Jesus, but because he made a decision to trust God.

If our relationship with God was dependent on our feelings, it really wouldn't be our choice, would it? We can't choose how we're going to feel. But we *can* choose to trust, to believe, and to have faith. We are saved by *faith*, the Bible says. But many of us have a very distorted picture of faith.

"I just don't have faith to believe," we say, and what we really mean is, "I don't *feel* sure."

Faith and feelings are *not* the same.

Now faith is the assurance, the confirmation, the title-deed of the things we hope for, being the proof of things we do not see and the conviction of their reality - faith perceiving as real fact what is not revealed to the senses (Hebrews 11:1 Amp).

Faith does not originate in our emotions, our feelings, or our senses. Faith is a matter of *will*. We decide to believe as truth what is *not* revealed to our senses.

To be saved by *faith*, means that we accept Jesus Christ as our Savior by an act of our will, not by our emotions or feelings. We are born again by faith, saved by faith, and that means we take God's promise that it has happened once we've accepted Christ into our hearts. We may not *feel* saved or *feel* born again, but that doesn't change the fact that we *are*.

We've talked about how easy it is for our understanding to be a stumbling block to faith. It is just as dangerous to try to measure our faith by feelings. We've been confusing feeling with fact for so long that we think we *are* what we *feel*. I *feel* sick - so I must *be* sick. But our feelings are changeable and can be affected by the weather, by our diet, by our sleep, or the mood of our boss. Our feelings are a poor test of reality. When we apply them as a test of our relationship with God, we get into trouble.

Jesus said, "Pray in faith, *believing* you have received." We can't pray the prayer of faith if we insist on measuring the results by our feelings. We may discover that God's truth in the Bible often says we should do the exact opposite of what we feel.

"Love your enemies," said Jesus.

Doesn't He know how we *feel* about our enemies? Sure He does. But He's telling us that we don't have to let our feelings boss us around anymore. We're free to choose to love even our enemies!

We are also free to accept God's Word as fact, regardless of what our emotions, our senses, our intellect, or our feelings try to tell us. Our new life in Jesus Christ is a life in *faith*. That means a life of freedom from the tyranny of our emotions, intellect, and senses. We don't have to pay attention to them anymore!

The Bible tells us we can be saved by faith, healed by faith, justified by faith, shielded by faith, walk in faith, stand in faith, live by faith, inherit the promises of God by faith, be rich in faith, pray in faith, overcome the world by faith, praise God by faith.

Our salvation experience becomes an accomplished fact when we accept it by faith. God isn't looking at our feelings, but at the decision we make. We may be feeling terrible, but as long as we accept Christ by faith, God considers the transaction done. Whatever you may feel or not feel immediately following your commitment makes no difference. God accepted your surrender of will, and you were born again by His Holy Spirit.

I'm concerned when people come to me and say, "Oh,

I just *know* Jesus touched me today, because I *felt* it." The same people will come back later and say, "I'm not sure I'm saved anymore; I don't *feel* the presence of God."

Praise God when you *do* have the wonderful experience of His presence, but don't let your faith depend on how you feel. A Christian who makes emotional experiences the test of his salvation will always be torn by doubts.

One woman wrote me:

> I gave my life to Jesus Christ several years ago, but nothing happened. I didn't feel anything, and as time went on I lost my hope and quit trying to keep my promise to Jesus about living for Him. Since then my life has become unbearable. I'm so depressed I'm afraid I'll destroy my marriage . . . I've read *Prison to Praise* and know that what I feel is a deep hunger for Christ. I've prayed for forgiveness, and I want to commit myself to Him again. I accepted Jesus Christ as my personal Savior and I want very much to be a part of His kingdom. I don't feel any difference yet . . . please pray for me, because I can't go on feeling this way much longer . . ..

Another letter came from a young man in federal prison:

> I believe in Jesus Christ with what I hope to be all my heart; I received Him as my Savior two years ago. I really meant it, and I felt wonderful for two days. Then I slipped right back into my old ways. I've had moments since then when I've felt the same joy, but I can't make it last. I want to serve God, but I just can't seem to find Him. I've read *Prison to Praise* and I know I need what you wrote about. How do I find it? Do you think maybe I don't want it badly enough? How can I make myself want it more? I've made such

a mess out of my life. There's no meaning,
the way I'm going. I've taken many Bible
courses, and I still don't seem to be getting
anywhere. I so badly want to find Christ. I'll
be leaving prison soon, and I want to go out
in the world with His love. Please pray that
I may find Him and experience the joy He
promised in the Bible . . ..

I've received hundreds of letters just like these, and
wherever I go I meet people who say they aren't sure they
have really met Jesus.

The reason for their doubt is always the same: ''I don't
feel anything.''

They are prisoners of their feelings and have greater
faith in their feelings than in God's Word. Once we
surrender to Jesus, He says about us, *I give them eternal life
and they shall never perish. No one shall snatch them away
from me* (John 10:28).

How do we fight our feelings?

Paul wrote, *The only condition* (for salvation)*is that you
fully believe the Truth, standing in it steadfast and firm,
strong in the Lord, convinced of the Good News that Jesus
died for you, and never shifting from trusting Him to save
you. This is the wonderful news that came to each of you and
is now spreading all over the world* (Colossians 1:23).

When doubts and feelings come to attack our faith, God
tells us to stand firmly on His Word.

One lady I know has a very practical way of doing it.
When a doubt comes along, she finds a verse in the Bible that
tells the truth about the matter. She copies the verse on a
piece of paper, and when the doubt comes, she quotes the
verse to herself.

The thought would come to her when she felt discouraged, *Are you sure God heard your prayer when you
accepted Jesus Christ as your Savior?*

In her Bible she found the verse, *And this is the
confidence which we have in him, that if we ask anything*

*according to His will He hears us. And if we know that he
hears us in whatever we ask, we know that we have obtained
the requests made of Him* (I John 5:14-15 RSV).

She copied it down, and underneath she wrote, "On
January 14, 1969, I confessed my sins and asked Jesus Christ
to come into my life as Savior and Lord. I know it happened
because my request was in agreement with God's plan and
will for my life."

She placed the paper by her bedroom mirror, and when
the doubt came, she pointed to the paper and said out loud,
"There is it. I *know* I was born again. I *know* God has
accepted me, because I accepted His Son as my Savior on that
day. I never have to wonder about it again."

When she felt guilt over a specific sin she had already
confessed to God, the temptation came to doubt that she'd
really been forgiven. She checked her Bible and wrote, *If we
confess our sins to Him, He can be depended on to forgive
us and to cleanse us from every wrong. And it is perfectly
proper for God to do this for us because Christ died to wash
away our sins* (I John 1:9).

Underneath she wrote down the sin she had confessed,
with the date and the words, "Hallelujah, I'm forgiven!"

Gradually her doubts ceased completely.

You can fight your doubts and feelings by keeping a
written, dated record of your prayer-transactions, along with
the Bible verse stating God's promise.

If you've been a Christian for several years, but still
have recurring doubts about your salvation, don't let your
doubts and feelings fool you any longer. Make a
commitment right now and put it in writing with today's
date. Some people record important spiritual milestones in
their Bibles.

The Christian life is a continuous journey in faith. It is
a good idea to keep a record of the way we've come. It serves
as a useful reminder on dark days when we feel sure we
haven't moved at all. Looking back, we can praise and thank
God for the way He's brought us.

Our faith is built on God's fact, not on feeling. But God's promise is also that we will experience more and more of His joy and peace in our lives as we go along. Rejoice when that happens, but rejoice also when you feel dry and empty.

Your salvation is still a wonderful fact. Throw the switch of your willpower in God's direction and say, "I will to believe, God. I stand on your Word."

Do it, and discover that your old dependency on feeling will gradually fade away. You will be free to believe!

You will know the truth, Jesus promised, *and the truth will set you free* (John 8:32).

Accept God's Word as truth - and you will be free!

Chapter 3

Power Unlimited

When we give our trust over to Christ, what actually happens? *God...has blessed us with every blessing in heaven because we belong to Christ* (Ephesians 1:3).

Because we belong to Christ, we are children of God. We have entered His kingdom, and all the power, privileges, and responsibilities belonging to the children of God are ours.

Just look at all the provisions our Father in heaven has made for us - *every blessing in heaven*. Not because we are worthy, but *because we belong to Christ*!

A human baby doesn't grow by stretching himself. He doesn't have to be good to deserve his daily care. He is fed, clothed, loved, and cared for by his mother and father, simply because he is their child. They know his every need, and they provide for him. His growth comes about naturally, effortlessly, as long as the child accepts his food and gets his proper rest and exercise.

Can you imagine a human child refusing to eat and sleep, telling his mother, ''I'm not ready yet. Mom, I'm over here stretching. When I've grown five inches on my own, I'll be ready to eat.''

That is exactly the way many Christians behave. God has made all the provisions; He's prepared everything we need to grow - food, rest, love, care. But we're over in the corner, struggling and stretching, trying to grow so we'll be worthy to receive.

God decided to do this for us long before you and I were born. *Long ago, even before he made the world, God chose*

*us to be his very own, through what Christ would do for us;
he decided then to make us holy...*(Ephesians 1:4).

Wait a minute! **Who** is God making holy? Has He made
you holy yet? Do you know anybody that has been made
holy? Is He behind schedule?

Read further: ...*without a single fault....*

Do you think it is possible for God to decide to make
Christians be without a single fault and yet fail so miserably
with all the people you know?

But read on: ...*in His eyes!* God has made us holy and
without a single fault ...*in His eyes.* He has done a great thing
for us. He has changed us ...*in His eyes. He* sees us
differently. *He* alone has the power to see the new man. Who
can see through the eyes of God? No one but God Himself.
He has made a new creation for His own glory and praise.

When others look at you, they may see the same old you.
They are not God. You may look at yourself in the mirror
and be convinced that you are not holy or without a single
fault, but remember that *you* are not God.

Do you dare say that God cannot see what He wants to
see? Would you rather perceive yourself as holy, or would
you rather God see you as holy? Thousands of Christians are
trying to force themselves into a holy mold because they
believe they need to do this themselves. When they fail, as
they inevitably must, the pangs of discouragement overcome
them. I've seen their unhappy faces all over the country and
heard their confession of failure so often that I know what is
coming before they even begin.

How did God do such a fantastic thing as to make us holy
in His eyes? Paul says, *We who stand before him covered
with his love* (Ephesians 1:4). A blanket of love! He drops
it over us and then stands back to look. What does He see?
His own love!

Others may see you. You may see you. God sees His
own love! Isn't that enough to start the joybells ringing in
your heart, turning your life into thanksgiving and praise?

Why did God do such a marvelous thing for us? *He did this because He wanted to* (Ephesians 1:5) Paul stated matter-of-factly. God *wanted* to wrap us in a blanket of His love. Don't you believe that He has the authority and the power to give us *anything* He wants to? Every blessing in heaven? Thousand-dollar gifts?

Why did He choose to do it Himself? I am convinced that this was the only way He could be sure that His work would be perfect. If He had to depend on you and me doing it right, He would never have had anything worthwhile to present to His Son. The end product was to be for God's glory and not for man's.

Paul wrote, *God's purpose in this was that we should praise God and give glory to him for doing these mighty things for us* (Ephesians 1:12).

The result of placing our complete faith in what Christ does for us is glorious.

Now we can come fearlessly right into God's presence, assured of his glad welcome when we come with Christ and trust in him (Ephesians 3:12).

Too many prayers are made with a whining, self-effacing, false humility. We don't need to apologize to God for being human. He knows all about what we're like. He has watched billions of human beings and knows all of our weaknesses. Now He wants us to believe that through Christ we have the *right* to approach Him and ask for whatever we need.

God wants to bless us with *good* things; He wants us to be happy; and this is sometimes hard for Christians to understand. I grew up in poverty and our family often received gifts of charity. I grew up resenting it when people wanted to give me things or do something for me. I wanted to earn or deserve everything I got. This carried over into my relationship with God. Somehow I wasn't able to believe that God wanted to give me anything more than my immediate needs. *After all*, I reasoned, *why should He*? My vision of God's boundless love and concern for my well-being was rather limited.

Then one day when I was stationed at Fort Benning as a chaplain, I found myself far away in another state without any means of getting back to carry out my duties. Bad weather had canceled the flight I had planned to take, and the next scheduled flight would not get me home on time. To go by car was out of the question. I was grounded, and quite unhappy about it. As long as I had been chaplain, I had never accepted any speaking engagement that would keep me from my regular duties, and now it looked as if I would have to neglect my job.

I prayed, "Lord, you know I've never been late before; I place this entire situation into your hands. I know you've got a perfect plan for me. I thank you and know that you will meet my needs."

At the meeting where I was speaking, I met an Air-Force pilot. He was stationed nearby, and when he heard of my plight, he said, "I'm going to call my commander and see if anything can be done."

The commander responded to his request, "Why sure. I need to get in some flying time myself; I'll be glad to fly the chaplain to Fort Benning. Bring him to the airfield at 0600 tomorrow morning."

I spent the night as a guest in the pilot's home, and the next morning at 6 am we walked onto the airfield. I felt refreshed, and rejoiced that God had met my needs. Just how abundantly He had met them, I didn't quite realize yet.

I looked all over for the plane I expected to see. A row of huge four-engine planes was lined up, but nothing that looked like it was ready to be taken up on a routine flight just to put in flying time. I expected something small and not too comfortable, just something to get me home on time. That was all I needed, I thought.

My pilot friend stopped and said, "Here it is Chaplain, step aboard."

I looked up. Before me was the biggest airplane on the runway! It seemed to be a block long.

This can't be for me, Lord! I thought. I walked up the steps in a half-daze and followed the crew member who showed me to a comfortable seat in a large lounge. I was the only passenger, and the plane was outfitted with every possible convenience. This was no cargo or transport plane.

The commander came back to introduce himself and said he hoped I would enjoy the flight. I could only mumble my thanks; I was still overwhelmed. I knew that God had provided the plane to bring me back to Fort Benning on time, but why this huge luxury plane? Why hadn't he just picked a small, adequate plane?"

I felt very undeserving, and a quick thought that such a big plane was really a waste went through my head.

"What does it all mean, Lord?" I asked, bewildered.

"Only that I love you," came the concise answer. "I want to show you that this is how I want to provide for all my children who trust me."

"I am beginning to understand, Lord," I mused, joy welling up in me as the thoughts continued.

"I want you to tell everyone who will listen to be thankful for every detail of their lives, and I will open the windows of heaven and pour out more blessings than they can ever ask or hope for."

"Thank you, Lord," I chuckled in my seat.

"And remember," the voice continued in my mind, "you can never deserve my blessings. You cannot work for them or earn them. I give everything to you as a free gift, because of my own goodness, and you must learn to understand and accept that!"

Whenever I traveled on commercial planes, I landed ten miles from my office, but the huge four-engine plane landed at Fort Benning, within a few hundred yards of where I had an appointment. As I entered the building, I looked at my watch. I had arrived *exactly* on time. Not one minute early or one minute late.

God *does* provide for our needs, and He does it abundantly and free. All we have to do is ask. The very *first* free gift God wants His new children to ask for is the baptism in the Holy Spirit.

That's right. The baptism in the Holy Spirit is provided as a ''first feeding'' for newborn believers. They need it to grow.

The Holy Spirit comes to dwell in the new believer the moment He accepts Jesus Christ as his Savior. He is born of the Spirit. But Jesus also told His disciples that they would have to wait until they were *baptized* with the Holy Spirit before they could be His witnesses and spread the Good News with power and authority (Acts 1:5 & 8).

The disciples waited in Jerusalem, just as Jesus had told them, and on the day of Pentecost we read that there came the sound *like the roaring of a mighty windstorm in the skies above them and it filled the house where they were meeting. Then, what looked like flames or tongues of fire appeared and settled on their heads. And everyone present was filled with the Holy Spirit and began speaking in languages they didn't know, for the Holy spirit gave them this ability* (Acts 2:2-4).

This was the beginning of the Christian church. The timid disciples of Christ were now transformed into fearless, bold witnesses; they began immediately to preach the Good News with power and authority, and the same miracles that had followed Christ, followed them.

Jesus said, *Truly, truly I say to you, he who believes in me will also do the works that I do; and greater works than these will he do, because I go to the Father* (John 14:12 RSV).

New believers were added to the church by the thousands, and when we read the Book of Acts, we see that the baptism in the Holy Spirit usually followed immediately after their conversion. When Peter preached to the household of Cornelius in Acts 10:44, the Holy Spirit overwhelmed the listeners as soon as they accepted what Jesus had done for them - even before they received water baptism.

When the gospel was preached in Samaria, many Samaritans accepted Jesus as their Savior, and were baptized in water.

Peter and John were sent from Jerusalem, and *as soon as they arrived, they began praying for these new Christians to receive the Holy Spirit* (Acts 8:15).

Peter and John didn't tell the new Christians to wait awhile, or to study scriptures and pray and make themselves ready. The apostles from Jerusalem were concerned that the Spirit had not yet overwhelmed the new believers, and right away, *Peter and John laid their hands upon these believers, and they received the Holy Spirit* (Acts 8:17).

The baptism with the Holy Spirit had been promised to everyone who believed in Jesus Christ. Jesus said, *If anyone is thirsty, let him come to me and drink. For the Scriptures declare that rivers of living water shall flow from the inmost being of anyone who believes in me. He was speaking of the Holy Spirit, who would be given to everyone believing in him* (John 7:37-39).

The baptism in the Holy spirit is a free gift. It cannot be earned. Jesus, who provided our salvation, also provided the Holy Spirit.

I will ask the Father and He will give you another Comforter, and he will never leave you. He is the Holy Spirit, Jesus said...(John 14:16-17).

Jesus is the One who sends the Holy Spirit; He baptizes us in the Holy Spirit.

God spoke to John the Baptist when he was baptizing in the river Jordan. *When you see the Holy Spirit descending and resting upon someone - he is the one you are looking for. He is the one who baptizes with the Holy Spirit* (John 1:33).

Then why do so many Christians struggle so desperately to receive the baptism in the Holy Spirit? All over the country I've seen them, sad-faced and unhappy.

"What's wrong with me?" they say, "Am I just too worthless, too weak? I so desperately need the power of God in my life."

A Sunday-school teacher wrote:

> I need the power of the Holy Spirit in my
> life. I try so hard to become more obedient
> and Christlike. I thought maybe I wasn't
> reading enough in the Bible, and I've been
> getting up earlier to read for an hour and then
> pray for half and hour. But I still don't see
> any power in my life, and I haven't been able
> to receive the baptism in the Holy Spirit. I've
> confessed every sin I can think of. I've been
> a Christian for twenty years, but I am so sadly
> lacking in Christian virtues that I sometimes
> wonder if I'm even saved...

Such people are like little babies standing over in a
corner trying to stretch and grow so they can eat the
wonderful meal that's been prepared for them. They've got
miserable hunger pains, but they don't want to eat until
they've outgrown their pains.

Christians in the early church had the same problem.
They kept thinking they had to make themselves good
enough to receive God's free gifts.

Paul wrote:

*Oh, foolish Galatians! What magician has hypnotized
you and cast an evil spell upon you?...Let me ask you this one
question: Did you receive the Holy Spirit by trying to keep
the Jewish laws? Of course not, for the Holy Spirit came
upon you only after you heard about Christ and trusted Him
to save you. Then have you gone completely crazy? For if
trying to obey the Jewish laws never gave you spiritual life
in the first place, why do you think that trying to obey them
now will make you stronger Christians?* (Galations 3:1-3).

The Galations had already received the Holy Spirit as a
result of having trusted Jesus Christ to save them, but the
temptation to think of themselves as responsible for their
own Christian growth had caused them to turn from a life of
faith.

At all stages of our spiritual life we are tempted to take credit for our Christian growth. Satan tempts us in two obvious ways. He may whisper, "My, you're getting spiritual! Just try a little harder, and you'll have *more* power." Or he says, "Look how weak and miserable you are! No wonder God can't trust you with more of His blessings!"

You may praise yourself for your spiritual accomplishments, or criticize yourself for your failure - it amounts to the same thing. You are placing the responsibility for your worthiness on yourself instead of on God - where it belongs.

A minister had a weakness he couldn't control, no matter how hard he tried. Finally he ended up in prison convicted of forgery. The minister was a born-again Christian; he was crushed by his own failure, and sincerely repented of his sin. He was able to believe that God had forgiven him, but he was convinced that God could never again use him to preach the Good News.

One day a friend sent him *Prison to Praise*. There he read that God uses everything, even our mistakes, for our good. With new hope he dared to thank God for his own mistake and imprisonment. He wrote:

> Praise God, my life has changed completely. The old regrets, guilt, and remorse that held me bound are gone. I can praise and thank God for every detail of my life, just as it is. I never before understood the depth of God's mercy. I once thought of myself as 'good' enough to be used of Him. What a joy it is to die to my old prideful self so that Christ and nothing but Christ can live in me!

The minister's cell soon became a temple of praise, and other prisoners were drawn to accept Christ.

When we think of ourselves or others as good enough or not good enough to be used of God, we're falling into a

dangerous trap. Jesus warned us to not judge and criticize
and condemn others, so that we will not be judged and
criticized and condemned ourselves.

Only God is qualified to judge, and He has already
declared that we are holy and without a single fault in His
eyes when we are covered by His love.

How do we dare set up a standard to measure ourselves
and others by? Only God is qualified to deal with our sins.
However wrong we or others may be, that is a matter for God
to deal with.

When we do judge each other, we are often completely
wrong. We judge each other by our manner of dress, amount
of makeup, our smoking or drinking, what kind of movies we
go to.

How do you select a Sunday-school teacher? Imagine
two Christians side by side. One is of average height and
weight, and you know he smokes. The other weights at least
three hundred pounds; he's a mountain of a man, but he has
a kind smile and never forgets to bring his Bible to church.

Now which one of the two would you choose to teach
on the subject "How to develop self-discipline as a fruit of
the Holy Spirit"?

Smoking is a bad habit, harmful to our health, and it
speaks of a lack of self-discipline. And what about the
overweight man? The Bible ranks gluttony with
drunkenness and says that they both deserve the death
penalty! (Deuteronomy 21:20-21). The glutton is hastening
his own death, and so is the smoker.

I don't recommend that you start judging overweight
people and smokers. We have no right to judge either one.

When the woman caught in adultery was brought to
Jesus, the Jewish leaders and Pharisees asked Jesus,
*Teacher...Moses' law says to kill her. What about it?...Jesus
said, All right, hurl the stones at her until she dies. But only
he who never sinned may throw the first!* (John 8:4,5, & 7).

Who among us qualifies to pick up stones of criticism,

judging, or condemnation? Measuring our "goodness" or "badness" is just another way to try to justify our standing with God by our good works instead of by faith.

When we discuss "faith" and "works," someone usually quotes the verse, *For we are his workmanship, created in Christ Jesus unto good works, which God hath before ordained that we should walk in them* (Ephesians 2:10 KJV).

Now doesn't that state plainly that we are born again to do good works for God?

But look at the two verses before that one:

For by grace are ye saved through faith; and that not of yourselves: it is the gift of God: Not of works, lest any man should boast (Ephesians 2:8-9 KJV).

Does Paul mean that we're saved by faith, but from then on we're on our own? That doesn't make much sense, does it?

Earlier in the letter to the Ephesians Paul said that we've *been made* holy and without a single fault in God's eyes, and that we've been provided with every blessing in heaven.

So what does Paul mean? Maybe he's got a different idea of "works" from what we do.

James wrote, *What is the use (profit) my brethren, for any one to profess to have faith if he has no good works to show for it? ...Was not our forefather Abraham shown to be justified - made acceptable to God - by his works when he brought to the altar as an offering his own son Isaac?* (James 2:14,21 Amp).

Now what kind of good works was that - walking up a mountain, preparing to sacrifice his only son on the altar just because God told him to do it?

James went on to say, *Can't you see that his faith and his actions were, so to speak, partners - that his faith was implemented by his deed? That is what the scripture means when it says: And Abraham believed God, And it was reckoned unto him for righteousness; and he was called the friend of God* (James 2:22-23 Phillips).

So what kind of "good works" are we supposed to do? The disciples once asked Jesus the same question: *What are we to do that we may habitually be working the works of God? - What are we to do to carry out what God requires?*

Jesus replied, This is the work (service) that God asks of you, that you believe in the One Whom He has sent - that you cleave to, trust, rely on and have faith in His Messenger (John 6:28-29 *Amp*).

And that is exactly what Abraham did. Abraham's "good work" was that He trusted God to keep His promises. He never wavered in his faith. And so God chose to make Abraham the father of Israel.

Jesus promised His followers that they would do even greater works than He did, and we know that after receiving the baptism in the Holy Spirit, His followers preached with power and great miracles.

Their part of the great works was to *believe*. The power to perform miracles didn't belong to them, but came from God through them because they believed.

Paul wrote, *Now glory be to God who by his mighty power at work within us is able to do far more than we would ever dare to ask or even dream of - infinitely beyond our highest prayers, desires, thoughts, or hopes* (Ephesians 3:20).

It is God who does the work in us, and it makes sense that the more we trust in Him and the less we depend on ourselves, the more He is able to do.

So what exactly *is* the baptism in the Holy Spirit?

Jesus sometimes referred to the Holy Spirit as the Spirit of Truth. *When the Holy Spirit, who is truth, comes, he shall guide you into all truth*...(John 16:13).

The Holy Spirit of Truth lives in all believers and guides them, but to be baptized in the Spirit of Truth means a great deal more. The word we translate as "baptize" in our English Bible actually means to immerse or saturate, and in Greek the same word is used to describe "waterlogged."

So to ask Jesus to baptize us in the Holy Spirit means that we surrender ourselves to be saturated - waterlogged with His Holy Spirit.

The baptism in the Holy Spirit is a cleansing, purging, stripping experience; it is total exposure to the searchlight of God's Truth into every little corner of our lives. The baptism is designed to flush out and empty us of our self-reliance, our pride, our shady areas of deception, and the excuses we've been holding onto - all the things that block our faith and the inflow of God's power and presence in our lives.

The baptism in the Holy Spirit serves a twofold purpose: the purging and preparing of the vessel to contain God's power and then the *filling* with that power.

Jesus said, *But you shall receive power - ability,, efficiency and might - when the Holy Spirit has come upon you...*(Acts 1:8 Amp).

He didn't mean that the power would belong to us, but it would fill us, and operate through us. We are the containers, the vessels, the channels. However hard we try, we can't become the contents. We are like glasses containing living water. The water can quench men's thirst, but an empty glass can't satisfy anyone.

Paul wrote, *But this precious treasure - this light and power that now shine within us - is held in a perishable container, that is, in our weak bodies. Everyone can see that the glorious power within must be from God and is not our own* (II Corinthians 4:7).

To say that we don't need the baptism in the Holy Spirit is to say that we don't need to be cleansed, immersed in, and saturated by God's Truth, nor do we need the fullness of His power operating in and through us.

Jesus told His followers, *You men who are fathers - if your boy asks for bread, do you give him a stone? If he asks for fish, do you give him a snake? If he asks for an egg, do you give him a scorpion? Of course not! And if even sinful persons like yourselves give children what they need, don't you realize that your heavenly Father will do at least as much, and give the Holy Spirit to those who ask for Him?* (Luke 11:11-13).

So we can ask Jesus to baptize us in the Holy Spirit and *know* that He does it.

Every week I get letters from people who say they've pleaded with God to baptize them in the Holy Spirit, but nothing has happened. What's wrong? The trouble is they are looking at their own feelings instead of at God's fact. The stumbling block is *always* feelings.

The baptism in the Holy Spirit, like every one of God's gifts, must be received by *faith*. That means you may not *feel* anything when it happens. Faith is an act of our will, not a response to feelings.

Some people experience dramatic physical sensations when they are first baptized in the Holy Spirit, just as some people have a dramatic, emotional encounter with Jesus Christ when they first receive Him as their Savior. But we don't get saved by feeling, and we don't get baptized in the Holy Spirit by feeling either. Whatever outward sensations you may or may not feel when you're baptized in the Holy Spirit, the sensations are *not* the baptism. The baptism is an *inner* transformation.

As a *result* of this inner transformation, we are told in the Bible, there will be plenty of evidence to follow. Increased power and authority in witnessing for Christ, the operation of the gifts of the Holy Spirit through us, increasing fruit of the Spirit - the love, joy, peace. All these things we'll experience with our senses and emotions, but these evidences follow our acceptance of God's promises.

We must decide to accept God's Word on faith and deliberately turn away from paying attention to our feelings. If we don't, we will never be able to exercise our faith.

Tell God that you *will* take His Word for it. You *will* believe Jesus baptizes you when you ask Him to. Stand firm in your trust and believe it has happened.

One young man wrote me:

> I am planning to enter seminary next
> fall, but my Christian life lacks power. I meet
> with a group of Christians who've
> experienced the baptism in the Holy Spirit.
> They pray and speak in tongues, and there are
> healings and miracles happening. I'm
> convinced this is all valid according to the
> scriptures, and I've prayed to receive it, but
> for some reason or other it hasn't happened
> to me. I know that the gifts of the Holy Spirit
> aren't given for our personal enjoyment, but
> for the work God would have us do. Still,
> God hasn't trusted me with this experience.
> What is lacking? I believe in the Lord Jesus
> Christ as my Savior and want to serve Him
> with all my heart. I've told Him so, many
> times. I've confessed my sins, and I know
> I'm forgiven and cleansed. I want to serve
> Christ, and I need the baptism in the Holy
> Spirit to do so effectively. Why then, hasn't
> it happened? Have I done something wrong
> so that God doesn't hear my prayer?
>
> Yesterday I knelt in our prayer meeting
> and asked that I be allowed to receive the
> baptism in the Holy Spirit. Several placed
> their hands on me and prayed that I might
> receive. But I didn't feel a thing...Please pray
> for me.

The Baptism in the Holy Spirit is a personal experience
between you and the Lord. When you ask Jesus to baptize
you in the Holy Spirit - whether you are alone or someone
prays for you with the laying on of hands - Jesus will baptize
you. Many people receive the Baptism in the Holy Spirit
while alone in prayer. However, our faith is often
strengthened when we have other people praying for us.

You may not feel anything, but there is one tangible consequence you can claim right away and experience the result. The gift of tongues was recorded as a consequence of the baptism in the Holy Spirit in the Book of Acts. It was the *first* operation of a spiritual gift in the newly baptized believers.

When I asked Jesus to baptize me with the Holy Spirit, I didn't feel a thing. A lady laid hands on me and prayed for me in tongues, but I felt no physical sensation then, and thought that nothing had happened. The lady told me to accept the baptism on faith, not to depend on my feelings, and to thank God that it was already done. So, I did, but felt a little ridiculous. Then the lady told me I could speak with tongues if I just opened my mouth and let the language pour out. I hesitated and thought that now I was really making a fool of myself. But I knew that the Bible said speaking in tongues *was* a gift of the Holy Spirit and - whether I could feel it or not - I could expect the Holy Spirit to operate in and through me. I did notice some strange "words" forming in my mind, and I opened my mouth and said them out loud. They sounded silly, and my instant reaction was to think, *You're faking it Merlin; you're just making up a bunch of gibberish.* Then I realized that speaking in *faith* meant I couldn't rely on my own senses to measure the results. I decided to accept God's word for it and not pay attention to what I thought.

Up to this point, I had still *felt* nothing, but I had made up my mind to *believe.* Later, I experienced an overwhelming awareness that Jesus Christ was my Savior and Lord. I knew from the Word of God that the Holy Spirit had been sent to witness about Jesus, and I was suddenly convinced more than ever before of Who Jesus was and what He meant to me. The second experience I had was a strong love for people. That, too, was foretold in God's Word. Love is a fruit of the Holy Spirit.

Since then I've experienced the operation of other gifts of the Holy Spirit in and through me as well. I haven't been given the ability to heal or to perform miracles or to prophesy. I only *believe* that God operates through me in the power of the Holy Spirit when I step out on faith, expecting Him to do so.

When someone is healed after I have laid hands on him and prayed, it is not because I've become extra spiritual. I'm just the channel. When I pray, I sometimes feel the presence of God's healing power and other times I feel absolutely nothing.

The results never depend on our feelings, only on our faith, that is, our deliberate choice to believe that God is at work.

When you open your mouth and begin to speak in tongues by faith, you will probably be tempted to think just as I did, that you are faking it and making up the words. Don't let that thought fool you into giving up the practice.

If you have sincerely committed yourself and your tongue to God, asking that the Holy Spirit give you the words to pray, then you can trust that He is doing just that, whether the words sound like made-up nonsense to your ears or not. It isn't really the words that matter anyway, but the fact that the Holy Spirit is praying through us directly to God.

But why pray at all - in tongues or in our native language - if God knows what we need before we even ask Him?

We pray, because this is God's plan for His children, and His explicit command to us as well.

Pray without ceasing (I Thessalonians 5:17 KJV).

It is very important that we take time to pray in tongues daily. Just think for a moment what we're actually doing. The Holy Spirit of Truth is speaking through us.

Jesus promised that *rivers of living water shall flow from the inmost being of anyone who believes in me* (John 7:38).

He was speaking of the rivers of truth flowing from our innermost being when we have been immersed in and saturated by the Holy Spirit of Truth.

We often think only of the truth that will flow out to others, but think now what the truth first must do in us. Truth is the power that sets our bound-up spirits free. It exposes every hidden lie, all guilt and fear, each dark area of our past lurking in the back of our memories, way back in our subconscious. We couldn't even begin to talk to God about those things *with our understanding*. And this is one of the reasons *God devised* this new dimension in prayer.

When we speak in tongues, we communicate directly from our spirit to God. The Holy Spirit prays *for us*, and we bypass the control-center of our own critical understanding. We speak words we don't understand, but the Holy Spirit of Truth searches out the deep areas of our beings. That's what gives speaking in tongues such great healing power in our lives. Later we'll discover that when we pray in tongues for others, we pray directly for needs that we don't know anything about with our understanding, and often the people we pray for have no idea what the root of their problem is either.

A housewife had suffered with serious mental and emotional problems. In her early teens she had accepted Christ as her Savior, but she did not experience a release from the deep tensions that plagued her. She studied what the Bible had to say about the baptism in the Holy Spirit and became convinced God wanted her to experience it.

One day she knelt in her living room and prayed, "I surrender all of me to you, Jesus. Cleanse me of everything that isn't of you, and baptize me in your Holy Spirit. I thank you, and I believe it has been done."

She felt no sensation of any kind and got up from her knees to continue with her housework, but over the next three weeks, something unusual seemed to be going on inside her. Weeping almost continuously, it was as if she was reliving again the early years of her unhappy childhood. Long-forgotten incidents came back to her memory, things others had done to leave scars of hurt and fear, and things she had done to hurt others. With each memory came a surge of tears, and she found herself asking God to forgive her and those who had hurt her and to heal the memories with His love.

She could think of only one explanation for all her tears, the verse in her Bible which read, *And in the same way - by our faith - the Holy Spirit helps us with our daily problems and in our praying. For we don't even know what we should pray for, nor how to pray as we should; but the Holy Spirit prays for us with such feeling and pleads in our behalf with unspeakable yearnings and groanings too deep for utterance* (Romans 8:26 TLB and Amp).

In between the crying sessions, she felt increasingly at ease. Then came one evening at the end of the third week when she cried and cried as if her heart was breaking.

"I felt as if the convulsions of tears were coming from the very pit of my being," she recalled. "Then suddenly it eased off, as if a storm had gone away, leaving behind a beautiful calm. Resting in that peace, I suddenly became aware of a light flowing gently over me. It could be felt more than seen, and I knew it was the love of God, surrounding me, holding me...."

Many of her tensions were gone - but not all. Over the next few days she felt lighter in heart than ever before, and she sang to herself as she did her housework or drove to town on errands. Over and over she sang a simple chorus she had taught her children. "Oh how I love Jesus, oh, how I love Jesus..." The song had suddenly taken on a new and happier meaning.

One afternoon she was driving downtown and realized that she was putting make-believe words to the tune she was singing.

"I didn't know what was happening," she said later. "I hadn't really paid much attention to what the Bible had to say about speaking in tongues, but there I was singing in a new language and I suddenly realized it wasn't 'make believe,' but it had something to do with being baptized in the Holy Spirit."

She continued singing in tongues every day, and as the weeks and months passed, her old tension and emotional distress vanished.

"The psychiatrist had told me that I would just have to accept myself as an emotional cripple," she said, "but praise God, Jesus healed me. I sang my way to wholeness - in tongues!"

If you have prayed to be baptized in the Holy Spirit, you can take God's Word for it, it is done. You may open your mouth right now and speak whatever words or sounds happen to come to your mind, trusting that it is the Holy Spirit who is placing them in your mind.

God will not force you to speak in tongues. With the baptism in the Holy Spirit, He has given you the ability - but only if you choose to do so. You use your mouth, your tongue, and your vocal cords, and you can begin speaking and stop speaking at will. If you feel no emotion or sensation of any kind, praise God *for* your lack of feeling. One day you *will* feel, but in the meantime He is giving you a wonderful opportunity to grow in faith.

In your Bible, read everything Jesus had to say about the Holy Spirit; read the Book of Acts and the letters to the young churches concerning the Holy Spirit, the gifts of the Spirit, and the fruit of the Spirit. All of this applies to you now.

Expect these things to happen in your own life. Tell God you are willing to be used as a channel of His love to others, and be ready to step out in faith when God provides the opportunities.

Praise God in all your circumstances, whether they seem good or bad to you; trust that God is using them to unfold His wonderful plan for your life.

Chapter 4

Count it All Joy!

Dear brothers, is your life full of difficulties and temptations? Then be happy, for when the way is rough, your patience has a chance to grow. So let it grow, and don't try to squirm out of your problems. For when your patience is finally in full bloom, then you will be ready for anything, strong in character, full and complete (James 1:2-4).

God has a very special plan for your life. It began long ago when He first created you. He formed you lovingly, carefully, exactly to His specifications, every detail just as He wanted it - your looks, your abilities, your place of birth, the family you were to be born into (or the lack of it). Nothing about you or your life has been accidental. In love he reached out and drew you to Himself through circumstances He had arranged just for that purpose. You were given a new birth, new life through His Holy Spirit when you accepted His Son, Jesus Christ, as your Savior, and were baptized, saturated with the Holy Spirit. And now God's plan is to make you full and complete!

For because of our faith, he has brought us into this place of highest privilege where we now stand, and we confidently and joyfully look forward to actually becoming all that God has had in mind for us to be (Romans 5:2).

God wants us to *become* something.

Why of course, we all know that! God wants us to become more loving, more kind, more patient, have more faith, peace, gentleness, kindness, humility, and self-discipline, so that we can be His witnesses wherever we are! Isn't that true?

Sure it is, but most of us think that means we have to embark on a rigorous program of self-improvement, trying to make ourselves more loving, kind, patient, humble, gentle, and disciplined. And the harder we try, the more frustrated we become.

God has to do the changing. He wants us to commit ourselves to Him and trust that He will transform us.

With eyes wide open to the mercies of God, I beg you, my brothers, as an act of intelligent worship, to give Him your bodies, as a living sacrifice, consecrated to Him, and acceptable by Him. Don't let the world around you squeeze you into its own mold, but let God remold your minds from within, so that you may prove in practice that the plan of God for you is good, meets all His demands and moves toward the goal of true maturity (Romans 12:1-2 Phillips).

How does God bring about the changes in us? *How* does He break the old habit-patterns of thought and action we've lived with for years? These are characteristics we've called "personality-traits," or "personal likes and dislikes," or "preferences," or "strong opinions." On closer examination, under the scrutiny of God's Holy Spirit of Truth, they are seen to be part of the self-centered, defensive, selfish behavior that for years has separated us from the love of God and the love of others.

What methods does God use to change us?

At present you are temporarily harassed by all kinds of trials and temptations. This is no accident - it happens to prove your faith, which is infinitely more valuable than gold...(which) must be purified by fire. This proving of your faith is planned to result in praise and honor and glory in the day when Jesus Christ reveals Himself (I Peter 1:6-7 Phillips).

So that is how our faith grows! And we read earlier how patience, endurance, and steadfastness grow when our life is full of difficulties, temptations, and problems.

I've heard some people say, "If that's the only way to get more patience and faith, I think I'd just as soon live with a little less of it!"

If that's the way you think, it is because you don't really trust God. Deep down you have doubts about His plan and His love for you.

When God showed His prophet Jeremiah that he would have to go with the Jews into Babylonian captivity for a lifetime, God also said, *For I know the plans I have for you, says the Lord. They are plans for good and not for evil, to give you a future and a hope* (Jeremiah 29:11).

The years of suffering in Babylon were part of God's plan for Jeremiah and the Jews. It was a good plan - God's plan - designed to give them a future and a hope.

God's plan for you and for me is a good plan. Can you take His Word for that?

Why can't our faith grow in pleasant, easy circumstances? It can, and as we come to trust and rely more and more on God's promises, it does. But the purifying, the testing of our faith, comes through circumstances that are a challenge to our determination to believe, trust, and rely on God's word, *in spite of* what our senses tell us. For too long we've trusted our senses, our emotions, and our intellect to dictate our beliefs. We must break that habit in order to exercise faith. Remember, faith means a deliberate determination to believe something we can't see or feel the evidence of.

So if God tells us He's working everything out for our good, and we see everything go wrong, our faith grows when we stand on God's word and thank Him for everything that happens.

How do you think Abraham's faith grew?

Would you have faith to walk up on a mountain with your only son, prepared to sacrifice him on the altar at God's command, and still believe that God was going to bless and multiply your decedents through that same son?

If you had been a friend of Abraham, and watched his crazy venture in faith, could you have praised God, believing that even if Abraham was making a mistake, God would still work it out for his good?

God alone can remake us, remold us from within. Our part is to follow Paul's advice to the Romans; to submit ourselves fully to Him, believe that He has taken over, and then accept eagerly and joyfully - with thanksgiving and praise - all the circumstances God uses to bring about his transformation of our lives.

There is the classic story of the pastor who prayed for more patience, and discovered the next day that his longtime efficient secretary had become ill. In her place was a volunteer who turned out to be the slowest office-worker the pastor had ever seen. He fussed and fumed in secret for a while, until he finally realized that the new secretary was an answer to his prayer. How else could he learn more patience? He began to thank and praise God for His choice of secretary and for the opportunity to grow in patience.

Faith and patience are essential characteristics of a Christian life and witness; yet there is another quality we must also have or else we've missed the point of the Good News.

Let love be your greatest aim, Paul wrote to the Corinthians (I Corinthians 14:1).

Your strong love for each other will prove to the world that you are my disciples, said Jesus, (John 13:35).

...that your joy...may be full, Jesus said, *this is my commandment, that you love one another just as I have loved you* (John 15:12, Amp).

Love...love...love...As Christians we talk a great deal about it. **God is love, Jesus loves you, I love you**. But sometimes we fall woefully short of really loving one another.

Jesus said, *I demand that you love each other as much as I love you* (John 15:12).

Love means more to us than anything else in the world. We were created to love God and to love one another. When we don't love, fearful things happen in us. We become hurt, resentful, afraid of each other, hateful, and guilt-ridden.

Our wounded emotions, our fears and frustrations, our defense mechanisms, our destructive ways - all come about from lack of love.

Educators, psychologists, sociologists, and all kinds of experts have told us what a difference love makes in the development of human beings.

A love that accepts, approves of, and believes in others, is patient and kind, never selfish or envious, never proud or seeking its own reward or way, not touchy or irritable. It doesn't hold grudges, and doesn't pay attention when it must suffer wrong. A love that is loyal, that believes the best and expects the best, is never glad when someone suffers wrong, but is always happy when truth wins out. Such a love endures without weakening in all circumstances.

This is the kind of love God has for us, and the kind of love He commands that we have for each other. This is the kind of love that heals the wounds of old hurts, casts out fears, melts away resentments and old grudges. This is the kind of love that makes us whole and able to love in return without fear of being rejected or hurt.

This is the love the Greeks called *agape*, a deliberate, reasoning, intentional, spiritual devotion. This is the love that is a fruit of the Holy Spirit, and when it is fully grown, it draws others to its source - God's love for us in Christ Jesus.

Every one of the gifts and manifestations of the Holy Spirit is given specifically to show God's love and concern for our every need. God heals because He loves us; He performs miracles because He loves us. God *is* love. His power reaching out through us is love - a supernatural, divine, intensely personal love for each individual in His creation.

His message to the world is one of love, and we are to be His messengers, the channels for His love. In order to accomplish this, His plan is to make *us* loving too.

If this kind of love can come only from God, if it is a fruit of the Holy Spirit, how can Jesus command us to love?

Mustn't we wait till He makes us more loving? Again we are faced with a promise in God's word that we must accept on faith.

Love is a fruit of the Spirit, and God's word says that the Holy Spirit dwells in us, therefore we can expect love to be present in our life. We have been given the ability to love, but we must step out in faith and choose to practice it.

Remember, *agape* is a deliberate, intentional love. We are told to love each other, even if we don't *feel* loving.

When we step out in faith, choosing to act on God's word, what happens then? We know that our step of faith releases God's supernatural power of love, and this power begins to transform us, *making* us more loving, while the power also flows through us to the person we've deliberately *willed* to love.

How does this actually work in practice?

I had prayed for God to make me more loving, and had come to think of myself as a rather loving sort of person. In fact, as I traveled and ministered to thousands of people all of whom seemed to be blessed, I rejoiced that I was able to feel more love for others all the time.

Then one day I was faced with an individual so miserable and repulsive that I cringed at the sight and realized to my horror that I felt no love for this creature, but only wished that she would disappear as soon as possible.

She was a girl who had been brought to my office with her soldier boyfriend. Her face was caked with old makeup and dirt, her hair hung like strands of wire, and her clothes were filthy and torn. Her legs were scarred and smeared with dirt, and the odor from her body filled the room. The expression on her face was sullen and hateful, and her eyes were swollen from crying.

This poor creature had come to Fort Benning to tell the soldier that she was expecting his baby. The boy admitted that he was responsible for her condition, but had flatly refused to marry her. The girl had flown into a rage and threatened to kill him and then herself. She had already had another baby out of wedlock, and this time she was determined to either get married or die.

I looked at her and thought I had never seen anyone so unlovable, so desperate, so frightened, and so lonely. Yet, the very thought of praying for her was offensive to me. I didn't want to touch her.

"Lord," I cried inwardly, "why did you bring her to me?"

"She's one of my children," came the answer. "She is lost and in need of my love and healing. I brought her here for you to love her and tell her of my love."

The painful realization hit me suddenly. I had congratulated myself on being able to love, yet now I cringed at the sight of one who desperately needed to be loved.

"O Lord," I cried inside, "forgive me, and thank you for showing me just how shallow and selfish my love is. Take my unlovingness and fill me with your love for her."

The girl was sobbing and her eyes looked dull behind the swollen lids smeared with mascara.

"Please, Sir," she said, "do something!"

"Do you believe in God?"

She nodded and whispered, "Yes, I do."

"Do you believe He can help you?"

She hesitated, then spoke slowly. "I know He *can* help me, but I don't think He'd want to. I used to be a Christian, but look at me now. Even if He wanted to help me, what could He do to get me out of this mess?"

"God *can* help you, and He *wants* to," I said with an assurance I didn't yet feel.

She shook her head and her shoulders sagged in utter hopelessness.

"Please," I said, "Try to understand that God loves you. He will fill you with His joy and peace and meet your every need before you leave my office today."

The girl stared, open-mouthed, and the soldier looked as if he thought I was going to force him to marry the girl.

"God has brought you here today," I continued. "He has permitted all these troubles in your life just so you could understand how much He loves you. He has a wonderful plan for your life, and if you begin to trust Him and thank Him for everything that has happened to you, you will discover that God is helping you right now."

"Thank Him for this?" Her eyes blazed in sudden anger again. "All I want is for this man to marry me so my child will have a name."

"Look at this." I showed her the underlined verse in my open Bible. *In everything give thanks, for this is the will of God in Christ Jesus concerning you* (I Thessalonians 5:18 KJV). I turned the pages to Romans 8:28. *All things work together for good to them that love God....*

Her eyes stared in blank mistrust, and I suddenly realized how futile it was to speak to this wounded creature about God's love or any kind of love. She didn't know the meaning of the word. Only God could light the spark of understanding in her mind.

"May I pray for you?"

She nodded dully. "Sure, why not?"

I moved to place my hand on her head, and as I looked down I saw just how dirty and in need of a scrubbing she was. A twinge of revulsion made me shudder.

"Oh, Lord," I whispered, "how endless your love is for us - so much greater than the little love we are capable of on our own. Please, God, let your love touch her now, and teach me to love her."

Then I placed my hand firmly on her head and began to pray out loud.

"God, I know it is your will that we praise you in everything. Nothing in this world can happen without your permission. This dear child of yours has been hurt. She feels bruised, forsaken, and unloved by man, but I know you love her. Thank you for all that has brought her to this day in her life. Help her, Lord. I believe you are helping her to see your love and to praise you right now...."

I felt the girl begin to tremble under my hand. God was touching her with His love.

"Can you thank God for everything now?"

"Oh, yes," she burst out. "I thank you, God. I really do thank you for everything."

I continued to pray. "God, I believe you are healing her broken spirit. You are putting new life into her; you are giving her joy in the place of sorrow, victory in the place of defeat."

When I stepped back, her face shone with tears.

"What happened?" she exclaimed. "I feel so different! I'm not all churned up inside anymore; it's so quiet in me. I've never felt like this before, I'm happy; I really am!" Her eyes were wide with surprise. "What did it?"

"God has done it because we believed Him and praised Him," I said, suddenly realizing that something equally miraculous had happened in me. I stared at the girl, and she looked like a different person. I wanted to put my arms around her. She seemed so beautiful, so clean, so holy!

"Thank you, Lord." I felt my spirit soaring upward. "I *love* that girl. Thank you for changing *me*, Lord."

I could never have made myself more loving by trying to change my attitude toward the girl. God had to do the changing. My part was to admit and confess my own lack of love, then submit in faith to God's transforming power.

The harder we try to change ourselves, the more frustrated we become, and the more guilty we feel about our own shortcomings.

God brings certain people into our lives just to show us how incapable we are of loving others in our own strength. He doesn't do it to make us feel bad; He does it to give us an opportunity to experience His transforming love in our life and in the lives of the people He has called us to love.

Do you thank Him for the people in your life who are difficult to love? Do you have a cranky neighbor? A difficult boss? Praise God for them, because He loves you and wants to make your joy full, by making it possible for you to love them. He loves them too, and wants to use you as a channel for His love to them.

I think perhaps the most wonderful and most challenging opportunities to love come in our own homes, right where we live. Does your husband or wife have certain qualities that rub you the wrong way? Are your parents difficult to live with? Your children rebellious?

Love one another, Jesus said. Accept one another; thank God for one another.

It isn't easy to thank God for an alcoholic husband or for an indifferent, rebellious child. It isn't easy to love someone who says he doesn't want our love.

It isn't easy to admit that beam in our eye, the self-righteousness, the self-pity, the role we've played as a long-suffering martyr. Can we thank God for bringing these people into our lives to show us the beam in our eye?

Can we thank God for them, just as they are, and especially for the things that make them hard to love? Can we confess our inability to love them *for* their irritating habits? Can we tell God we *want* to love them and then submit ourselves to Him to be remolded, so that we *can* love them, according to His will for us?

Then we can confidently expect God to work a miracle in us. It may happen instantaneously; we *may* feel a wonderful spark of love, and of course we rejoice and praise the Lord for that. But watch out and don't become dependent on feelings. That first spark may die down, and we may sit around waiting for a second touch without doing anything in the meantime.

To love, deliberately and intentionally as Christ loves us, always requires the setting of our will. Whether or not we *feel* any love doesn't change the fact that we *do* love. God will show us practical and specific ways to communicate that love to the person He has placed in our life, and soon we will experience a deeper love than any we've ever felt before. Our love will be stable and consistent, because **it flows from**

a source beyond our own limited resources. It is God's love filling us to overflowing, spilling over to others through us. This is what it means to be rooted in God's love; and in that fertile soil, our own ability to love will grow and grow.

That is how the Holy Spirit bears fruit in our lives.

A Christian woman had been married to an alcoholic for many years until finally he got into trouble with the law and ended up in prison. The wife had struggled to raise their children on the meager welfare allowance they received from the state. Faithfully she had brought them to church and enjoyed the sympathy and respect of her community.

"Poor Edna," her friends would say. "She's raised those kids alone, never missed a Sunday in church, and never a word of complaint. While that good-for-nothing husband of hers never has been able to hold down a job, lying drunk most of the time to the disgrace and shame of his fine family...."

While her husband was in prison, Edna felt justified in getting a divorce. Now at last, she would be free to raise her children in a better environment.

One day a friend brought her a copy of *Prison to Praise*. It seemed an almost impossible task to thank God for all the years of misery she had suffered, but she read how praise had changed the lives of others, and she decided to try it.

"Thank you for Al and his drinking," she prayed. "Thank you for the years of poverty and fear and loneliness."

Soon she heard that her former husband had been released from prison and had gone back to his old drinking habits. Still she continued to thank God for her circumstances.

Slowly she became aware of some things in her own life that she had never seen before. As she continued to thank God for her ex-husband, asking God to help her love him and accept him just as he was, she began to realize that for years she'd been guilty of a sin that was equally as serious as his drinking.

She'd been looking at the speck in her husband's eye and been totally unaware of the beam in her own. She had judged him for his drinking, feeling self-righteous and worthier than he was, and at the same time she'd lived each day steeped in self-pity, depression, and joyless martyrdom.

"Oh, Lord," she finally cried out one day, "I see that my sin has been just as evil as Al's. You gave us the commandments to love one another and to rejoice in our trials, and I haven't obeyed either one. Forgive me, Lord, and thank you for putting Al in my life so I could see myself. Now make it up to him. Heal the hurts he's suffered, and touch him with your love."

From that day on, Edna found it easy to rejoice in her circumstances. She *knew* God had brought them about as a part of His plan to fill her life with love and joy. As she continued to praise Him, all the old feelings of self-pity and depression rolled away; each day became a new, joyous experience, and she was aware of the presence of Jesus Christ in a new, exciting way.

Before long her former husband stumbled into a church service, accepted Christ as his Savior, and was completely healed of the alcoholism which had held him bound for fifteen years. Edna and Al remarried, and Al enrolled in college to start a brand-new life of serving God.

A difficult relationship or a trying set of circumstances may be God's loving way of providing us with an opportunity to grow, to exercise our spiritual muscle or it may be His loving way of exposing a particular weakness or sin in us.

Whatever the reason, we have grounds to rejoice. Any weakness, however well hidden, is like a crack in the foundation of a building.

Therefore this iniquity and guilt shall be to you as a broken section of a high wall, bulging out and ready at some distant day to fall, whose crash will then come suddenly and swiftly, in an instant (Isaiah 30:13 Amp).

Sooner or later, a crack in the foundation will cause the entire building to fall down. The cracks we are aware of, we can do something about. We can confess all our known sins and weaknesses and be assured that once they are confessed, they are also forgiven, and God's love covers and heals the scars and the memories. But what about the hidden cracks, the hidden sins that come to the surface only as a vague sense of restlessness, insecurity, confusion, resentment, or any number of such symptoms we all know from experience?

The particular iniquity Isaiah was referring to in the verse above was the Israelites' repeated refusal to act on God's Word; instead, they sought the counsel of their own seers and human advisers. They preferred to rely on themselves instead of on God.

Self-reliance and self-assurance are always serious cracks in our foundation. If God brings us into circumstances that reveal an area in our lives where we've been relying on ourselves, shouldn't we thank Him for our helplessness and rejoice in the power He can give us?

A young man in officer's training at Fort Benning, Georgia, found himself in circumstances he couldn't cope with.

"I need help, or I'll go out of my mind," he told me.

He had always been sure he could face every circumstance in life with success. His self-assurance bordered on cockiness. But since coming to Officers Candidate School, he had found himself unable to function as before, and his self-image and entire outlook on life was shattered.

The rigorous training for officer candidates is designed not only to teach the young men their duties as army officers, but is also meant to expose any weakness in the candidate that might endanger the lives of his men in combat. A certain stress is deliberately put on the candidates to test what "stuff" they are made of; if any are going to crack under pressure, it is better to find out before they are put in charge of troops.

The instructors had sensed that this particular candidate was unsure of himself under the mask of self-sufficiency he wore. The pressure had been put on. From early morning until late at night he was under surveillance. Every move he made was criticized.

"Can't you move faster, candidate?"

"Are you too dumb to follow instructions?"

"Do you always eat like a pig?"

"Don't you have any backbone?"

"Do you want your mother to help you?"

"Run around the building once more, candidate - maybe you'll learn to pick up your feet!"

The confidence the candidate had felt in himself was rapidly diminishing. Humiliated and helpless, he was at his wit's end, ready to desert the army and leave the country if necessary to get away from his persecutors.

As we talked, he told me that he'd never really believed in God, and the Bible had never made much sense to him. But if there was a God who could help him, he wanted to believe.

I shared with him what the Bible had to say about his circumstances: that God had a perfect plan for his life, that the trials he was going through were part of that plan, and that God would relieve the tension and stress if he would only turn over the reins of his life to Him and thank Him for everything.

The candidate looked drawn; his face and eyes showed the strain and lack of sleep.

"I've never been in this kind of spot before," He shook his head. "I'm at the end of my rope, and now you're telling me that God placed me in this predicament?"

"Let's say that God allowed it to happen," I said. I'm sure He would rather have had you turn to Him and accept His provisions for your life without having to go through all this suffering. But since you kept insisting you could handle your life without help, God chose the most direct, most loving way to show you that you need Him."

I turned to Paul's second letter to the Corinthians and read, *We would like you, our brothers, to know something of what we went through in Asia. At that time we were completely overwhelmed; the burden was more than we could bear; in fact we told ourselves that this was the end. Yet we believe now that we had this experience of coming to the end of our tether that we might learn to trust, not in ourselves, but in God* (II Corinthians 1:8-9 Phillips).

The candidate looked thoughtful, and agreed to let me pray for him, although he wasn't at all sure it would do any good.

I placed my hand on his head and began to praise God for the situation, asking God to give the young candidate a new understanding of His love and concern for every detail of his life. As I prayed, he began to tremble; then tears began to flow. After a while he began to laugh out loud.

"Praise you, God," he cried. "Thank you, God; I see you care; I believe you love me."

He turned to me, his face beaming.

"God really did bring me to officer candidate school, didn't He?" he said. "He knew this is where I'd find the answer. I feel like a new person."

And indeed he was. He accepted Christ as his Savior and went on to complete OCS with excellent standing.

The crisis point in his life had revealed a serious crack in his foundation. When he could acknowledge and thank God for His hand in the circumstances, the crack was healed.

Circumstances that rip out the walls of our own self-sufficiency are God's blessings in disguise. We can truly thank God for them and praise Him for every blow that removes more of the illusion that we have the ability to handle our own situation. The more we praise Him, the easier the transition will be. Our joy will increase, and the pain will hardly be noticeable. We'll also discover that the more trying the circumstances, the more we will realize that the real strength and power is Christ dwelling and growing in us.

Each challenge, each trial or opportunity for growth makes us better equipped to be channels for His love and power.

A young girl was faced with a series of tragedies. Her mother and two of her brothers died. Her father remarried, divorced, and remarried again. The girl was failing in college, and drinking heavily. Then she heard about Jesus and accepted Him as her Savior. For a time she was filled with joy, and as she shared her story, others came to know Jesus Christ. Her life was going smoothly, and she thought all the hard times were over.

Then the troubles began to pile up. She was in two automobile accidents and was injured in both of them. Next, a tumor appeared on her neck and had to be removed by a painful operation. One day she drank a coke and became seriously ill - the coke had been spiked with drugs. On her way to school she was badly frightened by an attacker with a knife; another day a man came after her with a gun. Prowlers came to her house at night; one of them broke in and raped her. At last she was fired from her part-time job because her boss was certain that she must be doing something wrong to get herself into all that trouble.

Through it all the girl struggled to hold onto her faith. The hardest burden to bear was the mistrust and suspicion of the church people she knew.

Then someone placed a copy of *Prison to Praise* in her hand. She read it and caught new hope. Perhaps God had a reason for permitting all the trouble she was going through. She began thanking Him for each calamity that had come into her life, and as she did, joy replaced the fear that had been gripping her.

"I suddenly realized that God is all I have," she told me. "Other people may have security. I have only Him, and everything that has happened has made me see this more clearly."

This young lady now goes about with a new, radiant

power to witness for her Savior. She has a deepened understanding and compassion for others who suffer as she has.

She has learned to trust that all the circumstances of her life are controlled by God's loving hand, and she can look at every new trial and say, "I know that God allowed it, so it must be for my good."

Another young woman lost her husband suddenly. They had no children, and she felt indescribably lonely. When she went to seek comfort and sympathy from her own family, they refused to speak to her, and behaved as if she didn't exist.

She couldn't understand this total rejection. Her family had never treated her like this before, and the anguish of being alone and unwanted was more than she could bear. Her body was in pain, she was unable to sleep, and she began to lose weight rapidly.

Day and night she cried alone in her house, until she began to lose track of time. She realized that her mind was slipping.

In despair she cried out, "God, are you there? Do you care about me?" She heard no answer and found no relief.

Then one day she saw *Prison to Praise* in a local bookstore. She read on the back cover that the author was an army chaplain and put the book back on the counter. He husband had been in the army when he died, and she was afraid of a fresh flood of memories. She went home empty-handed, but the title of the little book stayed in her mind all day, and one thought persisted: *Read it! Read it!*

She'd never felt such an urge to read anything before, and puzzled by the sense of urgency, she went back to the bookstore and purchased the little volume.

At home she began to read, and soon her tears stated flowing. At times she cried so hard she couldn't see to read, and at one point she realized that she had sunk to her knees on the floor and was still reading on.

She was certain that God was speaking directly to her through the book, yet the message was an incredible one. Was He actually telling her to thank Him that her husband was dead? How could God be so cruel? Everything in her seemed to rebel against the idea. Yet, as she read on, her sobs became more quiet and a new peace entered her heart. Slowly her thoughts began to take a new turn.

God has been in everything to help me she thought. *He knew that with my husband alive I would never have sought for Him! If my family had comforted me with kindness and love, I would have clung to them. Now I'm completely alone, and I'm coming to God. Oh Jesus, I feel your presence! You are here with me, and I praise and thank you, God for everything that brought me to you!*

The peace she felt in her heart was greater than anything she'd ever known before, and for the next several days her life radiated with a joy that completely astounded her friends and neighbors who had watched with growing concern how she had been broken down by grief.

Soon her brother came to see her with a tearful confession: "Can you forgive us?" he said. "There's been a terrible misunderstanding. Someone told us that you had told your neighbor that we had refused to give you any help when your husband was dying. We were foolish enough to believe them and felt so shocked and hurt that we didn't want to see you or talk to you." The brother was overcome with shame. "Today we learned that those people had been talking about another widow! And to think that we left you alone when you needed us the most."

"Don't be sorry," the young widow cheerfully replied. "Be thankful you made the mistake!"

"What do you mean, Sis?" The brother was not sure he'd heard right. "I let you down when you really needed me; do you want me to be thankful for that?"

"That's right," she laughed, "If you hadn't turned your back on me, I wouldn't have discovered just how much God loves me!"

This story is not meant to give an excuse for listening to gossip or for ignoring people who need our love. But God wants us to understand that when we trust our lives to Him, we can be sure that no one can treat us unfairly unless God allows it for our good. We can thank Him for every unkind word or sneaky, underhanded back-stabbing that comes our way.

God will bless you for this, if you endure the pain of undeserved suffering because you are conscious of his will. For what credit is there in enduring the beatings you deserve for having done wrong? But if you endure suffering even when you have done right, God will bless you for it (I Peter 2:19-20 Good News for Modern Man).

A rosebush must be pruned to bear perfect roses. Jesus said, *I am the true Vine, and my Father is the Gardener. He lops off every branch that doesn't produce. And he prunes those branches that bear fruit for even larger crops. He has already tended you by pruning you back for greater strength and usefulness by means of the commands I gave you* (John 15:1-3).

These are the commands Jesus gave: *Love the Lord your God with all your heart, soul, and mind. This is the first and greatest commandment. The second most important is similar: Love your neighbor as much as you love yourself* (Matthew 22:37-39).

The love Jesus spoke of was a deliberate love, one that required the setting of our will to love, a love exercised in faith. Jesus described the nature of this love when He said, *Love one another as I have loved you* (John 15:12 RSV).

Anything in us that prevents us from obeying His command must be pruned away. We're only hindering His work in us if we balk and complain about the painful pruning circumstances. These things don't come to us by accident or fate. They come because our loving Father is our loving Gardener. We can rejoice and thank Him, because He knows what is best for us.

A Christian officer candidate at Fort Benning received word that his wife had been committed to a mental hospital after a severe breakdown. The doctors gave a poor prognosis for her recovery and said that she would have to be in the hospital for an indefinite time.

When John came into my office, he could not speak at first. I watched his tall frame shake with sobs as tears coursed down his grief-lined face.

"Why, oh, why did this happen?" He fought to utter the words. "My wife and I have tried to live good Christian lives; why has God deserted us now?"

"God hasn't deserted you," I said. "He has a real purpose in letting your wife go to the hospital. Why don't we kneel and thank Him for it?"

John stared at me. "Sir, I'm a Lutheran, and I've never read anything like that in my Bible!"

"What about this verse?" I suggested. *Always give thanks for everything to our God and Father in the name of our Lord Jesus Christ* (Ephesians 5:20).

John shook his head. "I know that verse," he said. "I've always thought it meant to thank God for good things. Thanking Him for bad things just doesn't seem scriptural. I always thought Paul was a little extreme when he wrote about taking pleasure in infirmities."

"I used to think so, too." I said. "But I've become convinced that Paul is right. When he speaks about rejoicing in infirmities, he obviously doesn't mean we are supposed to find pain pleasurable in itself. But Paul had come to see his suffering from a different perspective. He had learned that his pain served a higher purpose and was part of God's loving plan for him."

John looked thoughtful. "I just don't know," he said slowly.

"Paul learned his lesson the hard way, too," I went on. "Remember his 'thorn in the flesh'?"

John nodded.

"Three times Paul asked to have it removed. He was obviously not rejoicing in his 'thorn' right then. And three times God answered him, *No. But I am with you; that is all you need. My power shows up best in weak people. Now I am glad to boast about how weak I am; I am glad to be a living demonstration of Christ's power, instead of showing off my own power and abilities* (II Corinthians 12:9)."

"Paul wasn't happy about his infirmities for their own sake," I continued. "He went on to tell the Corinthians, *Since I know it is all for Christ's good, I am quite happy about 'the thorn,' and about insults and hardships, persecutions and difficulties; for when I am weak, then I am strong - the less I have, the more I depend on him* (II Corinthians 12:10)."

John leafed thoughtfully through his Bible.

"I have faith that God is working in all things," he said at last. "But the rejoicing part is really hard for me."

"If we say we have faith but can't rejoice, doesn't that mean we haven't really committed ourselves to trusting that God is working in our situation, for our best?" I suggested.

John sat in silence, then he nodded with determination.

"I believe you're right," he said. "I want to try it."

We knelt together, and John's tall frame shook with sobs as he prayed, "God, I know you love my wife more than I do. I believe you're working out a wonderful plan for us."

The tears were flowing freely down his face, but his eyes shone with a new confidence.

"God is doing the right thing, Chaplain," he said. "I know it."

A few days later John applied for compassionate transfer so that he could be near his wife. The request was eventually granted, and he came to say good-bye.

"Wait till you hear the best part," he said excitedly. "God has promised to heal my wife the moment I see her if I place my hands on her head and say, 'in Jesus' name be healed.'"

I felt a twinge of doubt. What if John in his eagerness was jumping ahead of God? Then I, too, felt the assurance of the Holy Spirit, and placed my hand on John in a parting prayer.

"Father, you say that if two of us agree on earth concerning anything we ask for, you will do it for us (Matthew 18:19). So now I agree with John that the moment he touches his wife, you will heal her."

Two weeks later John's letter came.

> It happened just like Jesus told us it would. My wife was standing in the psychiatrist's office when I first saw her. She looked terrible. The lines in her face and the fear in her eyes almost convinced me she was beyond help. But I knew I had to obey what God told me, and so I walked over and put my hands on her. The moment I touched her something like a shock went through her, and I knew she was healed. I told the psychiatrist that she was healed, and he looked at me as if he thought I needed to be admitted. But they called me the next day, and the psychiatrist said, 'I don't know how to account for it, but your wife seems to be well!' My wife is home now, happier than she's ever been before. She has been strengthened by the afflictions she suffered, and she now joins me in being thankful for all things. We've learned how much of Christ's healing power is released when we praise Him.

God's strength can replace our weaknesses when we come to Him, recognizing and admitting where we fall short. But so often we're ashamed to confess that we are weak, afraid that others and God will not accept us as we really are. This kind of thinking is rooted in the wrong idea that we must earn or deserve God's love.

A Christian general came to me one day and confessed that the strain of presenting a perfect image before his men was about to kill him. As we talked, I realized that this man, whom I'd often admired for his outward poise and confidence, had never been able to accept himself as he really was. He was obsessed by the fear that if he should ever relax, he would grievously disappoint his family and his men.

I suggested that it would ease his tension if he would thank God for having created him exactly as he was.

"You mean, as I am today? Filled with fear and tension?" he asked, and I nodded.

"Do you think the God who created this universe and placed the stars in the heavens was any less careful when He created you? Nor has He been careless with the circumstances He has allowed into your life in order to show you how much He loves you."

The general came to several sessions in my office, and studied his Bible and read *Prison to Praise* with interest. Gradually he came to accept that God had a perfect plan for his life and that the continuous stress he'd felt was serving the purpose of bringing him to rely on God.

He began to praise God for his anxieties, and a sense of peace slowly replaced the old habits of fear. For the first time in his life he was happy to be himself.

"As long as I thought that God couldn't love me with my weaknesses, I tried to hide them and consequently drifted farther and farther from the truth," he told me. "As soon as I was able to admit I was weak, and thank God for having made me that way, His love began to transform me, and He began to fill me with His peace."

David wrote, *Let everyone bless God and sing his praises, for he holds our lives in his hands. And he holds our feet to the path. You have purified us with fire, O Lord, like silver in a crucible. You captured us in your net and laid great burdens on our backs. You sent troops to ride across our broken bodies. We went through fire and flood. But in the end, you brought us into wealth and great abundance...For I cried to him for help, with praises ready on my tongue. He would not have listened if I had not confessed my sins. But He listened! He heard my prayer! He paid attention to it* (Psalm 66:8-12, 17-19).

David wanted oneness with God, and he knew that anything unclean in him would prevent God's love from filing him and flowing through him. Therefore David welcomed the breaking and cleansing process God put him through. He rejoiced when the trials revealed the hidden sins of his own heart, sins he could confess and be healed of. God himself had shown David the way.

I don't need your sacrifices of flesh and blood. What I want from you is your true thanks...I want you to trust me in your times of trouble, so I can rescue you, and you can give me glory!...true praise is a worthy sacrifice; this really honors me. Those who walk my paths will receive salvation from the Lord (Psalm 50:13-15, 23).

The paths of God are the paths of praise!

Chapter 5

When Sparrows Fall

Not one sparrow - What do they Cost? Two for a penny? can fall to the ground without your Father knowing it. And the very hairs of your head are all numbered. So don't worry! You are more valuable to him than many sparrows (Matthew 10:29-31).

Jesus told his disciples that our Father in heaven keeps an eye on every sparrow and counts every hair on our heads; yet the fact remains that sparrows *do* fall. Tragedies *do* come to us. Innocent little children die under the wheels of cars driven by drunks. Someone we love is struck by cancer and dies in spite of our fervent prayers.

Could God have prevented the sparrow's fall? The tragedy? The child's death? The spread of cancer?

Most of us believe that God has the power to prevent such things *if* He wants to. We are then left to wrestle in our minds with the problem of *why* God permits what seems to us to be a triumph of evil over good.

Sometimes we draw the conclusion that God is calloused, uncaring, or partial; or we think that the victims of evil suffer because of their own or someone else's sin. Both conclusions are in stark contrast with the Good News that tells us God is love, and we don't have to be good enough to deserve His loving care.

It is impossible to praise God for *all* things if we think that He is not ultimately responsible for everything that happens, or if we think that He is sometimes indifferent to suffering.

Often I receive letters from people who ask me if it is right to thank God for something that is evil, when the Bible tells us to hate evil. They quote, *Ye that love the Lord, hate evil* (Psalm 97:10 KJV) and *Hate the evil, and love the good* (Amos 5:15 KJV).

What these scriptures mean is that we are not to approve of evil, practice evil, embrace evil, or submit to evil.

Praising God for evil circumstances does *not* mean that we approve of evil, except in the sense that Paul spoke of taking pleasure in his sufferings - because he *knew* that God was at work in and through it.

God does not want evil to control us. He created us with a free will and the capacity for evil. Evil remains in this world with God's permission, but is always subject to His will. Nothing evil can come near us without God's permission.

Because evil does exist, God sent His Son to die on the cross to break the power of evil in the lives of all who would believe in Him.

The evil bow before the good (Proverbs 14:19 KJV). We who believe have been given the power to overcome the world.

Every one who believes that Jesus is the Christ is a child of God...whatever is born of God overcomes the world; and this is the victory that overcomes the world, our faith (I John 5:1,4 RSV).

So what is this faith to be grounded on? What are we to believe in order to overcome? We believe in Jesus Christ, but there is more. To fully believe in Jesus Christ also means that we accept that God is the all-powerful God He says He is, and that nothing happens without His knowledge or permission.

If we set ourselves to firmly believe this, and to praise God for every circumstance of apparent evil around us, I am convinced that *every* difficult situation, *every* tragedy, will be changed by the hand of God.

When I say this, I know that some of you may jump to the conclusion that God is going to change a situation to what *we* think is good. But that is *not* what I am saying.

When we fully entrust an evil situation to God, thanking and praising Him for it, the power of God will be released. His power will overcome the plan of the evil inherent in that situation, transforming it to fit with the perfect plan of God.

We may not understand God's plan or recognize it as good, but when we praise Him for it, we release His power to work in the situation for our good.

Our ideas of good and bad are often sadly distorted. For instance, if a child inherits a million dollars, we say, "How wonderful!" But if a child dies and goes home to heaven, we say "How tragic!" Yet we know that a million-dollar inheritance can sometimes lead to a life of waste and dissapation, while going home to heaven can only be good.

If we praise God in all circumstances, I believe that some sparrows will be prevented from falling, some little children will not die, some cancers will be halted and leave. Yet this is *not* to be our motivation for praising God. Some sparrows will still fall, some children will die, and some people will succumb to cancer. Our praise must be *for* these instances also.

We are told to praise God for allowing evil to come into our lives, trusting that He has a plan and purpose for it, but what are we supposed to do next? How do we personally react to evil when we come face-to-face with it? There is a lot of fuzzy thinking on this point among Christians.

Jesus told his followers, "*Resist not evil*" Matthew 5:39. Yet we read that when He saw merchants selling cattle, sheep, and doves and exchanging money in the temple area, He *made a whip from some ropes and chased them all out, and drove out the sheep and oxen, scattering the money changers' coins over the floor and turning over their tables*! (John 2:15).

Here we see Jesus taking overt action against evil. Yet He did not resist the men who came to arrest Him in the

Garden of Gethsemane, and He reprimanded Peter who tried
to defend Him with a sword.

So there are times that God would lead us to take overt
action against a force of evil; at other times He would have
us submit without resistance. How do we know when to do
what?

We need to recognize that in ourselves we have no
power to overcome evil. The overcoming power is always
God. The essence of God's message to us is that we must
learn to focus our attention on Him, the source of overcoming power, and not direct our attention toward the evil
confronting us. He will then direct our action moment by
moment.

Paul told the Romans, *Do not let yourself be overcome
by evil, but overcome (master) evil with good* (Romans 12:21
Amp).

In the case of Jesus' arrest and crucifixion, **His
submission to evil broke the power of evil in the world**.

Jesus was showing us that there is a better way to deal
with evil than to resist it in the way that we normally do. Our
idea of resistance is to react in kind, using force against force,
and so we react to the evil circumstances opposing us, rather
than responding to God's presence and guidance in the
situation.

Anytime our action is prompted by the evil circumstances surrounding us rather than by our faith in God's
power and perfect control of the situation, we're allowing
evil to control us, rather than overcoming evil with the power
of God.

Jesus was not a pacifist. When He said, "*Resist not
evil*," He meant that we should instead *actively* recognize
the power of God over evil and recognize that God sometimes chooses to use apparently evil circumstances to bring
about His plan of good.

In such a case, to resist evil would mean that we were
working to thwart God's perfect plan. If the disciples had
succeeded in preventing the arrest of Jesus in the Garden of

Gethsemane, they would have meddled in God's plan, although it would have seemed to them that they were scoring a victory over evil.

Jesus came to teach us how to be conquerors, not how to lose without whimpering.

Both James and Peter tell us to stand firm in faith against Satan. If we look at the context of their message, it is clear that they are in complete agreement with Jesus and with Paul.

So give yourself humbly to God. Resist the devil and he will flee from you. And when you draw close to God, God will draw close to you (James 4:7). *Be careful - watch out for attacks from Satan, your great enemy...Stand firm when he attacks. Trust the Lord...*(I Peter 5:8-9).

Our defence against the power of Satan is the power of God. When we stand firm in our faith that God is in perfect and loving control of every detail of the circumstances surrounding us, God's mighty power is released. And we express our faith by praising and thanking Him for the situation.

We are told to be careful and watch for the enemy's attack, but our attention must be focused on God, not on Satan. We are to be aware of our enemy, but our protection doesn't lie in watching the enemy, but rather in our knowledge of God's power.

If we let fear and doubts and a preoccupation with the presence of evil take over our minds, we block the power of God from entering the situation. We must learn to see evil in the right perspective - **subject to the mighty power of God** - and then let that power work out everything for our good according to God's perfect plan.

Our part is to stand firm in faith, obedient to the promptings of the Holy Spirit, who will guide our outward actions in the situation. Inwardly, our part is *always* to keep our eyes on God and to praise and thank Him for His goodness and mercy in all things.

Standing firm in faith means that we set our will to believe God's Word that He is in charge, regardless of what our feelings say or how outward circumstances may seem.

The Bible firmly states that God is in charge of every rainstorm, earthquake, tornado or hurricane, every war, famine and pestilence, every birth or death, every flower in the field, every sparrow, and every hair on our heads. We will have to decide whether or not to believe Him all the way.

Some people say, "I can see that God is responsible for some things, but I can't accept that He is in charge of everything.

This is not an adequate basis for praise, and in particular areas where we refuse to see God's hand, we can not expect to see evidence of His transforming power.

Let us see what the Bible has to say about some areas where we have difficulty recognizing the hand of God.

Habakkuk was a prophet who complained about the conditions of his country much like some of us complain about the world today.

O Lord, how long must I call for help before you will listen? Habakkuk cried. (He didn't even think God was listening, and I'm afraid there are modern-day Christians who agree with him.) *I shout to you in vain; there is no answer. 'Help! Murder!' I cry, but no one comes to save. Must I forever see this sin and sadness all around me? Wherever I look there is oppression and bribery and men who love to argue and to fight. The law is not enforced and there is no justice given in the courts, for the wicked far outnumber the righteous, and bribes and trickery prevail* (Habakkuk 1:2-4).

Have you ever looked at twentieth-century America and voiced those thoughts? I confess that I have.

God answered the prophet, *Look, and be amazed! You will be astounded at what I am about to do! For I am going to do something in your own lifetime that you will have to see to believe. I am raising a new force on the world scene, the Chaldeans, a cruel and violent nation who will march across the world and conquer it* (Habakkuk 1:5-6).

God said that *He* would raise up a cruel and violent

nation to conquer the world. Do you think any of the armies we've seen rise on the world scene since then came up any other way?

God didn't just *allow* the Chaldeans to conquer, He *raised* them up. Are we willing to thank God for raising up evil - such as Communism - today? Can we accept His word that He is using evil - forcing it to work for our good? Can we praise Him for it?

Habakkuk was shocked when he heard what God intended to do.

O Lord my God, my Holy One, he cried, *you who are eternal - is your plan in all of this to wipe us out? Surely not! O God our Rock, you have decreed the rise of these Chaldeans to chasten and correct us for our awful sins. We are wicked, but they far more. Will you, who cannot allow sin in any form, stand idly by while they swallow us up? Should You be silent while the wicked destroy those who are better than they?* (Habakkuk 1:12-13).

Have you ever wondered why God allowed evil and cruel men to hurt innocent ones? I have.

Habakkuk continued, *Are we but fish, to be caught and killed?...Must we be strung up on their hooks and dragged out in their nets, while they rejoice?...Will you let them get away with this forever?* (Habakkuk 1:14-15, 17).

God didn't turn a deaf ear to Habakkuk's questions but told him to write down the answer for all the world to see and remember.

These things I plan won't happen right away. Slowly, steadily, surely, the time approaches when the vision will be fulfilled. If it seems slow, do not despair, for these things will surely come to pass. Just be patient! They will not be overdue a single day! (Habakkuk 2:3).

God is never late! His timing is perfect, but we sometimes complain - because it is *our* time schedule that is wrong.

Note this, God told Habakkuk: *Wicked men trust themselves alone (as these Chaldeans do), and fail; but the righteous man trusts in me, and lives* (Habakkuk 2:4).

The Chaldeans would fail in the end; they would be betrayed by their own arrogance, carried away by their own greed. Their apparent glory would turn to shame, as the consequences of their evil would catch up with them. The time would come when all the earth would be filled with an awareness of the glory of God (Habakkuk 2:14).

Now Habakkuk saw the greatness of God's plan, and he cried out in triumph, singing to God.

O Lord, now I have heard your report, and I worship you in awe for the fearful things you are going to do...I see God moving across the deserts...His brilliant splendor fills the earth and sky; his glory fills the heavens, and the earth is full of his praise! What a wonderful God he is! From his hands flash rays of brilliant light. He rejoices in his awesome power. Pestilence marches before him; plague follows close behind. He stops; he stands still for a moment, gazing at the earth. Then he shakes the nations, scattering the everlasting mountains and leveling the hills. His power is just the same as always! (Habakkuk 3:2-6).

Habakkuk was awed by the vision he had seen. He no longer questioned God's control over the fires, earthquakes, pestilence, famines, and wars. Habakkuk's lips quivered with fear, his legs gave way under him and he was shaking in terror, but he sang to God, *Even though the fig trees are all destroyed, and there is neither blossom left nor fruit, and though the olive crops all fail, and the fields lie barren; even if the flocks die in the fields and the cattle barns are empty, yet I will rejoice in the Lord; I will be happy in the God of my salvation. The Lord God is my Strength, and he will give me the speed of a deer and bring me safely over the mountains* (Habakkuk 3:17-19).

Habakkuk trembled in terror at the vision God had shown him of the future, but he also realized that God was a God of love, justice, and mercy, and he didn't hesitate to trust himself completely into His hands, praising Him for His perfect plan for Israel.

God's command to us is that we praise Him, too - even if our lips tremble in fear and we shake in terror over the outward circumstances of His plan for us.

Through the prophet Isaiah, God told His people that He intended to raise up King Cyrus of Persia to conquer and crush many nations. King Cyrus didn't know the Lord, but God intended to use him to bring the Jewish captives home from Babylon and rebuild the temple and Jerusalem.

Why would God choose Cyrus, a heathen king, to carry out His purposes? To those who would question Him, God answered, *I form the light and make the dark. I send good times and bad. I, Jehovah, am he who does these things...Woe to the man who fights with his Creator. Does the pot argue with its maker? Does the clay dispute with him who forms it, saying, Stop, you're doing it wrong! or the pot exclaim, How clumsy can you be?...Jehovah, the Holy One of Israel, Israel's Creator, says: What right have you to question what I do? Who are you to command me concerning the work of my hands? I have made the earth and created man upon it. With my hands I have stretched out the heavens and commanded all the vast myriads of stars. I have raised up Cyrus to fulfill my righteous purpose, and I will direct all his paths...*(Isaiah 45:7, 9, 11-13).

When we refuse to see God's hand in every situation around us, we are like the pot arguing with its maker. We say, "Now if *I* were God, I certainly wouldn't do it *that* way. I wouldn't send an earthquake to Peru or let that little girl die of leukemia or allow that preacher to thunder untruth from the pulpit, leading gullible people astray...and I certainly wouldn't allow drug-pushers to tempt little children!"

God knows how we feel about these things and how limited our understanding is. He spoke through the prophet Isaiah:

This plan of mine is not what you would work out, neither are my thoughts the same as yours! For just as the heavens are higher than the earth, so are my ways higher than yours, and my thoughts than yours. As the rain and

*snow come down from heaven and stay upon the ground to
water the earth, and cause the grain to grow and to produce
seed for the farmer and bread for the hungry, so also is my
Word. I send it out and it always produces fruit. It shall
accomplish all I want it to, and prosper everywhere I send it*
(Isaiah 55:8-11).

Our skepticism and disappointment in God's plan is
rooted in a distrust of God. We're not convinced that He has
our best interest in mind.

We question why God allows an innocent child to die
under the wheels of a car driven by a drunk in order that the
driver come to recognize his need for God. Does God care
more for the soul of the drunken driver than He does for the
child or the child's grieving parents?

We all ask countless questions like that, turning them
over and over in our minds, and while we are torn by the
questions, we have no peace and the situation remains
unchanged.

The only way out of our dilemma is to accept God's
Word on faith. To trust Him, in spite of what we think, feel,
or see. His Word is that He loves us, and that the death of an
innocent child *does* fit into God's loving plan for each of the
lives affected.

God's love for us can be accepted only by faith, just as
we accept every other promise in the Bible. We must decide
to believe in His love, because He says it is so, regardless of
whether we *feel* loved or not.

The Good News is that God loves us with a love more
kind, more patient, more long-suffering and concerned with
our happiness and well-being than any human love can be.
God loves us and has a perfect plan for our lives. He sent His
Son to die for us, to provide us with a new life full of abundant
joy and peace, in a world filled with suffering.

We can't possibly comprehend, with our limited human
understanding, the magnificent scope of God's plan for us
and for this world. Like Habakkuk, we are shocked that God
intends to use earthquakes and wars, suffering and death to

bring His plan about.

But God's plan is a perfect plan. It is the only plan that has ever worked on this earth where mankind's rebellion and evil has prevailed. Look at the bloody mess we've made in trying to order our own lives throughout history.

God's plan is not what we would work out, He told Isaiah, because His thoughts are so much higher than ours, His perspective is so much clearer.

God wants only what is best for us.

You will live in joy and peace. The mountains and hills, the trees of the field - all the world around you - will rejoice. Where once were thorns, fir trees will grow; where briars grew, the myrtle trees will sprout up. This miracle will make the Lord's name very great and be an everlasting sign of God's power and love (Isaiah 55:12-13).

God wants to shower us with blessings. He wants to take care of us in every way, down to every little detail of our daily lives. Yet we insist on looking at all the circumstances, the outward workings of His plan, and speculate on what they mean and how they all fit in, while His command to us is that we look to Him and trust Him.

We make our understanding - or lack of it - into a wall between us and God as long as we insist on figuring out and approving His plan before we dare trust ourselves to Him.

Here, just as in our first approach to God, acceptance of His will and plan must come before understanding. We must deliberately set aside our own desire for knowledge and comprehension of what God is doing, and throw the weight of our will into a decision to trust His Word.

His plan for us is good. Can we trust His Word for that?

His plan for Job was good, but it was a plan that tested Job's faith to the utmost and staggered his understanding.

Job was a good man. In fact, God said of him, *He is the finest man in all the earth - a good man who fears God and will have nothing to do with evil* (Job 1:8).

So what happened to Job? He lost everything he had. His cattle, his crops...and one day the roof fell in and killed all his children.

If that happened to you or to one of your neighbors, would you say it was God? Or Satan?

In Job's case it *was* Satan. But how did it come about? Satan came into God's presence and asked permission to bring the troubles on Job.

Satan may be the actor who acts out his role in the drama of our life, but God is still the Director.

So what was Job's response? He fell down on the ground before God and tore his clothes in grief.

I came naked from my mother's womb...and I shall have nothing when I die. The Lord gave me everything I had, and they were His to take away. Blessed be the name of the Lord (Job 1:21).

But that wasn't the end of Job's troubles. Satan came and asked permission once more to torment Job, and God gave it.

This time Job was struck with boils all over his body, until he became so disfigured that no one could bear to look at him. His own wife told him to curse God and die, and his neighbors, who had always respected him, now mocked him and turned away. Three of his best friends, who came to tell him that his suffering was caused by his sins, advised him to repent.

Job never doubted that God had brought his misfortune. He cried out for mercy, but was convinced that it was not his sins that had brought about his suffering. Job knew in his heart that he was a righteous man, and he trusted God.

Though He slay me, yet will I...trust Him. Nevertheless, I will...argue my ways before Him - even to His face (Job 13:15 Amp).

Job's faith that God was in charge never wavered, but his understanding questioned God's purpose and methods. Job's questions have been echoed by all of us, at one time or another.

"Why do you allow poverty, God? Why do you allow the innocent to suffer? Why are evil men living in ease and comfort? Why don't you listen to my plea? God, why don't you let me die so my suffering will end and I can rest with you?''

When God answered Job, it was the stern rebuke of a Father to a son.

Where were you when I laid the foundation of the earth? Tell me, if you know so much...Have you ever commanded the morning to appear, and caused the dawn to rise in the east?...Where is the path to the distribution point of light? Where is the home of the east wind?...Can you hold back the stars?...Can you ensure the proper sequence of the seasons?...Who gives intuition and instinct? Who makes the wild donkeys wild?...Have you given the horse strength, or clothed his neck with a quivering mane?...Is it at your command that the eagle rises high upon the cliffs to make her nest?...Do you still want to argue with the Almighty? Or will you yield? Do you - God's critic - have the answers? (Job 38-4, 12, 24, 31-32, 36; 39:5, 19, 27; 40:2).

Job replied, *I am nothing - how could I ever find the answers? I lay my hand upon my mouth in silence. I have said too much already* (Job 40:4-5).

God continued His impressive list of His creation: the animals, their ways and strength, God's power over all men.

Who can stand before me? I owe no one anything. Everything under the heaven is mine! (Job 41:10-11).

Job replied, *I know that You can do all things and that no thought or purpose of Yours can be restrained or thwarted...I was talking about things I knew nothing about and did not understand, things far too wonderful for me...I had heard of You only by the hearing of the ear; but now my (spiritual) eye sees You...I loathe myself and repent in dust and ashes* (Job 42:2-3, 5-6 Amp and TLB).

The Lord spoke harshly also to Job's three friends who had completely misunderstood the reasons for Job's suffering. God told them they had been wrong and instructed them to offer up a burnt offering and then have Job pray for them.

The three men did as they were told, and *when Job*

prayed for his friends, the Lord restored his wealth and happiness! In fact, the Lord gave him twice as much as before (Job 42:10).

It is interesting to note that God blessed Job **after** Job prayed for those who had accused him wrongly. Job had learned his lesson. No longer would he question God's operation of the universe. No longer would he see or hear or understand with his natural senses only, but with his new, spiritual insight, as well.

God had a perfect plan for Job. His trials were executed by Satan, but permitted by God to give Job greater faith and wisdom, and to show him just how great and loving God is.

God had a perfect plan for Ruth, the Moabite. Yet it looked for all the world as if misfortune followed her. First she lost her husband. Then she went with her mother-in-law back to Bethlehem and they were so poor that Ruth had to go into the fields of the rich farmers and glean whatever was left after the harvest. That doesn't sound like the outworking of a wonderful plan, does it? But Ruth trusted God, and there in the field she met Boaz, a rich relative of her dead husband. Boaz fell in love with Ruth and they were married. God's plan had worked, and Ruth became the grandmother of King David.

Or what about God's perfect plan for Joseph? God planned that Joseph would become Pharaoh's right-hand man in Egypt, because God intended to use him, at just the right time, to save the family of Israel from famine.

Joseph was sold by his brothers as a slave to a caravan of merchants on their way to Egypt. It was the first step in God's plan but Joseph's brothers had no idea that they were serving God's purpose. They hated their brother and meant only to harm him.

Later Joseph became the trusted servant of an influential Egyptian, and it looked as if he was on his way up the social ladder. But he was falsely accused of attempting to rape the Egyptian's wife and was thrown in jail. If that happened to you, would you think that the devil had won a victory? Or would you have accepted it as part of God's perfect plan?

It was in jail that God arranged for Joseph to meet Pharaoh's butler and interpret his dream. Joseph asked the butler to plead with Pharaoh to pardon him, and the butler promised, but later forgot all about it. Joseph spent another two years in jail, and that surely looked like an unfortunate quirk of fate. But God's timing was perfect. Pharaoh dreamed a strange pair of dreams that no one could interpret. Suddenly the forgetful butler remembered the fellow he'd met in jail a couple of years before. Joseph was brought before Pharaoh, and God told Joseph the meaning of Pharaoh's dreams. Seven years of bountiful harvests were to be followed by seven years of severe famine. Pharaoh accepted the interpretation of his dreams, and appointed Joseph to be in charge of the ingathering and storage of grain during the seven rich years, and in charge of the distribution of food during the seven lean years to follow.

When Joseph's brothers came to Egypt to buy grain, he revealed his identity, and they fell down before him, stricken with fear and remorse. But Joseph said, *Don't be angry with yourselves that you did this to me* (sold me into slavery), *for God did it! He sent me here ahead of you to preserve your lives...It was God who sent me here, not you!...As for you, you thought evil against me; but God meant it for good, to bring about that many people should be kept alive, as they are this day* (Genesis 45:5, 8; TLB and 50:20 Amp).

God **meant** it for good! We believe that God is able to make all things work for our good the way the Bible says, but we often think that God takes whatever happens to us and makes the best of it, sort of a secondhand blessing. But **God isn't on the defensive**. He isn't limited to making the best out of a bad situation. **God has the initiative!** We need to remind ourselves of that every so often.

God had the initiative when Stephen was stoned to death (Acts 7). Stephen was a man, full of the Holy Spirit, who served the Lord faithfully. When he was stoned to death, Saul of Tarsus, an angry young persecutor of Christians, was among the spectators.

Stephen obviously trusted that God was completely in charge of the situation, for he knelt down while the stones were being hurled at him, and cried out with a loud voice, "Lord, don't charge them with this sin!" And then he died. Stephen knew that although his persecutors meant evil against him, God meant it for good.

Would you be able to thank God for the murder of the most Christlike person you know and believe that God was using the tragedy for some great good?

Saul of Tarsus became Paul the apostle after a remarkable conversion experience on the road to Damascus. He experienced his share of what looked like mishaps in spreading the gospel.

Once when Paul and Silas came to Philippi, they were accused of corrupting the city and were stripped and beaten with whips until the blood ran from their bare backs. Then they were put in the inner dungeon of the prison with their feet clamped in stocks. (Acts 16:20-24).

But Paul and Silas didn't think that Satan had won a victory or that God had deserted them. They were convinced that God had called them to preach in Philippi, and that He was actively working in everything to bring about His perfect plan for them. So they didn't whine or complain or cry out to the Lord for help. They sat there in the dungeon with the blood stiffened on their sore backs, unable to stretch their aching legs, and they were praying and singing hymns of praise to God.

Suddenly, at midnight, there was a great earthquake, the prison doors flew open, and the chains fell off every prisoner. The jailer was horrified, thinking they had all escaped, and drew his sword to kill himself. But Paul called out, assuring him that all the prisoners were there, and the jailer came and threw himself down before their feet. "What must I do to be saved?" he begged.

God had a perfect plan for the city of Philippi. He sent Paul and Silas to be His witnesses there, and they had faith to believe that God was working out His plan, even if He used circumstances they could not have anticipated.

We are always trying to anticipate what God will do. Because He worked out a set of circumstances one way once, we draw the conclusion that He will do the same thing in every similar set of circumstances. But Paul wasn't always dramatically released from prison. Sometimes he stayed there for years.

Paul suffered many afflictions. He was stoned and left for dead, shipwrecked, bitten by a snake and suffered persecution but never once did he think that God had stopped directing every incident in his life. He counted it a joy and an opportunity to praise God. Paul knew that his suffering was working *for* him.

For years I suffered with excruciating headaches. In vain I searched the Scriptures, clinging to God's promise of healing, but I couldn't find a clue to the reason for my agony, nor did they go away.

In the meantime, I was tormented with doubts. Over and over I allowed myself to speculate *why* this particular suffering had come my way. The thoughts whirled in my head. *"Why doesn't God do something about your pain? You're praying for others who get healed, but your own pain is still with you."*

As I suffered and tossed through long, sleepless nights, the thoughts persisted. *Look how miserable you are! If God is a just God who knows about your suffering, - He surely wouldn't hold it against you if you ended your life. Just be careful how you do it, and no one will suspect suicide, no one will be hurt, and you'll be free from the pain...*

Like the arguments of Job's friends, these thoughts can sound very reasonable when you are racked with pain. But of course, they are a bunch of lies, invented by the master deceiver, Satan himself, who comes near only by permission of God.

Our accuser and tormentor must flee when we draw near to God and take our stand on His Word of truth.

My headaches didn't suddenly go away, but I determined to believe that God wouldn't permit anything to happen to me unless it was for my good. Therefore, the headaches had to be for my good, and I began to praise and thank God for them every time they came. As I did, something wonderful began to work *for* me. The more I hurt, the more thankful I became, and with the thanksgiving I experienced a new depth of joy radiating through my entire being.

Richard Wurmbrand tells what happened when the physical pain and mental agony of a Communist prison became more than he could bear. Three years of solitary confinement and torture was threatening to rob him of his sanity, but as he reached the extremity of his endurance, Richard still trusted God and praised Him for His ever-present mercy and love. He tells how, at this point, joy began to radiate through his being, and filled his cell.

God meant his suffering for good. Richard Wurmbrand's ministry is now influencing the entire world *because* of what he suffered.

As for God, his way is perfect, said the psalmist: *the word of the Lord is tried: He is a buckler to all those that trust in him* (Psalm 18:30 KJV).

The way may lead through fierce battles, raging storms, through fire or flood; yet the Bible tells us, that God's presence goes with us, and His hand guides us.

How can we doubt it? He created the soldier and his weapons, the storm, the fire, and the waters of the flood. They are all under His control.

Why did God cause a storm on the lake when Jesus was there in a boat with His disciples? So that His power and authority over the storm could be demonstrated (Mark 4).

Why did God cause a man to be blind from birth?

Jesus and His disciples were walking along when they saw a man who had been blind from birth. *Master, his disciples asked him, why was this man born blind? Was it a result of his own sins or those of his parents? Neither, Jesus answered. But to demonstrate the power of God* (John 9:2-3).

Then Jesus went on to heal the man.

The disciples looked at the blind man from the viewpoint of human reasoning and understanding; Jesus saw the situation under the perfect control and power of God.

Our viewpoint makes all the difference.

I've received hundreds of letters from people who've read *Prison to Praise*. Seventy-five percent of the letters come from people who tell me how they've started praising God for a difficult situation, with amazing results. Twenty-five percent of the letters come from people who tell of the same kinds of situations, but they are not able to believe that God is at work and can't praise Him for it. They are defeated, discouraged, and desperate.

The difference is not in the situation, but in the viewpoint, and consequently in the outcome.

Many write about the death of a close friend or relative.

> Tom suffered so terrible, wrote one lady. We had taken him to healing services and prayer groups all over the country. He seemed better for a while, and our hopes soared. Then the cancer came back, and after months of agony he died. How could God be so inconsistent? I can't believe it was His will that Tom die so young. He was a Christian and wanted to serve God. If God did it all just to teach the rest of us a lesson, why did Tom have to suffer? I can't believe I'm supposed to praise God for what has happened.

Here is another letter:

> Charles accepted Christ less than a year ago. He was a radiant witness for the Lord. After six months he developed cancer. He had two operations, but the growth in his lungs returned. He called the elders of his church; they anointed him and prayed for his

healing. When he went back for his checkup,
the growth had disappeared. Charles
rejoiced and praised the Lord. Then a few
months later he had severe headaches. He
went into the hospital for a checkup and was
dead in two days. Brain cancer.

A Pastor friend of the family flew in to
preach at the funeral. On the plane he sat
down next to a youth. They began to talk; the
pastor shared Charles' story and the young
boy gave his life to Jesus Christ before the
plane landed. In New Orleans the pastor
changed flights. On the next leg of his
journey he sat next to a young woman. She,
too, inquired where he was going, and he told
her the story about Charles. Before the plane
landed, she had accepted Jesus Christ as her
Savior. The funeral was an occasion to praise
the Lord for all He had done in Charles' life.
After the funeral, two men accepted Christ
on the sidewalk outside the chapel. Charles'
body was flown to his hometown for burial.
During the ceremony, I couldn't take my
eyes off the face of the young widow. She
was radiant with an inner peace and joy.
During the past year she and Charles had
come to know the joy that comes from
praising God for all things. She told me,
Death is swallowed up in victory (I Corinthians
15:54). I have no reason to weep. Praise
God!

The two letters told of similar circumstances, but what
a difference. One is a story of defeat, the other of victory.
One sees from the human viewpoint, the other from the
viewpoint of Christ.

The Bible tells us that we *can* have the viewpoint of
Christ.

Let this mind be in you, which was also in Christ Jesus (Philippians 2:5 KJV). *And be constantly renewed in the spirit of your mind* (Ephesians 4:23 Amp).

Paul wasn't suggesting an impossibility. The key words in his passages are "let" and "be renewed". When we read, study and meditate on God's Word, we wash and renew our minds. As we spend time in His presence, our minds are changed to have the same attitude, the same perspective that Christ had...to be a humble servant of the Lord.

David wanted to be surrendered to God's will for his life, and he desired to change his rebellious heart. He cried out to God: *Keep me from deceitful ways; be gracious to me through your law. I have chosen the way of truth; I have set my heart on your laws...I run in the path of your commands, for you have set my heart free* (Psalm 119:29-30, & 32 NIV).

David knew that his part was to choose the right way. David did his best to follow God, and trusted God to do what he could not do.

God will do the same for us if we choose to trust Him, standing firm in faith, believing it is done. Whatever circumstances come into our lives, we are to praise and thank God for them, because they are His way of working out His perfect plan for us. The circumstances are His way of removing the dross, purifying us, and giving us a willing heart.

Praise releases the power of God into our lives and circumstances, because praise is faith in action. When we trust God fully, He is free to work, and He *always* brings victory. It may be a victory that changes circumstances, or a victory *in* the circumstances. Death may be turned away, or made to lose its sting.

Praise is acceptance of what God has brought into our lives. We enter this attitude of praise by an act of our will, by a decision to praise God regardless of how we feel.

What time I am afraid, I will...trust...You, wrote David. *By the help of God I will praise His Word; on God I lean, rely and confidently put my trust* (Psalm 56:3-4 Amp).

My heart is fixed, O God, my heart is fixed: I will sing and give praise (Psalm 57:7 KJV).

Chapter 6

Good-bye Grumblings

Have you ever stepped outside your door on a beautiful, clear, sunny day, taken a deep breath of fresh air, and thanked God for His wonderful creation?

But what if the next morning is gray and rainy? Does it automatically make you feel a little depressed as you look out the window? Maybe you don't say it out loud, but how do you feel?

Are you in the habit of thanking God only for what you want? And are you in the habit of grumbling when things don't go the way you like?

So what's wrong with a little complaining? It's no big thing. What difference does it make?

It can make *all* the difference in the world. *Everything* depends on how we respond to the little things in life.

A marriage counselor will tell you that a marriage usually breaks up over little things. It takes only a small nail to puncture a tire. A tiny mistake by a mechanic can cause the crash of a giant airliner. A misunderstanding can start a war. One angry word can lead to a shooting. Little things mean a lot, because this is the level where we live, down at the nitty-gritty of our attitude at the breakfast table, or in the long check-out line at the supermarket on a Friday afternoon.

Grumbling comes so easily to all of us that we often don't realize what we're doing. But grumbling is the very opposite of thanksgiving; a complaint is the opposite of trust; a murmur against your wife when she burns your toast is the opposite of loving acceptance.

The dictionary defines a complaint as an accusation. By complaining and grumbling we are actually accusing God of mismanaging the details of our day. The attitude of praise releases the power of God into our lives, and the attitude of murmuring and complaining blocks that power.

And don't murmur against God and his dealings with you, as some of them did, for that is why God sent his Angel to destroy them. All these things happened to them as examples - as object lessons to us - to warn us against doing the same things; they were written down so that we could read about them and learn from them...(I Corinthians 10:10-11).

Paul was speaking about the behavior of the Israelites on their wanderings from Egypt to the Promised Land. So what did they do and what were the terrible consequences?

The people were...complaining about all their misfortunes, and the Lord heard them. His anger flared against them because of their complaints...(Numbers 11:1).

Moses had led the Israelites out of Egypt, and God had given them some remarkable signs of His presence and concern for them. He had parted the Red Sea, allowing them to walk across on dry land, and later brought the water back over the heads of the Egyptian soldiers pursuing them. God promised to lead His people to the Promised Land; He promised to feed them in the wilderness, and to drive their enemies out before them - if they would only trust Him. As a sign, God's presence went with them in the form of a pillar of cloud in the daytime, and a pillar of fire at night.

But the Israelites didn't trust God. They complained bitterly, first because of a lack of food and water, and later because they didn't like the taste of the water God gave them. They grew tired of the diet God had provided for them. They fussed and complained about petty little things. And what were the consequences?

Patiently, God humored His murmuring children. Again and again He met their needs, until it became obvious that they would not learn. When they got tired of the taste of manna, and wanted meat instead, God said that He would give them meat, not just for one day or two days, *but* (for) *a whole month, until you are satiated and vomit it up violently, and it comes out at your nostrils, and is disgusting to you; because you have rejected and despised the Lord*...(Numbers 11:20 Amp).

Forty years the Israelites wandered and every time something went wrong, they complained bitterly and wanted to go back.

Why did it take them forty years to cover less than two hundred miles? Even with women and children and cattle, they could have covered the distance in a few weeks. They were delayed because they murmured and refused to trust that God would keep His promise to take care of their every need.

When the Israelites first came to the border of their Promised Land, they discovered that giants already lived there, in fortified cities. Instead of rejoicing at the obstacles, praising God who had promised to drive all their enemies out before them, the Israelites turned against Moses and demanded to be taken back to Egypt. They accused Moses of having deceived them.

Only two men, Joshua and Caleb, who had seen the giants and the fortified cities, trusted that God would keep His promise and give the Israelites the land. But no one listened to Joshua and Caleb.

This was the last straw. God vowed to let the Israelites stew in their own complaints. Not one of the complainers would live to set foot on the Promised Land. Instead, the nation of Israel would wander in the wilderness for forty years, until a new generation would grow up. *They* would be allowed to enter, led by Joshua and Caleb, the only two who would survive the wilderness years.

God was patient with them for forty years, though they tried his patience sorely; he kept right on doing his mighty miracles for them to see. But, God says, I was very angry with them, for their hearts were always looking somewhere else instead of up to me, and they never found the paths I wanted them to follow (Hebrews 3:10).

Petty complaining kept the Israelites out of their Promised Land.

Our complaints and murmurings against God in the little things can keep us from entering into the perfect plan He has for our lives.

Beware then of your own hearts, dear brothers, lest you find that they, too, are evil and unbelieving and are leading you away from the living God (Hebrews 3:12).

The cause of the Israelites' murmuring was unbelief, and unbelief is at the root of every one of our little complaints.

Unbelief kept the Israelites out of Canaan. But God wanted to do more for them than just bring them into a geographical location. God's Promised Land was also to be a place of rest, of trust and peace of mind.

Although God's promise still stands - his promise that all may enter his place of rest - we ought to tremble with fear because some of you may be on the verge of failing to get there after all...For only we who believe God can enter into his place of rest. He has said, I have sworn in my anger that those who don't believe me will never get in (Hebrews 4:1, 3).

God has a place of perfect rest prepared for us. And I don't mean after death, I mean *now*. It is that state of perfect trust in Him that we can all enter. But in order to do so, we must give up our sin of unbelief, our grumblings, murmurings, and complaints. Unbelief is a serious offense against God.

The world's sin is unbelief in me, said Jesus (John 16:9).

Unbelief, like all sin, is an act of rebellion against God. We can choose to believe or not to believe.

Webster defines unbelief as a "witholding of belief: incredulity or skepticism: a rejection of what is asserted."

If unbelief is a deliberate witholding of belief, then we are responsible for our action, and we must do something about it.

The first step in dealing with any sin is confession.

For years I had proudly told myself that I rarely grumbled, that is, I rarely grumbled out loud. I had cultivated and maintained a smiling facade, but I was a habitual grumbler inside. Of course, as long as I didn't think I was guilty of grumbling, I never improved.

I thought *my* kinds of complaints were legitimate. I grumbled when I didn't get enough sleep and had to get out of bed in the morning without feeling rested. I grumbled under my breath if the bathroom was messed up by another member of my family and I grumbled over my hurried breakfast. I grumbled when things went wrong at the office, and when people didn't do what I expected of them. I grumbled over bills, and when my car wouldn't start, or when I hit a red light on my way to anywhere. I grumbled when I had to work late at the office and didn't get to bed on time; and the next morning I started all over again.

When the Holy Spirit began to show me what the Bible had to say about thanking God for everything, I began to realize that I'd been complaining for years and never thought a thing about it.

The first step toward rehabilitation was to admit to myself that I was a habitual grumbler.

I believe the most effective way to deal with our sins is to be specific about them. We confess them, repent, and ask God's forgiveness, and make a clear-cut decision not to fall into that sin again. We then ask God to remove the sin from us and to give us increased faith and strength to withstand temptation. At last we thank Him for it and proceed on faith, knowing that it has been done.

Once we make an agreement with God not to grumble, and promise instead to thank Him for every little thing that used to make us complain, we can expect Him to go to work.

We can't change ourselves from unbelieving grumblers to thankful, cheerful believers. God has to do the changing. We make the decision to stop complaining and start thanking and praising God, but it is God's power that works the transformation. Our job is to keep our eyes on Jesus and thank God for what *He* is able to do.

In practice, we will find that God will bring into our lives the very kinds of circumstances that used to trigger our grumbling. When we see them coming, we can thank and praise God, because He's using those very incidents to bring about the change in us. Before, they made us stumble; now they will show us God's strength. They will serve to increase our faith.

Accepting every little thing that happens with an attitude of thanksgiving will release the power of God in and through us, and we will soon experience a feeling of joy as well. But don't look for the feeling as a sign. Our praise and thanksgiving must be based on faith in God's Word, not on our feelings.

One of the things I'd grumbled about for years was my lack of musical talent. Whenever I heard beautiful music, I failed to enjoy it fully, because it always made me wish I could play an instrument or sing beautiful solos.

Then one day I was listening to a concert, and the question came into my mind, "Are you thankful that you can't play a musical instrument?"

I recognized the source of the question as the Holy Spirit and squirmed in my seat.

"No, Lord, I guess I'm not."

"Are you willing to be?"

"Yes, Lord, I'm willing, and I understand that this is your will for me. You could have arranged to give me a musical talent and have it trained if you wanted to, so I thank you for me, just as you wanted me to be."

As I said it, a great peace flowed into me, and I realized that I was actually happy to be as I am.

"What I wanted you to learn is this," the Holy Spirit said: "If you could make beautiful music, you would please some people, but when you give praise you always please God."

My lack of musical talent was never a shortcoming in

God's eyes, only in my own. *I* was the one who was dissatisfied with the way God had made me. He was never dissatisfied.

There are people who spend their lives wishing they could have a special talent and an opportunity to develop it. They grumble and complain inside because they are sure that given the right breaks in life, they might have become a movie star, TV personality, baseball hero, business tycoon, or doctor.

Do you have a favorite grumble about your own life? Do you say to yourself that if you could only have a chance to live it over again, you'd be in a different profession, a different neighborhood, a different marriage?

Can you accept and declare to yourself that God has you exactly where He wants you? That He hasn't overlooked a thing? That He wasn't helpless to interfere back when you made what you think of as your wrong choice?

Sure, there is such a thing as a wrong choice. We've been talking in the book about our responsibility to choose and the consequences of the right and wrong choices. But the promise of God is that He makes all things, including our own wrong choices, work for our good when we trust Him.

It is possible that you are in a job or in a situation God plans to move you out of. Still, it is essential that *right now* you accept your present situation with joy and thank God for it. As we thank God for every difficulty, submitting to His will at every turn, He is able to move us into the spot where He wants us.

Remember, He was able to move the heathen King Cyrus into the right spot at the right time even though Cyrus didn't know God. So you can be sure that if God had wanted you to be somewhere else at this very moment, He would have had you there. Your task right now is to thank Him for where you are right now!

If God, by His Holy Spirit, shows you that you made a wrong choice fifteen years ago when you deliberately chose to go against what you then knew to be God's will for you, confess that wrong choice to Him now, ask His forgiveness, thank Him for it, and ask Him to guide you in making right anything you may have done to wrong others. Then turn the rest of your life, as of this moment, completely over into God's hands and trust that He now is in complete charge. *Now* praise and thank Him for your *present* circumstances exactly as they are in every detail.

You may discover God's power working to move you out of your present circumstances very quickly, or you may find that God's power is transforming you in the midst of the circumstances. Whatever happens, continue to thank Him, for He is in charge.

A Christian businessman made a deeper commitment of his life to Christ, and shortly thereafter found himself laid off from his highly-paid job as an executive. The man searched for another job, but cutbacks in the industry made positions scarce. His family suffered from the financial stress, and his anxieties increased as the bills mounted and his prayers seemed unanswered.

He had been unemployed for a year when he heard me speak one Saturday night about being thankful for all things. It suddenly dawned on him that God probably had a good reason for not having led him to a job, and he began to thank God for his unemployment and for every hardship he and his family were suffering as a result.

All day Sunday he continued to praise God, and he discovered that his fears and resentments concerning the situation were decreasing. In their place, he felt genuine joy.

Early Monday morning the phone rang. Another executive wanted to know if he could go to work for him.

"Yes, I'm available," said the man.

"How soon can you start?"

"Tomorrow."

"Then be here at 9 am, ready to start."

His new job gave an excellent salary, but more important, he was in direct contact with groups of business-men daily. His witness for Christ led one man after another to accept the Lord as his Savior.

The businessman told me, "As long as I carried a spark of fear and resentment over my situation, I was blocking God from doing what He wanted with my life. As soon as I was able to trust Him and praise Him for my life exactly as it was, He was able to take over and place me where He wanted me."

A young teacher was spending her summer vacation in the mountains when a letter was mailed from the superintendent's office telling her to report for a conference concerning next year's assignment. She didn't get the letter, and when she didn't show up for the conference, her job was given to someone else.

When she returned from her vacation, she discovered that she was unemployed.

Her first impulse was to panic and go home to her parents in another state. School was to start in two weeks; there were no job openings in the district; and she had heavy financial obligations from her college days.

This young lady had just read *Prison to Praise* and recognized her present situation as an opportunity to practice what she'd learned. She deliberately quenched the impulse to panic, thanked God that He had allowed her to lose her job, and thanked Him for His perfect plan for her life.

For two days she praised God, fighting back every temptation to despair. On the third day a neighbor talked to her across the back fence.

"You know, you really ought to be teaching in a Christian school," she said. "Why don't you call the principal of the school where my son goes?"

The young teacher did, and discovered to her surprise that a position as first-grade teacher had suddenly been left vacant. She was interviewed and got the job.

"I know that God was able to take over the situation because I trusted Him enough to praise Him," she said. "If I'd pulled my usual old trick of panicking and running home to Mom and Dad, I might still have been unemployed and fussing at God for not looking after me.''

Her new job suited her far better than the old one. She was able to freely share her faith in the classroom, and could openly pray with any of the children who had problems.

God had a perfect plan and a perfect place for the young teacher and for the Christian businessman. He closed the doors to the jobs they had held and thought they wanted, and He opened the right doors when they trusted Him and praised Him *for* their unemployment.

Resentment and fear, grumbling and complaining, cause delays in the unfolding of God's plan for us. He has a perfect time plan, and we must realize that His timing doesn't always coincide with ours.

I had always been punctual, and was proud of my ability to organize and make proper use of ''the Lord's time.'' Then one day I found myself on a plane enroute to El Paso, Texas, where I was to speak at a convention of businessmen. I was glancing nervously at my watch. It was moving toward 2:30 pm, and I had planned to be at the meeting at 2. ''Now what possible good can come out of my being late for an engagement?'' I wondered.

''Why are you letting this happen, Lord?'' I asked, with just a trace of irritability. The only answer was another question:

''Are you thankful you are late?''

''That's not the point,'' I argued back. ''Those people who arranged for me to come, and paid my expenses, are expecting me there on time. They are the ones who'll have to learn to be thankful.''

"Are you thankful? '' The thought persisted.

The truth suddenly dawned on me. I wasn't really moved by concern for the people at the meeting. I was the one who was upset. I wasn't trusting that God was handling the situation right. I was fussing and arguing over His management of ''my'' time.

''I'm sorry, Lord,'' I whispered. ''I *do* believe you know best how to manage my time. If you're letting me be late, it must be part of your perfect plan, and I thank you for it. I turn the management of my time over to you and trust you to work it out for good."

I leaned back in my seat and drew a breath of relief. My watch said 2:45, but I felt perfect peace. At that moment the stewardess walked past, and her watch came into sharp focus before my eyes. It read 1:45.

I sat up. "Miss, your watch says 1:45. Are you sure that is correct?"

"Yes, sir, it is. We've just crossed into another time zone, and it is now 1:45."

I chuckled to myself. "Thank you, Lord, for teaching me how silly it is to worry about the time."

As the plane flew on, the time moved past 2, and I felt a twinge of anxiety again. At 2:15 we were coming in for a landing at El Paso, but it looked like I would still be a few minutes late.

"Lord, I'm sorry I'm impatient," I muttered. "But I've never been late to a meeting before, and I don't understand why you're letting it happen now."

"Are you thankful?"

"All right, Lord," I said. "I *will* be thankful. Thank you that it is now 2:20, and I'm exactly where I am."

When I walked off the plane, my watch said 2:25.

I pulled the convention schedule out of my pocket to check on the address, and my eyes fell on the time for the meeting. It said 2:30!

I ran to the nearest cabstand. *This is beautiful, Lord*, I thought. *You've been able to teach me a lesson about trusting your management of my time.*

The cabdriver looked at me expectantly. "Where to, Sir?"

"The El Paso Hilton Inn," I gasped. "I need to get there as quickly as possible!"

The cabdriver chuckled and pointed across the street.

"There it is, right in front of you!"

I walked through the door into the convention hall and

glanced at my watch. It was exactly 2:30. The men were walking up to the speakers' table, and I filed up behind them to take my seat.

God's timetable is precise to the minute. How great it is to know that we're on His schedule.

Release the timekeeping of your life to Him. He will get you where He wants you, when He wants you there, if you trust Him. His schedule is good for every appointment and every hour of our lives. God doesn't force His time plan on us, but if we give our days and hours to Him, it is His business to get us where He wants us on His time.

That doesn't mean we can sit down in our soft seats and say, "If the Lord wants me there, He'll have to get me there. I'm just going to sit here and doze until He moves me."

We've got to do our part, but that is *not* to worry about the timekeeping. We do our best, get up on time in the morning, prepare in time for appointments, then thank Him for whatever happens - even if we get delayed unexpectedly, or are interrupted by a talkative neighbor or demanding child.

God has a double purpose in teaching us to trust and praise Him in everything. It releases His power into our situation, and it also draws others to Him.

I once worked with a choir-leader who was a perfectionist.

Every detail of the music for each service was planned and performed with precision, but the choir-leader always performed under a strain, and his tension was transmitted to the choir. They sang with excellence, but without joy.

One day the choir-leader dropped by for a chat in my office.

"Bob, I think you would be more relaxed and experience greater joy in your music if you began to thank God for everything that happens." I said.

He looked at me in silence for some time, then said. "I've been watching you these past six months. At first I thought you were putting on a front. No one could be that joyful all the time." He smiled. "I made several mistakes with the choir, and you always reacted with joy...I don't understand how you do it, but I'd like to have the same attitude."

We talked until the time for choir-rehearsal, and Bob left my office in a hurry. He hadn't had time for any preparation, and I wondered how he would respond to the unexpected challenge.

Later he told me, "I was getting really tense thinking about all the music and equipment I hadn't prepared, when it dawned on me: this was exactly the kind of situation we'd talked about thanking God for, so I thanked Him. Just then, four members of the choir came to the door. They were early for rehearsal and asked, 'What can we do to help you get ready?' Nothing like that has ever happened in all the months I have led the choir."

"I was amazed. 'Thank you, God,' I prayed. 'You really took care of that problem quickly'!"

The rest of the day Bob had wandered in a half-daze. He had never realized before that God was personally concerned with the details of his life, and that God's power would be released as soon as he relaxed and was thankful in every circumstance. The discovery completely changed Bob's attitude to his music ministry.

The next time he sang a solo, he made several mistakes, something that ordinarily would have plunged him into despair. But instead of getting more tense with each wrong note, he offered up thanks to God who allowed it to happen. As a result, he experienced increasing joy as the song progressed, and we who listened could see the happiness radiate from his face and hear the new dimension of joy in his singing.

Bob's relationship with the congregation also changed markedly. He had been greeting us with a glum "Hello," now he beamed and said, "Good morning! Isn't it a beautiful day!"

Wearing a glum face may not seem like a sin, until we consider the fact that it expresses the very opposite of happy, abiding faith, and as such is actually an attitude of unbelief.

We all know the expression, "Well, we all have our bad days and our ups and downs." This is careless, even dangerous thinking, because it suggests that bad days and ups and downs are a normal part of the Christian life. The Bible says that our *outward* circumstances may go up and down, be bad or good, but our *inner* attitude is to be a permanent state of rejoicing in Christ.

...I have learned the secret of being content in any and every situation...(Philippians 4:12 NIV).

The consequences of our failure to be thankful in the little things are not always apparent to us, but once I was taught a stern lesson.

It was a busy morning in our chaplain's office at Fort Benning, and everything seemed to go wrong. The senior man in charge had not shown up for work, and none of the others seemed to know what to do. Telephones were ringing, work was piling up, and I began to feel impatient with the man who had not reported for duty. Of course, my attitude didn't make him arrive, nor did it improve the situation. I grumbled under my breath through most of a miserable day.

The next day the man returned and explained that he had gone to the hospital where he was told that he had a cancerous growth in his sinus. Overcome at the news, he had gone home to spend the day in bed, not caring if he ever got up again.

I was overwhelmed with remorse. I'd fussed over the insignificant delays at the office, instead of thanking God for the man who was absent. My grumbling had effectively put me out of commission as a channel for God's love and power flowing toward the sick man.

It is important that we learn to respond with trust and praise in all situations, whether or not the consequences are apparent to us. As we learn to push the praise button instead of the panic button, our lives and our attitudes are changed, whether the situation confronting us is a dramatic event or a minor irritation.

Once a man was driving home from work on icy roads. He misjudged the road conditions and slid through a stop sign and into another car. No one was injured, but the cars were badly damaged, and the responsible driver was angry with himself for having made a stupid mistake. Then he remembered having read recently about praising God for everything.

"Thank you for this accident, Lord," he prayed.

Immediately a silent voice whispered in his head, "Don't be stupid. You've made a bad mistake already. Are you going to make it worse by pretending you're glad about it?"

"But God has promised to make it work for good," he argued back.

"You'll never see anything good come out of *this*!"

"If I thank God, I will," the man persisted.

He continued to be thankful for the accident, yet nothing outwardly dramatic happened as a result. The other driver wasn't led to Christ, and no one seemed to react to his joyful attitude at the garage.

So what difference did it make how he reacted?

As the day progressed, something very remarkable was happening *in* that man. The more he thanked God, the more a new kind of peace spread inside him. Toward noon he discovered that something like bubbling laughter kept welling up from within, and each time he repeated his thanks to God for the accident, he could feel something being released, like the untying of tight knots, deep within him.

He had been an average Christian but from that day on his life was never again the same. He had entered a new dimension of victorious living in Christ - all because of his determination to recognize God's hand in something he had first thought was his own stupid mistake and a stroke of bad luck.

Another man heard me speak about praising God for

everything and promised God from that moment he would
be thankful for everything that happened to him.

He and his family drove home from the meeting through
a snowstorm in below-zero weather. They arrived home late
at night, and the moment they stepped in the front door, they
knew something was wrong. The house was ice-cold, and
the furnace was dead.

The family huddled upstairs while the man walked
down to the basement to check the furnace. He knew nothing
about furnaces and had no idea what might be wrong.

He stood staring at the cold, silent furnace, and his first
impulse was to pray that God would help him get it going
again. Without heat in the house, He would have to take his
family to a warm shelter for the night.

Then the thought came to him, "Are you thankful
now?"

"I'm sorry, Lord, I forgot," he prayed. "But I know you
must have planned this for our good, so thank you, God, for
this furnace, just as it is."

At that moment a very distinct suggestion came into his
mind: "Check the fan!"

"The fan? I don't even know where it is!"

"Look behind the plate on the right side," came the
thought.

He found a screwdriver and began removing the plate.
The whole scene suddenly struck him as ridiculous. Was he
just imagining things? Was the fan really behind the plate?
But if God was really at work giving him this direct kind of
help, he couldn't stop now, he reasoned.

His fingers were numb with cold, but the plate came off
- and there was the fan.

Now what? he thought.

"Look for the fan belt; it is off."

It was too dark to see inside the furnace, so he got a
flashlight and directed the beam down the small opening in
the furnace. There was the fan belt, lying loose. He slipped
it over the drive shaft on the fan and removed his arm from

the narrow opening. The furnace remained cold and silent.

"What now?" he prayed.

"Turn the furnace switch," came the suggestion.

As soon as he turned the switch, the furnace came alive with happy dancing flames, and the man ran upstairs to share with his family how God had blessed them with a cold furnace.

Had the man *not* responded to the crisis by praising God and expecting Him to work it all for good, he and his family would have suffered inconvenience and hardship. The cold furnace was a God-given opportunity to learn that praise releases the power and guidance of God.

Following the furnace incident, the man's life was changed. He began to listen for the voice of God in all situations, and today has developed a rare sensitivity to the promptings of the Holy Spirit. His open ear to the guidance of God has made him a channel for God's power in the lives of others also.

The first step was an act of faith, believing that a cold furnace on a dark, snowy night was an expression of God's loving concern for him and his family's welfare. He could have passed up that first opportunity, and I am sure that God would have provided other challenges. You and I are confronted with many opportunities to recognize God's hand in the situations of our daily lives. How many opportunities do we pass up?

The results of our reactions are cumulative. With each positive step of faith, it becomes easier to believe. In the same way, each time we allow unbelief to deny God's presence and love in a difficult situation, the negative results heap up, and it becomes increasingly difficult to muster our will to exercise any faith at all. The more we grumble, the more we become entangled in the web of defeat. Many little grumbles can add up to overwhelming mountains of depression.

A Christian nurse wrote of years she had spent in misery. It seemed like little things always upset me and caused irritation. Gradually my life was getting more and more miserable. I prayed for God to help me, but nothing happened. I started taking pills to get going in the morning and pills to go to sleep at night. Every day began with the agony of having to get out of bed. I couldn't cope with my own housework. At the hospital I was breaking under the strain of caring for the patients.

Each day was worse than the one before. I couldn't even do little things I had been able to do with ease a few months before. I was sinking into such a depression that I prayed for God to let me die. Living was sheer hell.

Then one day she read *Prison to Praise*.

It was like a light of hope had been turned on inside me, she wrote. She determined to praise God for everything, and made a long list of things to be thankful for, beginning with the circumstances that had caused her so much strain. The results soon began to show up.

All I can think of now is, *What a wonderful change in my life there has been - since Jesus came into my heart*! I no longer have a horrible fear of failure hanging over me. Things don't irritate and upset me. When something appears to go wrong, I just look up and say, 'Thank you, Lord!' and it really puts a song in my heart!

Whether you are surrounded by what seem to you like mountains of accumulated misery, or just irritating little molehills, the turning point is the same. Confess your complaining and murmuring as a sin, and promise God that you'll be thankful from now on.

You make the decision and determine to stand on it in faith; God will furnish the strength to do it. Once you've made your commitment, the opportunities to thank God may come in little or big packages, but they'll come.

At a retreat near Fort Benning, several young people made a promise to thank God for all things. The next day one of the soldiers was notified that a favorite uncle had been killed in a tractor accident on the farm. Immediately the thought came to the soldier, "Now see what happened! You made the silly commitment to praise God. Your uncle wasn't even a Christian!"

The soldier recognized the source of that thought, and resisted the temptation to complain to God about his uncle's death. Instead he prayed, "God, you know how much I loved my uncle, but you love him more, so you must have had a good reason for letting him die. I'll just thank you and praise you for doing what was best."

The soldier felt a peace about his uncle's death, but was unable to shake off a concern for his cousin who had just recently accepted Christ as his Savior. How was he taking his father's death? The soldier wanted to go home for the funeral in order to encourage his cousin, but he was unable to get leave.

"Okay, God," he prayed. "You know all about my cousin, so I'll just thank you that I can't go." He thought he would call home and ask his parents to convey a message to his cousin, and stepped into a phone booth to make the call.

When a voice answered at the other end, he immediately recognized his cousin. "How are you?" he blurted out in surprise.

"I'm praising the Lord," came the answer. "We're all so glad that Dad accepted Christ several days before the accident. He had time to tell everybody what God had done for him, and we know it was God's will that he go to heaven now."

The soldier returned to the retreat to share with the others what had happened. A chaplain's wife who was there, promised God she would thank Him for everything in her life.

Driving home that evening, she had her first opportunity. In eighteen years of driving, she'd never had a traffic ticket. This time she was asked to pull over to the side of the road and an MP who'd been following her at a distance gave her a ticket for going through an intersection without making the required stop.

She explained to the MP that he had made a mistake. Another car looking just like hers had failed to stop at the intersection, speeding past her as she came to a careful halt. The policeman did not accept her story, and her first impulse was to be angry and complain about the injustice. Then she remembered her promise to be thankful in everything.

"God, I trust this is your will," she prayed. "I will praise you for the whole experience." Suddenly she discovered that her inner being was flooded with joy.

The next day she returned to the retreat and told us what had happened.

"Isn't it marvelous?" she said, "We don't have to worry about being treated unfairly or taken advantage of. Even *those* circumstances become a source of joy and strength when we see God's hand in them and give thanks."

Others are drawn to Christ when we praise God. If we grumble and complain as bitterly as our non-Christian friends over the many little upsetting incidents of our days, others conclude that our faith does no more for us than having no faith does for them. Unless they can see, in the nitty-gritty of our daily lives, that Christ makes a difference, how can we expect them to believe when we say they need Jesus?

It isn't what we say, but what we are and what we do that draws others to the Christ-life in us. Nowhere is this more apparent than in our daily lives. How do we react to delays and difficulties on the job, in emergencies, in everyday encounters? Do we react in such a way that no one sees anything different about us? Or does our reaction cause them to stop and say, "Something is different about that person. He's got something I need?"

One couple read *Prison to Praise* and were convinced that God wanted them to be thankful for everything. One night they were awakened at 2:30 am by the sound of breaking glass. The man looked outside and saw that all the windows in his car had been smashed by a group of kids who were fast disappearing around the corner.

The couple agreed that God had given them an opportunity to praise Him, and they knelt by their bed, giving thanks for what had happened.

The next morning the man took his car to a garage and explained what had happened.

"Thank God," he said. "I'm sure He has a wonderful purpose behind it all."

The owner of the garage shook his head.

"If something like that happened to me, I'd see to it that those young punks were made to pay," he said.

The customer smiled. "That isn't necessary," he explained. "God is in charge of the situation; I don't need to be upset about it."

The garage-owner stared at him for a moment, then said, "I've been a Christian for years, but I never heard about praising God for vandalism."

They talked on, and the customer told the garage-owner about the baptism in the Holy Spirit and the power of God released through praise.

"Hold it," said the garage-owner. "I've heard about the baptism in the Holy Spirit till I've gotten sick of it. I have one customer who talks about nothing else. But tell me more about praising God. That sounds interesting."

The customer explained that he thought the two subjects were one, since both had to do with complete trust and commitment to God. Finally the garage-owner accepted an invitation to attend a meeting of Spirit-filled businessmen, and at the meeting he experienced the baptism of the Holy Spirit for himself.

Next he committed himself to praising God for everything, and the first item on his list was his business. It had been sliding toward bankruptcy for two years.

The next afternoon one of his employees came with bad news; he had been in an accident, wrecking their truck. This could be the last straw, toppling the business.

The garage-owner looked at his young employee, who stood pale and trembling, obviously expecting an outburst of temper from his boss. Instead the garage-owner smiled, put his arm around the young man's shoulders and said, "Let us praise God for this accident and believe He will work it out for good!"

A routine insurance claim was submitted, and to the garage-owner's amazement, the settlement enabled him to pay urgent bills. The accident marked the turning point in his business, and his profits began to show a marked increase. It was an even more important turning point in the life of the garage-owner who had experienced increasing joy and peace in every area of his life. In turn, a steady stream of customers came to know Jesus Christ as their Savior because they were impressed with his obvious joy.

When the joy of Christ is released in our lives, others are drawn to Him.

Once, after a late meeting, I walked into a restaurant and asked for a glass of milk. The waitress smiled and went to the kitchen to get my order. A moment later she reappeared with an angry frown on her face.

"I'm very sorry, sir, but someone has locked the refrigerator, and I can't get any milk for you."

"Thank the Lord!" I responded automatically. The waitress looked puzzled.

"Why did you say that?"

"I have learned to be thankful for everything, because I believe that God works in everything for our good if we let Him."

"What religion are you?" she asked incredulously.

"Methodist."

"Well, I'm a Baptist, but I have never heard of being thankful for things like that!"

"Are you a Christian Baptist?" I asked.

"Well," she hesitated, "I think I am, but I've never been sure."

"You can be absolutely sure," I said. "Jesus came into the world to give us eternal life as a free gift. All we have to do is ask Him to forgive our sins and then believe that He does. I'd like to pray with you and ask God to give you this free gift if you want it."

The waitress nodded eagerly. "Yes, sir, I would like that!"

I touched her shoulder with my hand, we bowed our heads, and there in the empty restaurant, a few minutes after midnight, I prayed that God would release her faith and give her assurance of eternal life through Christ.

Tears were running down her face.

"I've never felt like this before in my life," she said. "I feel as if a great burden has rolled off my back. I really do believe I'm a Christian now."

It may seem inconsequential to make a point out of being grateful for not getting a glass of milk when you want it, but as you learn to thank God for every little thing, God will use your praise to draw unhappy, weary people to Him. And He can turn their burden of worries and anxieties into pure joy and peace.

I was sitting in the Atlanta airport, waiting to board a plane, when a stranger suddenly picked up the briefcase I had placed on a low table beside me. I had left the latch open, and the contents spilled all over the floor. Papers flew in all directions, and I noticed my toothbrush, thrown out of its case, lying on the dirty floor. I stifled the impulse to be upset with the clumsy stranger and muttered under my breath, "Yes, Lord, I do thank you for this and I know you have some good reason for letting it happen."

The embarrassed stranger apologized and hastily began to pick up my scattered belongings. When I joined him, he looked up and said, "You don't remember me, do you?"

"No, I'm afraid I don't."

He explained that we had met briefly several months ago and that he had just now been walking through the terminal feeling tired and discouraged, asking God to lead him to someone who could help.

"I saw you and picked up your briefcase in order to sit down on the table next to you," he explained. "Now I know God led me to you. Will you please explain how you could remain completely undisturbed when I spilled your things all over the floor?"

I was more than happy to tell him how glorious it is to trust that all things work for good if we love God, and that little experiences like an upset briefcase are opportunities to thank God and watch Him work.

The man was amazed and asked several questions. When the time came for my plane to leave, he said, "Would you consider coming to Fort Lauderdale, Florida, as my guest, at your earliest convenience?"

It was my turn to be amazed. I had been praying that God would provide a way for me to go to Fort Lauderdale. I had heard much about what God had been doing in the lives of Christians there.

Paul wrote to the Christians at Philippi:

In everything you do, stay away from complaining and arguing, so that no one can speak a word of blame against you. You are to live clean, innocent lives as children of God in a dark world full of people who are crooked and stubborn. Shine out among them like beacon lights, holding out to them the Word of Life...Whatever happens, dear friends, be glad in the Lord. I never get tired of telling you this and it is good for you to hear it again and again (Philippians 2:14-16; 3:1).

It is our lack of complaining as well as our happiness in Christ that enables us to shine like beacons, holding out the Word of Life in a dark world. It was true in Philippi, and it is true today.

Let's quit our grumblings and praise the Lord for every dark and crooked thing we see around us. Do it, and watch God's light penetrate that darkness.

Chapter 7

The Joy of the Lord

The joy of the Lord is your strength, said the prophet Nehemiah (Nehemiah 8:10).

No wonder Jesus desired so strongly that His disciples understand that He had come, not only to purchase their salvation through His sacrifice on the cross, but also to provide them with the sustaining power of His joy.

You haven't tried this before, He told them, *but begin now. Ask, using my name, and you will receive, and your cup of joy will overflow* (John 16:24).

The joy of the Lord is ours for the asking!

Jesus prayed for us: *That My joy may be made full and complete and perfect in them - that they may experience My delight fulfilled in them, that My enjoyment may be perfected in their own souls, that they may have My gladness within them filling their hearts* (John 17:13 Amp).

Every born-again Christian knows that his salvation is a free gift. He was born again of the Holy Spirit when he accepted Jesus Christ as his Savior, *by faith*. Many Christians have come to discover that there is much more to God's free gift than being born again as a child of God. The baptism in the Holy Spirit can be claimed by *faith*. But few of us seem to have realized that Jesus has also provided us with His joy. It is there to be claimed *by faith* with the rest of the package.

If the joy of the Lord is our strength, then it is obviously not something that comes last in a long line of attainments, sort of like the whipped topping on the cake. It is something we need from the start, something to sustain us and strengthen us in our task of carrying the Good News around the world.

Paul wrote to the Corinthians, *When I come, although I can't do much to help your faith, for it is strong already, I want to be able to do something about your joy: I want to make you happy, not sad* (II Corinthians 1:24).

Paul didn't mean that He would make them happy by bringing nice gifts or providing pleasant circumstances. He intended to remind them of the joy they had already been given. He wanted them to practice rejoicing to cultivate the joy planted in them by the Holy Spirit.

Paul knew that the outward circumstances for a strong Christian would always be filled with trials and suffering. The Christian's source of joy was to be his inward abiding in Christ.

The Holy Spirit clearly...affirms to me in city after city that imprisonment and suffering await me. But none of these things move me; neither do I esteem my life dear to myself, if only I may finish my course with joy, and the ministry which I have obtained of...the Lord Jesus, faithfully to attest the good news...of God's grace... (Acts 20:23-24 Amp).

If joy has already been given us by Jesus, why do so many Christians live such joyless lives?

Jesus prayed that His joy would be perfected in us. What He means is that we can't make ourselves joyful anymore than we can save ourselves, give ourselves peace, or make ourselves more loving. What we *can* do is choose to accept what Jesus has done for us and allow Him to perfect His joy in us.

In practice, this means that we deliberately set out to practice joy, regardless of how we feel, trusting that God then goes to work, transforming our sorrows into pure joy, just as He has promised.

Love, joy, and peace are all fruit of the Holy Spirit. Jesus told his disciples how they were to cultivate this fruit.

I have loved you even as the Father has loved Me. Live within my love. When you obey me you are living in my love, just as I obey My Father and live in His love. I have told you this so that you will be filled with my joy (John 15:9-11).

The source of joy was not to be found in happy circumstances, but in knowing Jesus' commandments, obeying them, and abiding in Him.

Jeremiah wrote, *Your words were found, and I ate them, and Your word was to me a joy and the rejoicing of my heart* (Jeremiah 15:16 Amp).

Joy is certainly something we are meant to feel. It is to be a happy, overflowing, pleasant experience. But joy does not depend on feeling. We are not to rejoice because we feel joyful, rather we can expect to eventually feel joyful as a result of our rejoicing.

David had learned the secret of rejoicing. *Rejoice...with trembling*, he wrote in Psalm 2:11. *And now shall my head be lifted up above my enemies round about me; in His tent will I offer sacrifices and shouting of joy; I will sing, yes, I will sing praises to the Lord* (Psalm 27:6 Amp).

For a long time I thought that joy was something I would experience when I was satisfied and things were happy around me. Now I realize that joy doesn't spring up in my emotions, but is triggered by my will and is part of the life of praise.

Let all the joys of the godly well up in praise to the Lord, for it is right to praise Him, wrote David in Psalm 33:1.

Joy, thanksgiving and praise belong together, and our commitment to praise and thank God for everything does not become complete until we've committed ourselves to rejoice in everything as well.

An elderly woman who had been filled with the Holy Spirit and had been an active Christian worker for years became crippled with arthritis. Years of pain had robbed her of any joy in living; the smallest household chore was an agony, and she experienced increasing depression.

She believed that God could heal, and had gone to healing meetings, but her condition only grew worse. One day she heard about the power in praising God for everything, and made up her mind to try it. Her task wasn't easy,

since now every moment of her days and nights were filled
with pain. But she was willing to be genuinely thankful for
every part of her life, including her pain.

One day she moved slowly across her kitchen floor,
carrying a tray of utensils. Suddenly the tray dropped,
scattering items over the entire floor. Her painful back and
stiff fingers made it impossible for her to bend over to pick
anything up from the floor. Her usual reaction to dropping
an object was to break down in tears of self-pity. But this
time she remembered her promise to praise God.

"Thank you, Lord," she prayed, "for letting me drop
everything on the floor. I believe you're working it to my
good."

In a flash she became aware of other beings in the
kitchen besides herself. She had been alone - yet now she
sensed others present. Startled, she realized she was
surrounded by angels. The angels were laughing and
rejoicing, and she knew their joy was for her. Suddenly she
understood.

Jesus told His disciples, *There is rejoicing among the
angels of God over one sinner whose heart is changed* (Luke
15:10 Phillips).

She was certainly a saved sinner whose heart had been
miraculously changed. For years she had been filled with
self-pity and complaint against God for letting her suffer.
She had begged Him to heal her, and inwardly had felt that
God had let her down. At last she had seen that her grumbling
was rooted in unbelief, and there was rejoicing among the
angels when she trusted God enough to praise Him for the
mishap with the tray of utensils.

She stood in the middle of her kitchen floor and felt
herself saturated by the joy that filled the room. With a heart
rejoicing she could thank God sincerely for allowing the
suffering that had brought her such joy.

A short time later she attended a service where they
offered prayer for the sick. Confidently, she walked
forward. Always before, the painful awareness of her

disease had crippled her ability to believe. Now her faith was not anchored in her feelings. She was free to believe, no matter how intense her pain was. That night she was instantly healed. All pain left, and the twisted joints became straight and whole.

We are such creatures of habit. For too long we've let our feelings dictate our reactions. But Christ came to live in us so that His joy can become full and complete in us.

The more we allow our will to take the initiative for our actions, rather than giving in to our feelings, the more we'll discover that we become increasingly able to respond to any situation with praise, joy and thanksgiving. Our old dependency on feelings will grow weaker. As we persist in praising God, we'll discover joy originating in our will, and spreading to our feelings as well.

What is begun as an act of obedience to God's Word, will eventually bring about in us a state of being where we sense, feel, think, and experience a real, overflowing praise, thanksgiving and joy beyond anything we've ever known.

When we fully submit to God's will, so that all obstacles in us can be flushed away, and we can be molded, transformed, and renewed into perfect vessels for Him, then we'll also find that the joy of the Lord *is* complete in us.

For nearly twenty years I suffered with stomach trouble. Many foods gave me extreme discomfort. I'd gone the rounds of doctors and taken all kinds of medicines, but nothing helped.

I prayed and tried to believe that God would heal me, with no apparent result. Others prayed for me - Christian leaders well-known for their effective ministry in healing, prayer groups, and friends - but the problem continued.

I claimed the promise Jesus gave in Mark 16 that not even poison could hurt me, and frequently ate whatever foods were served to me. But "apparent disaster" struck again and again, and I would be miserably ill, unable to sleep, and feel extremely sorry for myself.

I finally decided to accept on faith the fact that I had been healed by Christ's death for me, and to believe that the symptoms would go away when He was ready. For several years I rested on that assurance and thanked God for working in my life in this way for whatever good He wanted to accomplish.

Before I retired from the army, the doctors decided to operate on my stomach. They found nothing obvious to explain the years of pain I had gone through, and consequently could do nothing to improve my condition.

As I lay in my hospital bed after the operation, the pain increased in severity beyond anything I had endured before. Pain-killing drugs had no effect. Hour after hour I lay without sleeping, feeling as if the darkness of the room was closing in on me. I thought I could almost reach out and touch the dark power of evil hovering around me, and I fought against the temptation to give in to the terror I felt. I didn't want to die but dreaded living in such misery.

At the moment when the blackness seemed darker than ever, I cried out, "Lord, I don't care what happens or how miserable I am, I thank you for this entire experience. I know you are going to bring something good out of it."

Instantly the darkness of the hospital room was shattered by a brilliant, white light, brighter than the sun. It was as bright as the light I'd seen in a vision several years before. At that time, the Holy Spirit had explained the vision to me. There was a dark cloud hovering over a meadow, and above the cloud was a bright, white light. Up above the cloud was the state of joy and blessing Christ had already secured for us, but to get there, we had to climb on a ladder straight through the dark cloud of confusion and pain. Inside the cloud it was impossible to know what direction to take through the use of our ordinary sense perceptions of sight, hearing or feeling. The ladder could only be climbed by faith, and by praising God each step of the way. Climbing through the dark cloud, we would be stripped of our dependency on our senses and learn to trust God's Word. The ladder of praise would lift us right up into the heavenlies, to take our place there with Christ Jesus.

As I lay on my bed in the hospital room, my entire body flooded by that wonderful, brilliant light, I suddenly realized that what had once been a vision, now was a reality.

The years I had walked by faith, believing that God was using my pain for good, were years of climbing through the cloud of darkness and uncertainly. Without the cloud, I would never have learned to let go of my reliance on my senses and feelings. Now I could wholeheartedly thank God for every circumstance of my life that added to the dark cloud. How else could I have learned to utterly trust in Him? How else could I have come to experience this beautiful saturation of light and joy?

When I returned home from the hospital, I discovered that God had done something about the condition of my stomach as well.

The foods that had once sent me into hours of pain no longer bothered me. I rejoiced in my new freedom to eat strawberries, apples, bananas, ice cream - all the things I had tried to stay away from for years.

Over the years, others had been healed instantly as I prayed for them, but God had chosen to strengthen my faith by letting me trust in His Word.

Praise does release the power of God to heal, but the healing is of secondary importance. As long as we're primarily concerned with our own comfort, our desire to be healed and free from physical pain, we've got the wrong perspective. Our concern actually amounts to a questioning of God's plan for us.

For years I'd been afraid of some day losing my teeth. Then one day my dentist told me that my gums were badly infected, and the bones around my teeth were deteriorating. Initial X-rays showed a sad picture; I would soon lose my teeth!

Downhearted, I left the dentist's office. Of course I knew that I ought to be thanking God for my condition, but I wasn't very happy about it.

"Thank you, Lord," I said, "I'm grateful that you've allowed my teeth to get into such bad shape. I'm sure you know better than I do what's best for me, so I praise you, Lord."

Even as I prayed I began to feel more thankful, and when a friend came along, I told her about my new occasion to praise the Lord.

"Have you prayed for healing?" she asked.

"No," I said. "I've just now realized that losing my teeth isn't anything to fuss over, since it can't happen unless God allows it."

"I think God wants you to have perfect teeth," my friend said, placing her hand lightly on my shoulder. "Dear God," she prayed. "Thank you for letting Merlin's teeth get in such rotten shape. We praise you and ask that you be glorified in this, so touch Merlin now and heal him completely."

Three days later I was back at the dentist's to have a complete set of X-rays done. I watched while he studied my new X-rays carefully. He had a concerned, puzzled look on his face, and once put the X-rays down to take another look in my mouth. He shook his head and muttered under his breath, and I thought, *Maybe they're worse than he expected.*

Finally the dentist stepped back, looked me over from head to foot, and asked, "What in the world have you done to your teeth?"

"Not a thing!"

"Then I don't understand." He looked from my old X-rays to the new ones. "Your bones are perfect, your gums are no longer infected and swollen - in fact your whole mouth looks perfect!"

I chuckled. How wonderful to know God had healed me - but even better, healing was no longer the real issue. That little gnawing fear I'd carried with me about having false teeth was gone. I knew that with or without teeth of my own, it was the perfect union with Christ and trust in God's loving concern for every detail of my life that really mattered.

Recently I had a letter from a dear lady in New Hampshire. She lives alone with her teen-age son, and when she wrote me, she had been flat on her back and in constant pain after two major operations. She wrote:

> Praise God for His great faithfulness! I was very discouraged after my last operation, but someone gave me *Prison to Praise*. I decided to praise God for my illness and keep looking to Jesus. Since then my pain has not gone away, but I have come to know my Savior in a deeper way, and the Holy Spirit has ministered to me so wonderfully.

> Some of my friends have told me that God made me suffer in order to punish me. But I know this isn't so. Jesus has never accused me; instead He has taught me much about His love. These past months He has used His Word to show me things in my heart and life that shouldn't be there, feelings and thoughts unlike Christ. God in His wonderful love has forgiven me and healed every scar of the old hurts in my life.

> I've learned to thank Jesus for the hard places, and even for the pain. I love Jesus with all my heart. I don't understand why He leads the way He does, but if I can be happy and 'take pleasure' in my infirmity (II Corinthians 12:10), and in going this way for God, I certainly praise Him for it.

> I have to go back to the hospital for a possible third operation. I thank God for it, knowing that He will work in it for my good. I know He can heal me, and I thank Him for whatever He decides in His love is best for me.

Her letter overflowed with genuine joy and gratitude. Her physical body was still in pain, but she had experienced a healing of her emotions and inner being and had entered into a wonderful relationship with God in Christ. Everything else, even her healing, had become secondary.

Oneness with God in Christ was the goal Paul was pressing toward. Jesus knew that His purpose for coming to earth was to remove the sin barrier between man and God, so that once more the Creator could be united with His creation, just as He had originally intended.

Before His crucifixion Jesus prayed for us:

I am not praying for these alone, but also for the future believers who will come to me because of the testimony of these. My prayer for all of them is that they will be of one heart and mind, just as you and I are, Father - that just as you are in me and I am in you, so they will be in us, and the world will believe you sent me. I have given them the glory you gave me - the glorious unity of being one, as we are - I in them and you in me, all being perfected into one - so that the world will know you sent me and will understand that you love them as much as you love me (John 17:20-23).

Jesus prayed, and we know for certain that His prayer was answered. We can be assured that Christ dwells in us. We are one in Him with the Father.

When we begin to grasp the full significance of these accomplished facts, everything else in our lives begins to take on the right perspective. The outer circumstances that once loomed out of proportion to our relationship with Christ and captured most of our attention can now be seen fitting perfectly into the plan that God is working in our lives. We still don't see the plan, but we *do* see Jesus Christ as Lord and Master, and we *know* that God has a plan and that it is good.

Many letters have come to me from people in prisons and jails across the country since *Prison to Praise* was published.

One fellow wrote from death row:

> I've been sentenced to die in the electric
> chair. I know I have to die, and for a long time
> I had no hope for anything beyond death.

Fear controlled all my thoughts, and I felt forsaken by God and man. Then I read *Prison to Praise*. It was as if my mind had become alive again. I dared believe that God is for real and is working in every life to draw us to accept His Son as Savior and Lord.

I looked back on my own sordid life and realized that everything had happened with God's permission so that I might come to the point of reaching out for Him. I did reach out, and in one blinding instant I knew that God does work in all things for our good and His glory. For the first time I knew that my entire life was being blessed by God, and that by faith in His Son I belonged to Him. Now I am truly free and filled with His peace and joy.

Another prisoner wrote:

I had learned to hate everyone and everything. No matter how hard I tried, I couldn't see any reason to be glad I was alive. Someone gave me *Prison to Praise*, and when I first read it I thought it was a bunch of nonsense. But the more I thought about it, the more I was tempted to try thanking God for my messy life. After all, I was at the bottom; what did I have to lose?

I began to go over the events of my life, one by one, as they came back to my memory. I thanked God that each incident was a part of His plan for me. The whole program seemed pretty foolish, but I forced myself to keep going. As I stuck with it, something began to happen inside of me. I began to think of God being personally involved in my mixed-up life. Could it really be true that He was interested in *me?* Events I'd forgotten pounded their way back into my mind. I'd

thought of them as tragic before; now I began
to see them as part of God's faithful drawing
to convince me that I needed Him.

I praised Him for every detail of my life;
I thanked Him for the people who had hated
me, mistreated me, lied about me, and
betrayed me. I thanked Him for the ones I had
hated, mistreated, lied about, and betrayed.

A glowing peace began to flood me.
God was healing all the bitter memories. The
prison walls melted, and peace surrounded
me instead. The walls and the bars can't
make me a prisoner anymore. I'm free in
Christ, praise God!

Another letter came from a Christian in a top-security
penitentiary in the West:

Praise God! Attendance at our church
and evening Bible study groups is swelling.
Last week three men accepted Christ as their
Savior. Imagine what it would mean if three
souls came to Jesus every week inside these
walls! (A later letter told that in the next
month twelve men accepted Christ and four
received the baptism in the Holy Spirit.) We
really appreciate the prayers of the brothers
at Fort Benning. The Lord is making His
presence felt in this institution like never
before...God is answering our prayers and
we will someday see many souls belong to
Jesus among the prisoners here. What a
blessing it has been to read *Prison to Praise*.
We rejoice over the possibility of a tape-
ministry inside the prison walls so that we
can actually hear some of the teachings of our
Christian brothers on the outside.

God is so great! Eight years ago I
walked through these prison gates with a

fresh ten-to-eighty year sentence for armed robbery. I thought my future held nothing but a policeman's bullet or oblivion through alcoholism. I had tried all rehabilitation programs, but when I went out on parole I was drunk for a solid three months and twenty-five days until I was put back in prison. I'd honestly tried to change myself, but it was no use.

Then six months ago, in an instant, Jesus Christ did the changing for me. I was transformed, just like it says in the Bible. *Therefore, if any one is in Christ, he is a new creation; the old has passed away, behold, the new has come* (II Corinthians 5:17 RSV). Since then, Jesus Christ has been working to clean up my life, letting His light shine over all the murky, cobwebby corners. Praise God! Nobody has a rehabilitation program worthy of mention, compared to the one Christ has to offer. Man cannot change the inner man, only Christ can!

Praise the wonderful Jesus. He poured over me the light of God's love. The joy of living with Jesus becomes deeper day by day.

Thank you for joining us in prayer for a continuing awakening among the prisoners, and for a strengthening of the new converts...Love from the brethren in Jesus.

That Christian brother is living and praising God in circumstances most of us would call dark and difficult. Yet for him, the perspective has become totally changed. He knows the joy of abiding in Jesus Christ, and everything else in his life has become secondary. He has learned to: *rejoice evermore. Pray without ceasing. In every thing give thanks: for this is the will of God in Christ Jesus concerning you* (I Thessalonians 5:16-18 KJV).

John Wesley wrote in his comments on that passage, *"Rejoice evermore* - in uninterrupted happiness in God. *Pray without ceasing* - which is the fruit of always rejoicing in the Lord. *In everything give thanks* - which is the fruit of both of the former. This is Christian perfection. Farther than this we cannot go; we need not stop short of it. Our Lord has purchased joy as well as righteousness for us. It is the very design of the gospel, that being saved from guilt, we should be happy in the love of Christ. Thanksgiving is inseparable from the true prayer: it is almost essentially connected with it. He that always prays is ever giving praise, whether in ease or pain, both for prosperity and for the greatest adversity. He blesses God for all things, looks on them as coming from Him, and receives them only for His sake; not choosing nor refusing, liking nor disliking anything, but only as it is agreeable or disagreeable to His perfect will" (*Notes on the New Testament*).

To live a life of uninterrupted happiness in God, looking on every circumstance as coming from God, and thanking Him for it - that is Christian perfection.

There is nothing haphazard about God's plan for our lives. Nothing, absolutely nothing, however strange, inconsistent, or evil it may seem to us, happens to us without God's specific consent.

One lady wrote me her amazing story illustrating that point.

She had been born with only one hand, and from the time she was old enough to realize that she was different from other children, she had worn a scarf or a stole over the stump of her arm to hide her handicap. She was always painfully conscious of her deformity, and as a young woman she began to drink to hide her hurt.

She was fifty-six years old at the time she wrote me:

> Six months ago I visited my sister, and she played a tape where you spoke about praising God for every problem or tragedy in your life. As I listened, I felt like someone

had hit me in the stomach. I felt sick. After
all the years I'd blamed God for my misfortune, I wasn't ready to thank Him for it. I said
Lord, forget it. I thanked you for freeing me
from alcohol, but I can't thank you for this
other thing.

But no matter how hard I tried, I couldn't
get the thought of thanking God off my mind.
It bugged me day and night. Finally I said,
'Lord, why don't you get off my back - I'll do
anything for you, but not that! I just can't.'
Still, I couldn't find any rest. At last I played
the tape once more. This time I heard something I'd missed before. You said that when
the young soldier and his wife found themselves *unable* to thank God for the terrible
thing they were threatened by, they at last
said they were *willing* to try. The rest seemed
to come easy. About that time, I'd reached
the point where I was willing to try almost
anything, just to get some rest. So I told God
I was *willing* to try, even if I was sure I wasn't
able. As soon as I'd said it, it seemed like a
load of many years just rolled off my
shoulders. I started to praise the Lord - my
tears flowed - and it was like the song says,
'Heaven came down and glory filled my
soul!' In the middle of all this rejoicing, the
Lord spoke to me and said, 'Wait a minute;
I'm not through with you yet!' I sat up. What
possibly more could there be? I'd just made
the supreme sacrifice and thanked God for
the deformity I'd hated all my life! But very
clearly the words formed in my head:

'You are not to carry a stole or a scarf
over the stump of your hand anymore!'

I felt an instant tightening-up inside.

'No, Lord,' I muttered. 'That's going too far. Don't ask me to do that.'

'As long as you're hiding it, you're not really thankful; you're still ashamed,' came the gentle reproach. Tearfully, I conceded.

'I'm willing to try,' I promised. 'But You've got to make me able.'

The next time I had occasion to leave the house was when I was called for jury duty. I dressed and automatically reached for my stole. Instantly the warning came. 'No. No!'

I said, 'All right, God, I'll start out without it, but I am not going to promise I won't come back for it!'

For the first time in my life I stepped outside the front door without the protective covering to hide my missing hand. As soon as I closed the door behind me, all embarrassment, the shame, and the sense of guilt were washed away! I knew for the first time in my life what it was like to be really free. I knew that God loves me just as I am. Praise the Lord!

God permits every circumstance of our life for a good reason. Through it, He intends to bring about His perfect and loving plan for us. God permitted that lady to be born without a hand because He loves her. God permitted Satan to harass Job because He loved Job. God permitted Christ to hang on the cross because He loved us. God allowed the darkness and evil forces of this world to gain *apparent* victory - apparent to our senses - yet all the while God's perfect plan for the salvation of the world was being worked out.

No one knew this better than Jesus. Some readers have written me, stating that Jesus complained when He hung on the cross and cried out, *My God, my God, why hast thou forsaken me?*

But to think that Jesus complained is in complete contradiction with everything Jesus said and did about His crucifixion.

No one knew better than Jesus every detail of God's plan to save the world. Jesus had often told his disciples about His coming crucifixion and resurrection, and He had quoted for them passages from the Psalm's and Prophets foretelling His sacrifice on the cross. Jesus even urged His disciples to rejoice over what was to happen.

Remember what I told you, He said. *I am going away, but I will come back to you again. If you really love me, you will be very happy for me, for now I can go to the Father, who is greater than I am* (John 14:28).

He had also told them that no one could take His life without His consent.

The Father loves me because I lay down my life that I may have it back again. No one can kill me without my consent - I lay down my life voluntarily. For I have the right and power to lay it down when I want to and also the right and power to take it again. For the Father has given me this right (John 10:17-18).

The disciples had been told the real truth, but when the going got rough, they reacted to the apparent victory of evil and rushed to defend Jesus against the soldiers who came to arrest Him.

Jesus stopped them. *Put away your sword*, He said. *Don't you realize that I could ask my Father for thousands of angels to protect us, and he would send them instantly? But if I did, how would the Scriptures be fulfilled that describe what is happening now?* (Matthew 26:52-54).

Jesus knew that God's Word, the Scriptures, must be fulfilled. *No* circumstances or actions on our part can change the final outworking of God's Word. Jesus Himself was subject to the Word, although He *is* the Word become flesh.

The Jews who surrounded the cross where Jesus hung were familiar with the passage in the Old Testament foretelling the coming of their Messiah who would be crucified for their sins.

The words Jesus cried out, *My God, my God, why hast thou forsaken me?* were the introductory words to the well-known Psalm 22, a psalm of praise and victory, telling of the crucifixion and the future reign of the Messiah King.

Jesus' agony on the cross was very real. The nails that pierced His hands hurt Him as much as they would hurt us if we were hanging there. But Jesus knew that his suffering was not a victory for Satan and the forces of evil, but part of God's plan. Jesus praised God *for* the suffering, because He knew it would bring victory over evil in the world.

My God, my God, why have You forsaken me? Jesus cried out, and the Psalm continues, *Why are You so far from helping me, and from the words of my groaning?...But You are holy, O You who dwell in...the praises of Israel...Our fathers trusted in You; they...were confident - and You delivered them...But I am...the scorn of men, and despised by the people. Everyone who sees me mocks and sneers and shrugs. 'Is this the one who claims the Lord delights in Him? We'll believe it when we see God rescue him!'...I am surrounded by fearsome enemies, strong as the giant bulls from Bashan. They come at me with open jaws, like roaring lions attacking their prey. My strength has drained away like water, and all my bones are out of joint. My heart melts like wax; my strength has dried up like sun-baked clay; my tongues sticks to my mouth, for you have laid me in the dust of death. The enemy, this gang of evil men, circles me like a pack of dogs; they have pierced my hands and feet. I can count every bone in my body. See these men of evil gloat and stare; they divide my clothes among themselves by a toss of the dice. But be not far from me, O Lord; O my help, hasten to aid me!...I will praise you to all my brothers; I will stand up before the congregation and testify of the wonderful things you have done. Praise the Lord, each one of you who fears him; I will say. Each of you must fear and reverence his name. Let all Israel sing his praises, for he has not despised my cries of deep despair; he has not turned and walked away. When I cried to him, he heard and came. Yes, I will stand and praise you before all people. I will publicly fulfill my vows in the presence of all who reverence your name.*

The poor shall eat and be satisfied; all who seek the Lord shall find him and shall praise his name. Their hearts shall rejoice with everlasting joy. The whole earth shall see it and return to the Lord; the people of every nation shall worship him. For the Lord is King and rules the nations. Both proud and humble together, all who are mortal - born to die - shall worship Him. Posterity shall serve Him; they shall tell of the Lord to the next generation. They shall come and shall declare His righteousness to a people yet to be born, that He has done it (Living Bible and Amp).

Jesus had often referred to the prophet Isaiah who foretold with amazing accuracy His life and death and future reign.

But He was wounded and bruised for our sins. He was chastised that we might have peace; he was lashed - and we were healed! We are the ones who strayed away like sheep! We, who left God's paths to follow our own. Yet God laid on Him the guilt and sins of every one of us! He was oppressed and He was afflicted, yet He never said a word. He was brought as a lamb to the slaughter; and as a sheep before her shearers is dumb, so He stood silent before the ones condemning Him. From prison and trial they led Him away to His death. But who among the people of that day realized it was their sins that He was dying for - that He was suffering their punishment? He was buried like a criminal in a rich man's grave; but He had done no wrong, and had never spoken an evil word.

Yet it was the Lord's good plan to bruise Him and fill Him with grief. But when His soul has been made an offering for sin, then He shall have a multitude of children, many heirs. He shall live again and God's program shall prosper in His hands. And when he sees all that is accomplished by

*the anguish of His soul, He shall be satisfied; and because
of what He has experienced, my righteous Servant shall make
many to be counted righteous before God, for He shall bear
all their sins. Therefore I will give Him the honors of one who
is mighty and great, because He has poured out His soul unto
death. He was counted as a sinner, and He bore the sins of
many, and He pled with God for sinners* (Isaiah 53:5-12).

Jesus knew that His crucifixion was not a thwarting of
God's plan, but a fulfillment of it. The disciples, however,
didn't understand. They saw the crucifixion of Jesus as an
end to all their hopes and dreams for the future. They didn't
remember Jesus' words when He had told them, *You have
sorrow now, but I will see you again and then you will rejoice
and no one can rob you of that joy* (John 16:22).

The disciples weren't looking forward to seeing Jesus
again, and when they were told that He was no longer in the
tomb, they thought His body had been stolen.

Later that day, two of Jesus' followers walked along the
road from Jerusalem, to Emmaus. They were talking about
Jesus' death when suddenly Jesus Himself came and walked
beside them. But they didn't recognize Him.

He looked at their sad faces and said, *What are you so
concerned about? One of them named Cleopas, said you
must be the only person in Jerusalem who hasn't heard about
the terrible things that happened there last week* (Luke
24:17,18).

Jesus listened as they poured out their sad tale to Him,
about the wonderful Jesus of Nazareth who had done such
great miracles that they were sure He was the Messiah who
had come to rescue Israel, but the religious leaders had
handed Him over to the Roman government and He had been
crucified. The men spoke as if they had just witnessed the
greatest tragedy the world had ever known. On top of it all,
they said, the body of Jesus was missing from the tomb, and
some women said they'd seen angels who told them that
Jesus was alive. The men seemed certain that the last bit of
news could only be a fairy tale.

Then Jesus said to them, You are such foolish, foolish people! You find it so hard to believe all that the prophets wrote in the Scriptures! Wasn't it clearly predicted by the prophets that the Messiah would have to suffer all these things before entering His time of glory?

Then Jesus quoted them passage after passage from the writings of the prophets, beginning with the book of Genesis and going right on through the Scriptures, explaining what the passages meant and what they said about himself (Luke 24:25-27).

By this time they were coming near Emmaus, and since it was getting late, the two men asked the stranger to spend the night with them. They still hadn't recognized Him!

Jesus came home with them, and when *they sat down to eat, He asked God's blessing on the food and then took a small loaf of bread and broke it and was passing it over to them, when suddenly - it was as though their eyes were opened - they recognized Him!* (Luke 24:30-31).

At last they believed. But for so long they had been able to see only the outward circumstances and had completely missed seeing God's perfect plan unfolding.

The disciples had seen their leader crucified, an apparent triumph of evil over good, and they had taken it as proof that God was not present with them. Yet, had they believed God's Word spoken through the prophets, they would have taken the same circumstances as evidence that God *was* with them and working out His plan.

We, too, are like the disciples. When trials and sorrows come our way, our first reaction is, "Oh God, why have you forsaken me?"

But Jesus said, *Here on the earth you will have many trials and sorrows; but cheer up, for I have overcome the world* (John 16:33).

If we truly believed these words of Jesus, we'd see our circumstances as evidence of God's presence with us, and we'd praise and thank Him for them, instead of complaining and grumbling.

We shake our head at the world conditions as if to say, "Now *there* is plenty of evidence that God isn't doing much these days."

But Jesus told his followers to expect wars, earthquakes, famines, insurrections, epidemics, and so on down the list - a perfect picture of the world we live in, and a promise that it would be getting worse.

Jesus said, *Now when these things begin to take place, look up and raise your heads, because your redemption is drawing near* (Luke 21:28 RSV).

When things get worse in this world of ours, it is no evidence that God is absent or indifferent. Quite the contrary. All these signs are evidence that God is very near, that every part of His plan and purpose is being fulfilled, just as His Word has promised us.

Jesus told His disciples to rejoice with Him over His crucifixion. Had they been able to trust in His word, they could have experienced joy instead of grief. God's Word tells us to rejoice in our trials.

Peter wrote, *Though not seeing Him, you trust Him; and even now you are happy with the inexpressible joy that comes from heaven itself* (I Peter 1:8).

So what will you believe? Will you walk along your road as did the two men going toward Emmaus, saddened and preoccupied by the outward circumstances, convinced that God is far away? Or will you let your eyes be opened and be thankful?

Receive the love, the peace, and the joy that Jesus is offering you. Believe that Jesus is with you, and that God is working in every circumstance of your life to meet your need.

The very thing you think is painful proof of God's absence from your life is in fact His loving provision to draw you toward Himself - so that your joy may be full!

Look up and praise Him! He loves you, and He dwells in the praises of His people!

Bringing Heaven into Hell

MERLIN R. CAROTHERS

KINGSWAY PUBLICATIONS
EASTBOURNE

CONTENTS

1. What Is Praise?

For seven exciting years, I have written and taught about Praise, yet I am beginning to see that so far I am barely into the kindergarten of Praise myself. This is no statement of false humility. Each day I am more convinced that I know very little of all there is to learn about praising God. In fact, I am finding out that praising Him is one of the most important things I can learn while I am here on earth — because to praise Him, as he intends for us to praise, involves every aspect of my life.

Praise is meant to be the focal point of our relationship with God.

Over the years I have seen thousands of people approach the subject of praising God. For some, praise revolutionized their lives. For others, it meant nothing. I have observed the same contrast in my own life. Sometimes praise "works". Sometimes my words of praise fall flat and empty.

What makes the difference?

First of all: praise can never be a surface thing. It isn't saying, "Praise the Lord, Praise the Lord," all day long. The secret is something that flows from the center of what is really you. It is something that brings an immediate response from the heart of God.

This something is "true Praise." What does it consist of? What conditions must be present in our lives for our praise to be true? What conditions in our lives hinder praise? If I live to be a hundred years old, I expect to be still learning more about the answers.

Beyond the mechanics of praise lies the heart of praise and the way actually to bring Heaven into Hell. More than anything else in this world, I want to understand more of how God wants me to praise Him. More than anything else, I want my heart to flow in a continuous stream of worship to God.

Suffering draws people together. If you suffer, and think others do not, you will be convinced they could not possibly understand you. If you read my books and think, "Merlin doesn't really have to suffer because God always answers his prayers immediately," you wouldn't believe I could help you. But I do suffer, and God often permits me to wait a long while before He shows me the results of trusting Him. I was once charged with misappropriating church funds, and by someone I had loved and trusted. There was absolutely no basis for the charge and no evidence of even the slightest kind. A judge looked at the charge for a few minutes and responded with, "What is this doing here? There isn't any evidence of even a mistake in judgment by this defendant." But the vicious harm had been done. My reputation had been attacked, and this was all the accuser wanted to do. Many people would leap at the opportunity to declare, "I knew something was wrong all the time" or "Here is proof that praise pays — in dollars." On and on the accusations could go. But the point is — I want to learn obedience even as He learned it. "Though he were a Son, yet learned he obedience by the things which he suffered." (Heb. 5:8 KJV)

I pray that as I share with you some of the things I am learning, you, too, will want to stretch and grow and open your heart to the flow of praise that glorifies God and demonstrates His love and power.

2. From "Big-Shot" To Nothing . . .

The solid steel door clanged shut, and the prisoner was alone in the tiny underground cell. The words of the guard still rang in his ears, "Get in there, big-shot — we'll be back for you in fifty years!"

It was no nightmare. On the "outside" the prisoner had been a well-known criminal lawyer, enjoying the power and luxuries that money and the right connections could supply. He had lived what he believed: "If you like it — do it. If you want it — get it."

It was the liking for excitement that led him into big-time crime: smuggling dope, dealing in guns and explosives, bank robberies, and insurance frauds. His connections were big names in organized crime. At forty, when his power was rising fast, he was caught selling drugs. All was lost. His wife and two small children were left desolate. He faced a first sentence of fifty years with more charges pending. They would be added on if he lived long enough to be even considered for parole.

The walls of the cell were smeared with blood and human excrement. Some poor prisoner before him had kept track of the years with pencil marks on the concrete: ten years — twenty years — thirty years. There was no escape. The cell was dark and damp, and the silence only broken by the clanging of steel doors down the corridor and the screams of a prisoner pushed to the brink of insanity.

Stripped of the glamor and success of the outside world, suddenly completely helpless, the prisoner felt as if he were buried alive in a stinking grave, forgotten and alone. Overcome, he fell to his knees on the cold floor. Like a child he sobbed, "Oh, God — I don't even know if You exist, but if You're out there and can hear me — I am so very, very sorry for what I have done. Please forgive me. If you will only forgive me and give me one last chance, I'll give You my whole life — everything — every bit of me. Forever!"

The darkness remained silent, but something had happened. The fear and horror were gone. Instead he was filled with an overwhelming sense of being forgiven and loved. Warm tears of gratitude rolled down the prisoner's face. He felt like a small boy who comes to his father to ask forgiveness and is caught up in loving, strong arms.

The loathsome cell was no longer a place of loneliness and despair. Gone was even the desire to get away from there. "Never had I felt so free — so happy," the prisoner wrote me. "I thanked God from the bottom of my heart for bringing me into that stinking little hole to meet him."

The prisoner was Dr. Gene Neill. I first learned of his existence when he wrote to tell me he had received the book, *Power in Praise.* After surrendering his life to God, he eagerly studied the Bible someone had smuggled into his cell. More than anything he wanted to know God's instructions for his life. Reading *Power in Praise,* it became even clearer that God wanted him to be thankful in every circumstance.

So he thanked God for the lice and the cockroaches and for the abuses of the guards. He gave thanks for the stench of urine and filth. He praised God for his five-year-old son who would be a middle-aged man before his father was released from prison. He even praised God for the greed and callousness of his own heart that had driven him to destroy his family.

Praising God brought remarkable results in Gene Neill's life. Aside from his being filled with joy, others were affected, too. Fellow prisoners and guards turned their lives over to God.

Before long, Gene was transferred from the high-security prison to a prison-camp in the Florida swamps. Nearly eaten up by mosquitoes, he thanked God for the insects — and they stopped biting him. His fellow prisoners were certain he had smuggled in some high-powered bug-spray. Soon the other men began to respond to the power of God they saw demonstrated in Gene's life.

After two years, Gene was released from prison. A full pardon was issued from Washington, D.C. He was free to join his wife and family, who now lived nearby in poverty. Together they thanked God for their circumstances, and through a series of happenings, their daily needs were met. Once a stranger stopped them on the street to give Gene a sum of money without any other explanation than: "God told me to give you this!" Another time they were giving thanks for their meagre diet when someone knocked on the door of the old, converted bus the Neills called "home." He handed them a package of T-bone steaks and left.

Why did praise "work" in Gene Neill's case? What was that something that flowed from his heart and met with such immediate response from God?

The key is found in one word: forgiveness.

Gene asked to be forgiven — and surrendered his life into God's hands. God's response was instant. It always is.

True praise is the natural response from a heart that has been forgiven. Forgiveness is a necessary foundation for praise — it holds the key to our entire relationship with God.

No one knows our nature better than God who made us. He knows we are disobedient, and that our disobedience separates us from Him. He longs for a restoration of our broken relationship, and since He knows He can't depend on us to do anything right, He decided a long time ago to depend on Himself instead. Our disobedience deserves death, so God let His own Son, Jesus Christ, die for us. Thus our debt is paid and God's system of forgiveness has been set up.

"Forgiveness" means to give up the claim to compensation from an offender. We are the offenders. Based on what Jesus has done, God gives up all claims to repayment from us. He holds nothing against us. It sounds so simple, but it is obvious that we don't understand it fully. If we did, we would be overwhelmed with gratitude and filled with joy for the rest of our lives. Most of us undervalue God's system of forgiveness. We can only be thankful that He doesn't!

The plan of redemption is designed to restore our relation with God, but it doesn't work unless we accept it. You would think that the idea of being set free from all guilt would thrill us — instead, we balk — because our part in the system involves admitting that we are wrong. I think the hardest thing we human beings do is to admit that we can't do anything right. We do almost anything to keep from swallowing our pride and accepting what God has done for us.

Part of the reason is that we have been taught from childhood to "do our own share" — earn our own way. We are proud to be "self-made," and to say, "Look at Joe, look at Susie — they've made something of themselves in this world."

Pride in our own accomplishments separates us from God. We want to handle things on our own, and we struggle along until our problems and pain become unbearable. Even then, we try to resist God's solution and say, "I'd be ashamed to come to God like a beggar. I'll wait till I get myself out of this mess first!"

Some of us try a half-hearted confession. We *say* we are sorry, but our actions deny our words, and we go right back to doing what we did before. A vital ingredient is lacking in our repentance — the element of surrender to God's will. Surrender means to give up oneself into the power of another. To do anything less in our relationship with God is only to kid ourselves. It probably means we aren't really sorry for doing wrong, but only for getting caught.

The true forgiveness that restores our relationship with God hinges on our surrender to His will. Without it we will be like a runaway child who decides to come home when things get rough out in the world. He may say, "I'm sorry I ran away, and I want to come home. But I don't like your rules — I want to be independent, and I'm going to wear my hair and my clothes the way I like and do what I want."

Have you treated God like that? Do you say, "God, I'm hurting now, and if you'll get me out of this mess, I'll try not to do it again"? If you are not really sincere, God reads your secret thoughts: "But I like doing what I'm doing, and I'll keep on with it as long as I get away with it . . ."

We won't be able to have a close relationship with God that way, any more than a restless runaway will be content to stay with Mom and Dad for very long.

In contrast, the Bible tells a story about a father-son relationship that was completely restored. The son took his inheritance and left home. He lived in luxury in a far-off country until his money ran out and his friends left him. Hungry and alone, he begged a farmer for work and was allowed to feed the pigs. He ate what the pigs left and slept with them. It was not a very pleasant way of life, and one day the boy came to his senses and realized he had done wrong. In his father's house, even the servants lived in comfort and had plenty to eat.

Deeply regretting his mistake, he knew that he had spent his inheritance and no longer had a right to be treated like a son. But he decided to ask his father for a job on the farm. He was willing to do the most menial labor. With that in mind, he hurried home, and when his father came to meet him, he cried out, "I have sinned against heaven and you, and I am not worthy of being called your son!"

Instead of scolding him, the father was overjoyed. He embraced him, dressed him in new clothes, and placed rings on his fingers to signify that he was a rightful heir and son. Then he gave orders to kill a fatted calf for a big homecoming celebration. (Luke 15)

In the same way, God waits for each of us to return from our land of disobedience. When we admit that we have done wrong and are ready to let God order our lives, His response is like the father's in the story. He rejoices that we have come home, clothes us in new robes, and calls for a great celebration, because "my child who was lost has been found."

The Father's forgiveness is waiting — but some of us won't return home to accept it. What if the prodigal son had been sorry for his wrong-doing, but never came home to ask his father's forgiveness? There are some very unhappy people who bitterly regret the condition their lives have fallen into, and who cry with remorse for their guilt, but who will not ask God's forgiveness.

Judas was like that. He regretted his betrayal of Jesus and tried to pay back the thirty pieces of silver he had received for his act of treason. When that didn't work, his guilt drove him to hang himself. He never heard the words of Jesus on the cross: "Father, forgive them; for they know not what they do . . ." (Luke 23:34 KJV)

Are you so burdened by guilt that you try to destroy yourself? Psychiatrists say that unresolved guilt causes a self-destructive urge. We try to punish ourselves by becoming alcoholics, over-eaters, drug-users, or criminals.

We may think we are too undeserving to be forgiven, and our sins too terrible for God to accept us. Some of us may not understand that God *wants* to forgive us, but more often it is pride that makes us unwilling to accept God's full pardon. We want to take the responsibility for repayment on ourselves, and refuse to admit that God's forgiveness is the only remedy for our guilt.

There are some of us who take only the first step. We admit our faults to God and ask Him to forgive us, but somehow we are unable to believe that *He does*. Over and over again we say that we are sorry, never believing He heard us. Can you imagine the prodigal son in the story coming to his father: "Oh, Dad, I have sinned, please forgive me." Without waiting for a reply, he repeats, "Oh, Dad, I have sinned, please forgive me." Every day he cries it, over and over again, never accepting that his father forgave him the first time.

A prisoner wrote me who had spent most of his life behind bars. He had been to five reform schools, eleven prisons and countless jails. On the outside he could never be good enough to stay out of trouble, and he was convinced that God was punishing him for being bad by putting him in prison again and again. Finally, he reached the conclusion that the only way to get out and stay out was to make himself good enough to earn God's favor. So he began to read a Bible ten to twelve hours a day in his cell. "A thousand times a day I asked God to forgive me, and just as many times I tried to fight off the devil," he wrote me. "I thought God was a wrathful judge, and I was sure He didn't love a sinner like me."

Someone gave him the book, *Power in Praise,* but he thought the writer was a nut for suggesting he should thank God for putting him in prison. He continued the struggle to make himself worthy of God's forgiveness until, finally, one day he was too exhausted to keep fighting. Sobbing helplessly, he admitted his failure, "Lord, You'll have to forgive me, because I'm all fought out. If You want me like I am, come get me, God, and do what You like with me. But please don't hold it against me that I can't try to please You any more."

His pillow was wet with tears, but that night he slept like a baby. "The Lord and I are good friends now," his letter continued. "He's the best cell partner a guy can ask for. The words, 'Praise the Lord' even come to me in my sleep. Jesus is all right. He does love me. He is so real and such a friend when we give Him credit for what He did for us on the cross."

When we want to pay for our own sin, we refuse to give Jesus the credit for what He has done. We want God's forgiveness on our terms. Our guilt is an unnecessary burden, carried only because we are too prideful, too self-willed to lay it down in God's waiting hands. God's father heart yearns for us. He says, "My child, I know what you have done. I know every ugly act, every evil thought. You have sinned against me and others, but I forgive you. Come home. Let me clothe you and feed you and shower you with blessings. Let me love you and heal your wounds and your broken heart."

Our rejection of His forgiveness may not be so obvious. We may say we admit our wrongs and accept His forgiveness, but behave as if we are paying the penalty for our own sins. Many people in that category become Christian workers. They give their lives in service to God as pastors, Sunday school teachers, lay leaders, nuns, or priests, but they labor more out of a sense of duty than of love, and know little joy in serving Christ. All of us, at one time or another, behave like that.

Try to imagine the prodigal son coming home to his father saying, "Dad, I know you forgive me, but I don't deserve a homecoming party. You'll have to celebrate without me. I'm unworthy of living in your house and eating at your table, so I'll stay out in the barn. I promise to slave from sunrise to sunset to make up for the inheritance I wasted. I have no right to be happy ever again. You'll be proud of me, Dad, for the way I pay you back for the horrible thing I did."

Does that sound pious and self-sacrificing in your ears? How do you think it sounds to God when He's already made other arrangements to take care of our guilt?

We may look 'good' in the eyes of others as we play the martyr's role, paying God what we feel we 'owe' Him. But that isn't what *He wants* from us. We are refusing to give Christ credit for canceling our debts. We are rejecting Him as our Savior, and it is pride, not humility, that motivates us.

David addressed himself to God, saying, "You don't want a sacrifice; if You did, how gladly I would do it! You aren't interested in offerings burned before you on the altar. It is a broken spirit You want — remorse and penitence. A broken and a contrite heart, O God, You will not ignore." (Ps. 51:16,17)

It is a proud and unbroken heart that insists on paying for its own sins. Jesus said, "Come unto me, all ye that labour and are heavy laden, and I will give you rest." (Matt. 11:28 KJV)

There is no heavier burden in this world than trying to carry the penalty for our own sins. As long as we do, we will never know God's forgiveness. We will never know the joy of a cleansed heart. Our relationship with God can never be a close one. Our praise can never become more than empty words.

What a tremendous load rolls off our back when we learn to accept God's forgiveness completely. Our need for it should not be a source of despair, but of rejoicing. Only a heart that has been forgiven understands the love of God. The more we are forgiven, the more we love Him, and the more we are able to praise Him. Then we can sing with David, "What happiness for those whose guilt has been forgiven! What joys when sins are covered over! What relief for those who have confessed their sins and God has cleared their record . . . So rejoice in Him, all those who are His, and shout for joy, all those who try to obey Him." (Ps. 32:1,2,11)

3. Three-Way Forgiveness

Steve lost his Dad in a two-car accident. A policeman who was an eyewitness reported that the other driver was entirely to blame — and came away without a scratch. Anger and grief settled deep in Steve's heart.

A year later Steve became a Christian, but found no lasting peace. The grief over his father and bitterness against the man who had killed him preyed on his mind day and night. He begged God to take it away, but it only seemed worse.

Someone gave Steve *Prison to Praise*, and he haltingly tried to praise God for the accident that took his father's life. Now suddenly he could see that his grief and hatred were rooted in his unwillingness to forgive the other man. With eyes opened to his own sin, Steve asked forgiveness for his hatred and help to forgive. He wrote me, "It has been several months now, and I am actually growing to love the man who drove the other car. God loves him, and so should I. What a glorious peace I have found."

Praise opened the way to forgiveness in Steve's heart, but had he refused to forgive, his praise would have remained mechanical and brought no fruit. An unforgiving heart cannot be a heart of praise. Forgiveness not only holds the key to our relationship with God, but also to our relationship with others. In fact, God has made one dependent on the other. Forgiveness is a three-way proposition.

Jesus said, "Your heavenly Father will forgive you if you forgive those who sin against you; but if you refuse to forgive them, He will not forgive you." (Matt. 6:14,15)

God forgives us immediately when we confess our sins to Him. That is His nature. But if we don't go on to forgive others, we will suffer. Unforgiveness will rob us of peace, joy, and health. God made us that way. He built it into us, and we have no control over it.

A young woman came to me with a problem that threatened to ruin her marriage. She found it nearly impossible to respond in love to her husband. Instead, she felt resentment and fear at his touch. She loved her husband, and could not understand her own behavior. No matter how hard she tried, she could not change herself.

As she talked, I began to get a picture of an extremely unhappy childhood. Her father had abused and beaten her repeatedly. When she tried to hide under the bed, he pulled her out by the hair to beat her some more. Fear and bitterness had festered in her heart for years, until she felt a repulsion towards all men, including her husband. In addition, she felt guilty for hating her own father, although she had repressed both her hatred and her guilt so that she seldom thought of it any more.

The young lady was able to accept God's forgiveness for her attitude of unforgiveness, and to understand that God forgave her father as well. When she was able to forgive her father, the fear and resentment towards her husband disappeared, and she was free to respond to his love.

Often the root of our present family problems can be found in painful experiences of our childhood. Perhaps a difficult experience with a parent, a sister or brother still haunts us. Old wounds dictate our behavior and until they are healed, we continue to hurt those we most want to love.

One man told how his suspicions and jealousy were about to drive his wife away. As a child he had burned with anger and shame over his mother's promiscuity, and had never been able to forgive her. The unforgiving attitude towards his mother caused him to watch every move his wife made, expecting to discover that she was unfaithful. As soon as he was able to forgive his mother, the suspicions towards his wife faded away.

Without realizing it, we can transpose our feelings from the past to our present relationships. With handicaps like that, no wonder many of us are having difficulties.

Not only are we imprisoned by the unsettled accounts of the past, but so are the people around us. They may react to us because our behavior rubs their old wounds. We need to ask God, "Is there any unforgiveness in me, Lord, that is making me ill or making me unhappy or that is hurting my family?"

We human beings can get ourselves into situations we think are unforgivable, but that simply isn't true. There is no need to repress old memories or keep old wounds covered up, because the Bible declares, "If the Son therefore shall make you free, you shall be free indeed." (John 8:36 KJV). Jesus came to guarantee our forgiveness for everything we've ever done or thought of doing wrong, and to make it possible for us to forgive everything that anyone else has ever done or thought of doing against us. Our sins or the sins of others have no power to bind us when we are forgiven and forgiving.

We can usually think of many reasons why we won't forgive others. "How can I forgive when the people who hurt me don't deserve to be forgiven?" It may be true — they don't deserve it — but we don't deserve to be forgiven either, and God forgives us anyway.

"Never pay back evil for evil . . ." wrote Paul. "Don't let evil get the upper hand but conquer evil by doing good." (Romans 12:17,21) Holding on to unforgiveness is just another way of paying back evil for evil, and by our attitude we give evil the upper hand over us. The only way to conquer evil is to forgive. That is how God overcomes the evil in us. Forgive and God conquers the evil in us by forgiving us. When we forgive and love those who hurt us, evil loses its power over us.

You may get hurt in your physical body if they hit you or torture you — Jesus didn't promise that we would never suffer physically — but they can't upset your peace and joy on the inside. In fact, I guarantee that if you respond to evil with real forgiveness and love, you will experience great joy.

"What happiness it is when others hate you and exclude you and insult you and smear your name because you are mine! When that happens, rejoice! Yes, leap for joy! . . ." (Luke 6:22,23) You can only leap for joy when you have forgiven those who hurt you.

Jesus said, "Listen, all of you. Love your *enemies.* Do *good* to those who *hate* you. Pray for the happiness of those who *curse* you; implore God's blessing on those who *hurt* you." (Luke 6:27,28)

To love your enemies you first have to forgive them. If that is difficult, try to think of it this way: God forgives even the worst offenders, and the greater our guilt, the more we have reason to be grateful for his forgiveness. If someone has hurt me; the worse it is, the more he needs to be forgiven, and the greater is my opportunity to be like Christ and to forgive him.

Maybe you don't want that kind of opportunity to practice Christian love, but just think of it; until someone hurts you, you will never know the joy of forgiving!

Sometimes we avoid the issue by saying, "Well, I would forgive that person if only he or she would ask me to forgive." God's forgiveness comes to us even before we ask Him. Jesus, hanging on the cross, said, "Father, forgive them, they don't know what they are doing." The people who mocked Him and beat Him and crucified Him didn't ask His forgiveness, or care if they ever got it. He forgave them anyway, because the Son of God could not do otherwise. And we cannot do otherwise either, if we want to do God's will. He wants us to forgive all those who have ever hurt us in our entire lives, whether or not they know what they did, or want our forgiveness.

Not only does it help us to forgive. God has arranged it so that it also helps those we forgive — even if they are unaware that we've forgiven them. When we ask God, "Forgive them for what they did to me," He does just that. He uses our forgiveness in their lives to begin freeing them from their bondage of guilt and draw them closer to Himself.

Paul was in the crowd watching Stephen being stoned to death. "So they stoned Stephen while he called upon God and said, 'Jesus, Lord, receive my spirit!' Then, on his knees, he cried in ringing tones, 'Lord, forgive them for this sin.' And with these words he fell into the sleep of death, while Saul gave silent assent to his execution." (Acts 7:59,60; 8:1a Phillips) I am sure God was working in Paul's heart that day, and Stephen's words of forgiveness hastened that work.

Our responsibility to forgive others is put to us plainly. Unless we forgive, we keep ourselves and those to whom we refuse forgiveness in bondage, blocking out God's love.

Bill, a prisoner, wrote to tell me how he had experienced God's forgiveness. The very next day in the mess hall, he was confronted with his worst enemy. The two men had tried to kill each other, and for ten years, prison authorities had kept them separated. Their files were stamped with the warning never to put them within reach of each other. But now there had been a slip-up and they were staring at each other across the breakfast table. Bill's first reaction was fear, but then the thought came, "Praise Me for this," and he responded almost automatically, "Thank You, Lord, for letting me face Ron this morning."

Ron was calm as they talked. Bill told about the change Jesus Christ had brought into his life, and the two men parted as friends. In the middle of the night, Bill was awakened with the words ringing in his head, "Forgive Ron!" He said, "Lord, forgive Ron!" and felt peace and a wonderful joy as he went back to sleep. The next morning he received word from Ron that he, too, wanted to meet Jesus.

Forgiveness unlocks our prisons of hatred and ill feeling towards others. Can you imagine what would happen if we all could forgive everyone everything that was ever done to hurt us?

Most of us put a condition on our forgiveness. We say, "Okay, I'll forgive you — if you'll change!" That is not real forgiveness. Forgiveness means to give up any claim to compensation or payment from an offender. That means he doesn't even owe us an apology, and we have no right to expect him to change. To forgive means to accept that person just as he or she is — even if he should continue to do the thing that hurts us over and over and over again.

Peter asked Jesus, "Sir, how often should I forgive a brother who sins against me? Seven times?"

"No!" Jesus replied, "Seventy times seven!" (Matt 18:21,22) If you add that up and say, "Okay — after 490 times I don't have to forgive him any more," you missed the message.

One woman wrote to tell an amazing story of forgiveness. She read the book *Prison to Praise* on the eve of an operation and decided to thank God for the pain she expected to suffer during her recovery. To her great surprise and the surprise of her doctors and nurses, she experienced no pain at all, and did not even need an aspirin for discomfort. Now she was convinced that praising God worked and decided to thank Him for whatever might come into her life from that moment on.

The big test soon came. Her husband announced that he wanted a trial separation. He told her he was contemplating a divorce, but first wanted to see if he could live away from their children. "I realized then that God had allowed me to see the power of praising Him just so I would have the strength to praise Him now," her letter stated.

After a month the husband came home. He could not bear to live apart from his children. However, he also confessed that for the past three years he had loved another woman and desperately wanted to marry her.

"It was agony to watch my husband's pain," the wife wrote. "He was miserable without the woman he loved, yet he could not bear to leave our children. He was in torment, not knowing which way to turn." Still she was determined to praise God for it all. "I began praising Him for the broken marriage vows, for the woman in my husband's life, for the fact that he did not love me and wanted a divorce . . ."

For a year she kept it up. Her husband remained at home all that time, and one day they discovered that they had a new and deeper love for one another than ever before. "It still amazes us both that our love continues to grow, but we have seen that anything is possible with God," she wrote. "He truly turned my mourning into joy and made even such a disaster as ours into something good and beautiful. Praise the Lord!"

The secret of the success in this woman's story does not lie simply in her determination to praise God for it all. The power was released through her praise because she was willing to forgive her husband and accept him just as he was.

Can you imagine how difficult it must have been? The husband did not ask his wife's forgiveness or promise to change. Each day she could see how his thoughts and longings were openly directed towards another woman, yet she was moved with compassion for his agony instead of pity for herself. Most of us would have understood more readily if her reaction had been indignation and bitterness.

I have received letters from other women telling similar stories, but without a happy ending. In those letters the unforgiving spirit was revealed by the bitter and complaining tone, "I have praised God for my situation, but my husband is as intolerable and mean as ever."

A common characteristic of unforgiving people is an unwillingness or perhaps an inability — to see themselves at fault. A lady in our church told me that for years her marriage had been going up and down like a roller-coaster. She and her husband had been divorced once and separated several times. She became a Christian and came to our church because she wanted to learn how to praise God for her husband — in order for God to change him. She thought that her husband's selfishness and demanding attitude caused all their problems.

However, her praise brought no results that she could see. During a three-day separation while she considered divorce again, she promised herself and God that she would make one last try. "I determined to be totally honest with myself and God and not pretend in any way," she told me.

She and her husband came to church the following morning, and during the sermon she became overwhelmed with the feeling that she needed God's forgiveness. Kneeling at the altar she wept and wept, and when she came back to her seat she asked her husband to forgive her as well. "Suddenly my heart just overflowed with gratitude for my husband," she said. "And the strange thing is that all the time I had thought he was at fault. I was angry because he never asked my forgiveness or admitted to being sorry for anything. Now at last I realize I had the whole thing turned upside down. *I* was the selfish and demanding one who needed forgiveness."

Now her praise flowed freely from a heart filled with love and peace. The old restlessness was gone completely.

Jesus told the parable of the servant who owed the king the equivalent of ten million dollars. He could not pay and pleaded for mercy. The king forgave him all his debt, but as soon as the servant was released, he went to a man who owed him the equivalent of two thousand dollars, grabbed him by the throat and demanded instant payment. The man didn't have the money and fell to his knees begging for a little time, but the king's servant refused and had the man thrown in jail until the debt could be paid in full. When the king heard, he called the servant and said, ". . . 'You evil-hearted wretch! Here I forgave you all that tremendous debt, just because you asked me to — shouldn't you have mercy on others, just as I had mercy on you?' Then the angry king sent the man to the torture chamber until he had paid every last penny owed. 'So shall my Heavenly Father do to you, if you refuse to truly forgive your brothers,' " Jesus warns us. (Matt. 18:32-34)

Unforgiveness is a deadly poison — and it is tearing up families every day. Our resentment grows over such little things, and as we hang on to it we don't realize that it masks a dangerous attitude of unforgiveness.

A teenager gets mad because Dad won't let him borrow the family car for the evening. "Why should I forgive him?" he says. "He doesn't trust me!"

Teenager, can you believe that God could change your Dad's mind if He wanted? And if He doesn't, it must be because right now God doesn't want you to take the car. Can you thank God for your Dad? And forgive him? If you do, I guarantee that the atmosphere in your home will be a hundred percent better.

Dad may even let you borrow the family car, but that is not the important point. What you will notice most is that you get rid of that ugly feeling inside that grows every time you think of how rotten and unfair your Dad is.

Sometimes we seem to take pleasure in refusing forgiveness even when we're asked to forgive. Does this scene seem familiar?

A husband complains because he doesn't like TV dinners three days in a row. The wife feels guilty because she neglected to plan her days better. The husband uses ugly words and slams the door as he leaves without eating, but soon he comes back to say, "Honey, I'm sorry I hurt your feelings. Please forgive me."

Here is the opportunity to heal the gap that has come between them, but the wife hides her true feelings behind a "sweet" smile and murmurs, "You didn't hurt me, there's nothing to forgive . . ." Behind her words lurks the resentment and unforgiveness — "You made me feel ashamed. Now I'll let you suffer awhile!"

How many times do we repeat that scene with minor variations when someone hits our sore points? We may use the words, "Sure I forgive you, it was nothing." But our actions make it only too clear that we haven't forgotten the nasty thing he did, and won't let him forget it either.

When someone asks your forgiveness, give it even if you don't think he has hurt you. Your forgiveness means a great deal to him, and is important in his relationship with God.

If we can begin by forgiving the members of our family continuously, what a difference it will make. Instead of being grouchy or irritable or cross with one another, we would say, "Thank you, Lord, that my Dad just broke his word to me for the millionth time. I forgive him, Lord, and please forgive him, too." Or, "Thank You, Lord, that my child forgot to make up his bed again this morning for the umpteenth time. I forgive him." Start reacting like that and the atmosphere in your home and at your dinner table will cause visitors to want to know your secret! Then you can introduce them to Jesus.

What a difference it makes when we start to forgive the difficult people we work with and thank God for them just the way they are.

Roy Wyman became a Christian and read my books on praising God for everything. His corporation was in financial difficulties, and there were ill feelings among the partners. At a board meeting plenty of harsh words were said until it was time for Roy to speak. Always he had been a man of quick temper and angry outbursts. During the entire meeting he had been talking to God under his breath, "Lord, I thank you for these men and for what they are saying. Forgive me my angry feelings, Lord, and I praise you for everything that is happening here." When he opened his mouth to speak, he was surprised at his own words, "All I have left to say to you fellows is that I love you!"

The corporation reorganized when the most difficult partner decided to sell out. Soon the profits began to rise and there were remarkable changes in the personnel, who came to know Christ as their Savior, one by one. Several months later, at a Christian rally in town, the former partner, who had left the corporation in anger, received Christ into his heart. Roy said, "I lost a partner, but, praise God, I soon gained a Christian brother."

Sometimes Christians even have trouble getting along with each other in church! Yet Jesus said, "That's how people will know you are my followers; because you love each other!"

When churches seem cold and Christians harsh and critical of one another, an unforgiving spirit may be quenching all joy and love. If you are in a church like that, start thanking God for putting you there and take a close look at your attitude.

Paul wrote, "Be gentle and ready to forgive; never hold grudges. Remember, the Lord forgave you, so you must forgive others. Most of all, let love guide your life, for then the whole church will stay together in perfect harmony. Let the peace of heart which comes from Christ be always present in your hearts and lives, for this is your responsibility and privilege as members of his Body. And always be thankful." (Col. 3:13,14)

If all Christians had lived up to their responsibility and privilege of loving and forgiving each other, we would have a lot fewer denominations today! It is our wonderful privilege to be forgiving and loving, to let our hearts be filled with peace, and always to be thankful.

If you feel that your spiritual life is at a standstill, then ask God, "What haven't I forgiven?" Do you sometimes think that God Himself has done you wrong? That He hasn't been helping you or hearing your prayers? Then you need to settle it with Him. Tell Him, "God, I don't understand why You have allowed these people to hurt me and these problems to pile up. I have been thinking you weren't concerned about me. You weren't bringing good things into my life. Please forgive me for thinking that way. I want to believe You love me and are working every problem in my life for my good."

My friend, Gene Neill, told me about Roy Roach, who was arrested for something he had not done and put in the same prison with Gene at Eglin Air Force Base Federal Prison at Fort Walton Beach, Florida. The false testimony of another man resulted in Roy's conviction. One day he heard that the other man had been caught for another offense and had landed in the same prison. Hatred and bitterness rose up, and Roy began to plot the murder of his false accuser. He confided in Gene, who suggested that Roy should give up his plans for murder and instead thank God for the whole situation. The idea didn't make any sense to Roy, who continued with his plot to murder.

One day he was told that his wife and daughter had both been diagnosed as having terminal cancer. In agony he pleaded with God to help them, and begged Gene to pray with him. Gene repeated his suggestion that Roy should thank God for everything. Despair had brought Roy to the end of his rope. On his knees he surrendered his hatred for the other man, asked forgiveness and was able to praise God for being in prison and for the illness of his wife and daughter. He was able to believe that God was using all these calamities for His glory and the family's good.

In two weeks an absolutely amazing thing happened. Roy's wife and daughter came with the report that all symptoms of cancer were gone. X-rays showed no trace of illness. Roy's forgiveness released the power of God to heal.

Are you treated unfairly? Suffering innocently? Can you believe God intends it for good? Joseph was sold by his own brothers into slavery in Egypt. Later he spent two years in prison for something he hadn't done. After he had been restored to freedom and put in the highest position in the land, next to Pharaoh, his brothers came to buy grain from him. They were horrified when they recognized him, certain that he would take revenge. But Joseph said, ". . . Ye thought evil against me; but God meant it unto good . . ." (Gen. 50:20 KJV)

It makes no difference that those who hurt you intend to do evil. God won't let any harm come to you unless He means it for good. If you can believe that, can you praise Him for it? Can you be so forgiving that you are actually glad they did it? A glad-glad, happy-glad? If you let yourself be that glad and that forgiving, God will bless you. He will cause the joy of the Holy Spirit to move inside you and get rid of that thing that has been hurting for so long — that ugly little lump of unforgiveness that has spread like cancer to rob you of joy and of health.

God knows us so well, for He made us. He knows even a little unforgiveness, nurtured in our hearts, will greatly harm us physically, emotionally, and spiritually. When we suffer like that, He lays it on the line for us: "Your pain is caused by your unforgiveness. If you don't forgive, then I cannot forgive you. But if you forgive others, I will forgive you, heal you, and set you completely free!"

4. How To Raise The Dead

An amazing example of praise at work is when Jesus raised Lazarus from the dead. Jesus was told that Lazarus was ill, but didn't go to him right away. He waited till Lazarus was dead, then told the disciples, ". . . Let's go to Judea." (John 11:7) The disciples didn't want to go. The people in Judea had tried to kill Jesus the last time they were there. Why should they risk their lives going to a funeral!

Jesus then said something that must have sounded strange to the disciples. "Lazarus is dead. And for your sake, I am glad I wasn't there, for this will give you another opportunity to believe in me . . ." (John 11:14,15). Jesus was glad Lazarus was dead. Everybody else considered it a tragedy, but Jesus had another perspective on things and was glad.

When they arrived in Bethany where Lazarus lived, the family, friends, and many prominent Jewish leaders had gathered to mourn the dead. There was wailing and weeping and not much praise and thanksgiving. When they saw Jesus, some got angry and said, ". . . this fellow healed a blind man — why couldn't he keep Lazarus from dying? . . ." (John 11:37)

Jesus was disappointed at their reaction and said, "Where is he buried?" They showed him, and he said, "Roll the stone away!"

Up to that point you or I could probably have done what Jesus did. We could have gone to the funeral, consoled the family, and if we believed what the Bible says, "All things work together for good to them that love God," we might have tried to tell the family it had all happened for the best. But in all likelihood, that is as far as you or I would go, even if we were challenged by the family of the dead; "You say you're a Christian and your God can do anything — how about asking Him to do something now!"

What did Jesus do? Did He ask God for help? Did He plead, "Father, will you hear me, please, because I've got a big problem here and I need help"?

No, He just stood there and said, "Father, I thank You that You've heard me, and that You always hear me." Jesus didn't ask God to do something. He thanked Him that it was already done. He was saying, "Thank you that the problem isn't a problem any more."

There was quite a crowd around the grave, mourning and crying. The disciples were looking over their shoulders, worrying about getting caught and killed. Jesus was the only one there without a problem. He didn't have anything to ask God. He only said, "Thank You, Father, that You always hear me." And then He looked straight at the grave and commanded, "Lazarus, come forth!"

Why can't you and I do the same? Didn't Jesus tell His disciples later, "In solemn truth I tell you, anyone believing in me shall do the same miracles I have done, and even greater ones, because I am going to be with the Father. You can ask Him for *anything,* using my name, and I will do it, for this will bring praise to the Father because of what I, the Son, will do for you. (John 14:12,13)

That is one of the verses in the Bible that often makes us a little uncomfortable. I haven't raised anybody from the dead yet, and you probably haven't either. We can't even handle some of the minor problems that confront us. But Jesus said we could — and He demonstrated how. He simply said, "Father, I thank You that You heard me."

That convinces me that praise and thanksgiving are meant to be the ultimate expression of my confidence and faith in God — that somewhere along the road of learning to thank God for everything, more of His power will be real in our lives. I know the secret is not in the words Jesus said. I could stand before an open coffin and say, "Father, I thank You that You heard me," over and over again, trying a different tone of voice each time. But that wouldn't make the corpse get up. It wasn't how He said it; it was something in the heart of Jesus that flowed directly to the heart of God. If that something could flow through our hearts, the love of God would be released into our lives and the circumstances around us as surely as sunshine flows through an open window to fill a room with warmth and light.

How do we learn to praise God the way Jesus did? I am sure there are different ways to begin, but you've got to start some place, and I started by thanking God for little things, like an old car that wouldn't run. At first it may seem a little silly, but the Bible says that we should be "Giving thanks always for all things . . ." (Eph. 5:20 KJV) That includes old cars, burnt toast, broken tools — everything.

In the beginning I didn't even mean it half the time, but giving thanks was an act of outward obedience to something God wanted me to do. That was the first step for me, and it took quite a long while before I saw many results. The change was gradual. Slowly I began to mean it more when I said, "Thank You"; slowly I began to notice that I was actually happy about some things that always made me upset or unhappy before. Also, I was becoming more convinced that God *was* in charge of everything that happened to me, and it was not so difficult to believe that He brought these circumstances into my life to show me that He loved me.

As I began to share with people and thank God for them in their difficult circumstances, the evidence continued to pile up; praise, as an expression of faith, brought more remarkable results than pleading with God. I found that praise was not just something I should be doing sometimes. The Bible tells us over and over that praise is the true expression of worship and love for God.

But before I understood that much I had to face some problems. At times praising God got me absolutely nowhere. Things looked darker than before I began. Depression settled over me. My words of praise — when I was able to say them — were empty and without meaning.

What was wrong? I tried new ways of praising. I used my will to stick with it, even when I wanted to give up. Still there was no breakthrough. So I finally thanked God for my lack of joy and lack of faith and asked Him to show me what was wrong. He showed me that I had reached a point where no amount of will power, no repeating words of praise, would bring me any closer to a solution. The problem was not what I was saying or doing, or even how I was saying or doing it. I was the problem.

When Jesus said the simple words, "Thank You, Father, for hearing me," the power of God was instantly released through Him, because *there was nothing between Jesus and God.* Nothing in the heart of Jesus blocked His relationship with the Father. They were one. We know that Jesus prayed for all who would believe in Him, "I have given them the glory You gave me — the glorious unity of being one, as we are — I in them and You in me, all being perfected into one — so that the world will know You sent me and will understand that You love them as much as You love me." (John 17:22,23)

Praising God as an act of outward obedience is a good thing, but it is only a beginning. Sooner or later we come to the point where our praise seems to break down. That usually means something more is required of us.

The price is high — and the paying often painful; we must give up that one thing in our heart that blocks our relationship with God. Although the reward is oneness with Jesus Christ, we human beings always resist letting go.

A Jewish ruler asked Jesus what he had to do to be sure of eternal life. "I have kept all the commandments since I was quite young," he said.

But Jesus told him ". . . 'There is still one thing you have missed. Sell everything you possess and give the money away to the poor, and you will have riches in Heaven. Then come and follow me.' But when the man heard this, he was greatly distressed, for he was very rich.

And when Jesus saw how his face fell, he remarked, 'How difficult it is for those who have great possessions to enter the kingdom of God.' " (Luke 18:18,22-24, Phillips)

The problem was not the riches the man owned, but his love for them. Jesus knew what was in the man's heart and put his finger on the one thing that blocked his relationship with God. Anything we will not give up for Jesus is clearly something we consider more important than our relationship with Him. It is a good test-question to ask ourselves, "Is there anything or anyone in my life I won't give up for God or for which I won't thank Him? Is there anyone or anything I won't forgive?" If the answer is yes, that something or someone stands between us and God.

Once a lady told me about her many problems. They included money, health, and family. "I want to turn the whole mess over to God — I have even tried thanking Him for it, but things just get worse. Tell me what I must do to break out of this deadlock."

"Is there anything you know God wants you to do that you *don't* want to do?" I asked.

She blushed and said, "Only one thing I can't forgive — I can't even talk about it."

"That is the one thing God wants you to do before anything else can happen."

She was crying, but her face was set. "Then I'll have to go on suffering — I just can't forgive."

Most of us do a pretty good job of hiding the real issues or denying them. Jeremiah knew something about human nature when he wrote, "The heart is the most deceitful thing there is, and desperately wicked. No one can really know how bad it is! Only the Lord knows! He searches all hearts and examines deepest motives. . ." (Jer. 17:9,10)

David was honest enough to say, "Search me, O God, and know my heart; test my thoughts. Point out anything You find in me that makes You sad, and lead me along the path of everlasting life." (Ps. 139:23,24)

If you pray like that, God will answer. He will remind you of what you are trying to hide. Often His clues are found in the painful circumstances under which we feel so burdened. We can thank Him for them because they aren't meant to punish us, but to bring us closer to Him.

When we know the truth, we must do something about it. "If I regard iniquity in my heart, the Lord will not hear me," (Ps. 66:18 KJV) David said. Anything we hold back from God is sin. As long as we cling to it, He can't hear us. The only remedy for sin is God's forgiveness, and that brings us back to the original basis for our relationship with our Creator; we confess our wrong and surrender it to Him, and He forgives.

As long as I live I will have to depend on His forgiveness. I am more aware of it today than ever before, and I hope I will become even more dependent on it in the future. Are you afraid or ashamed to ask His forgiveness over and over again? Do you think you are playing games with God and that He will get angry or tired of forgiving you? That is not humility. It is your pride that won't let you see how much you depend on God's forgiveness.

One day I stood by the ocean with the waves lapping at my feet. A little boy ran down to the water and filled his play bucket to the brim. Then he ran up on the shore to pour the water into a hole he had dug in the sand. Back and forth he ran, and I suddenly realized that God's forgiveness is as vast as the ocean. We can dip our little buckets again and again, and immediately the water rushes in to replace the little bit we dipped out. No matter how much we take from the ocean, it will be just as full as when we started. And no matter how many bucketfuls we pour into our little hole in the sand, the water will disappear and we will soon need another bucketful.

God's Father heart rejoices when His children come to receive His forgiveness. He does not give it grudgingly and say, "There you are back again. When will you ever learn!" No, each time He sees us come, He says, "I'm so glad you're back, my child. I forgive you and love you."

Our trips back to God, who forgives and forgets, are the lifeline of our fellowship with Him. Each time we honestly admit our wrong and surrender it to Him, Christ is given more control over that area of our lives. The change taking place in us may be gradual or instant, but we can be sure it is happening.

We cannot change ourselves; that is why Paul tells the Ephesians, ". . . be filled instead with the Holy Spirit. . ." (Eph. 5:18) Because ". . . when the Holy Spirit controls our lives, He will produce this kind of fruit in us: love, joy, peace, patience, kindness, goodness, faithfulness, gentleness and self-control . . ." (Gal. 5:22,23) Those are qualities we cannot produce in ourselves.

What does it mean to be filled with the Holy Spirit? It may be easier to understand if we think of it as a process instead of as an instant happening. When Paul said, *"Be* filled . . . ." he used a form of the word that does not exist in English. In the Greek it means something like, "be being filled continually." It is a continuous present tense action word you would use to describe a hose filled with running water. The hose is filled only as long as the water keeps running through it. If the tap is turned off, or something plugs the hose, it is no longer being filled. It is either empty or holding stagnant water.

You and I are like that hose, and we are commanded to be being continually filled with the Holy Spirit, who does not stand still, but is flowing through us. Turning the tap is our continuous attitude of surrender to Christ. Anything that stands between Him and us plugs up the hose. Now do you see

how important it is to keep the channel of communication open
between God and us? And now do you understand how dependent we are on His continuous forgiveness?

I know that I am not the same person today that I was five
years ago, and my relationship with God is not the same as it
was then. I hope I have grown and matured some, and that I
have surrendered new areas of my life to God so that He has
been able to be filling me more with His Holy Spirit. He can
only fill me as I am willing to be emptied, and as I am willing to
stretch and grow in new areas.

So you and I are like flexible, expandable water hoses,
meant to hold more of the Holy Spirit as our relationship with
God deepens and grows. A water hose can get clogged up, and
so can we. You may be being filled with the Holy Spirit and
then you lose your temper, or God shows you something you
need to give up, but you refuse. At that point, are you being
filled and flowing with the Holy Spirit? Or is the hose plugged?

Some folks talk about a person as "spirit-filled" in reference
to a particular experience of surrender to the Holy Spirit. From
that point on, they expect the "spirit-filled" person to be nearly
perfect. Nothing could be further from the truth. One who has
been open to be filled with the Holy Spirit and then plugged up
can be more difficult to live with and harder to understand
than anyone else. When we have tasted of a close relationship
with God and then back away, it is only natural that we
become irritable and unhappy. The Holy Spirit brings peace
within, and when that peace is gone, we can react very
unfavorably to everything and everyone around us.

If we use the term, "I am now being filled with the Holy
Spirit," instead of saying, "I am Spirit-filled," we are more
accurately describing the way the Holy Spirit works. Paul was
carefully directed by the Holy Spirit Himself to use the
continuous present tense form of the verb in the Greek. It
impressed the early Christians with their need to be continually filled. It isn't a one-time experience, but an on-going
process depending on the state of our relationship to God. Are

we continuously willing to confess our failings and ask His forgiveness? As we do, we are being emptied of our hang-ups and increasingly filled with Him.

Jesus was continually being filled with the Holy Spirit. He and the Father and the Holy Spirit were one. The picture He used of our relationship with Him was vivid. "Yes, I am the Vine; you are the branches . . . " (John 15:5) Branches cannot grow and produce anything when they are cut off from the vine. They need that life-giving sap flowing through them at all times. It is a picture of complete dependency. The sap, the lifeline, is the Holy Spirit. The more we surrender our lives and ourselves to Him, the more we experience the oneness we are meant to have with Jesus Christ.

True praise springs from a oneness with Christ and acts as a filter turning everything in our lives into joy and thanksgiving. Can you imagine having a praise-filter in your heart? You no longer see pain or problems or tragedy; only wonderful opportunities for God to demonstrate His glory.

Jesus was like that. Not only His tongue, but every fiber of His being was flowing with praise, so He could say at the funeral in Bethany, ". . . I am glad I wasn't there, for this will give you another opportunity to believe in me. . ."

Does part of your life seem dead and buried? Ruined and wasted? Maybe it's your marriage, your business, or your talents. "No use trying to resurrect that," you say. "It's gone forever." You are wrong!

Stop wailing and weeping. Instead say, "I'm *glad* it happened. It's for God's glory!" It is time for resurrection — "Come out, Lazarus!"

5. Give Up Your Shackles

A group of practical jokers made a gift for a friend; a heavy iron chain, with a fifty-pound iron ball fastened to one end. They locked the other end around the foot of their buddy, and threw the key away. "Now see how fast you can run," they teased him. Without hesitation the shackled fellow picked up the fifty-pound ball, cradled it in his armpit, and began walking without too much difficulty. "Thanks a lot, fellows," he grinned. "Just what I've always wanted — my very own ball and chain!"

Have you ever met anyone who enjoyed being shackled? Or I'd better ask, do *you* enjoy being shackled? Do you have your very own ball and chain you carry around? In the letter to the Hebrews the writer says, ". . .Let us strip off anything that slows us down or holds us back, and especially those sins that wrap themselves so tightly around our feet and trip us up; . . ." (Hebrews 12:1)

Most of us Christians have put away those obvious, outward sins that are easily seen: theft, murder, adultery. What we haven't given up is usually hidden in our minds and hearts. It might be our attitude toward those who steal, kill, or commit adultery.

Jesus wants to show us that the root of our problem is in the invisible, hidden thoughts of our hearts. He says, "For from the heart come evil thoughts, murder, adultery, fornication, theft, lying and slander."(Matt. 15:19)

Like the fellow with the ball and chain, we tell ourselves we can get along pretty well carrying our extra burden. We say, "I'm only human and I have my weaknesses, but at least I'm not as bad as that fellow over there . . . ." We can do that for awhile, but there comes a day when God will bring our hidden weakness to our attention in a way we can't ignore.

For years I struggled with immoral thoughts and lustful dreams. They always made me feel guilty, and I asked God to forgive me and deliver me from the temptation, but soon I was right back to where I started. It was a vicious circle, and I thought I would have to live with it for the rest of my life.

Then one day it came to me that what is most difficult for us humans is precisely what God wants to do for us. If I really *wanted* to give up my immoral thoughts, God would take them and give me Christ's thoughts on the matter instead. "Let this mind be in you, which was also in Christ Jesus" Paul told the Phillipians. (Phil. 2:5 KJV)

Of course I said immediately, "You know, God, I *want* to think only pure thoughts." But then a new idea presented itself: "Would you be willing to have all your thoughts projected on a screen over your head for everyone to see?"

I felt myself get hot under the collar. What if I wanted to keep a wrong thought for just a tiny little while before giving it up? I was suddenly not so sure I was ready to give my thoughts to God after all.

My problem was no longer a sin I could not stop, but a sin I was not sure I *wanted* to stop. Before, I had been able to consider myself a hapless victim of the tempter's snare, and had pleaded with God to deliver me. Now He was showing me that I could be delivered in an instant if I wanted. The truth of James's words burned in my mind: "Temptation is the pull of man's own evil thoughts and wishes." (James 1:14)

Shamefacedly I had to admit that I actually enjoyed my hidden thoughts. Surrendering them was not easy. Satan was busy whispering in my ear that from now on my life would be pretty dull. Finally I was able to say, "Lord, I thank You for all these thoughts that have taught me the truth about myself. Forgive me, Lord. Now take my mind; I surrender it to you, and if you want to project my thoughts on a screen that's all right with me. Only let me have the mind of Christ."

Satan's whispers had been unfounded. They always are. Instead of boredom, I experienced glorious relief, and whenever I saw a pretty girl I was only filled with joy and gratitude. Often tears flowed as I realized the clean, new pleasure God had given me. Now I could appreciate the beauty of God's creation that before had been marred by my own ugly thoughts.

I wanted to share my new freedom with the men in my church and was in my study preparing for the meeting, when suddenly a heavy gloom filled the room. It was as if the devil himself had entered and seemed to say, "Don't you dare talk about that! It's my territory. Keep out!"

When I stood before the men to speak, my throat constricted and the words came with difficulty. But I was able to give the same challenge to them that I had received myself. Many men joined me in surrendering our thoughts to God.

The next day Mary and I flew to Indiana on a speaking tour. There we met our good friends, Gene and Vivian Leak. Gene took me to his farm to see a new piece of equipment: a huge fan used to dry the grain. I leaned down for a closer look. Just then Gene turned on the fan, and a rat that had been hiding inside was shredded into a thousand pieces. The mess spewed over me. As the filth of blood and intestines filled my eyes and nostrils and mouth, and ran down the front of my clean shirt, it seemed I could hear the devil leer in my ear, "That's what you get for intruding on my territory, trying to clean up men's hearts!"

I realized with a burst of joy: Satan can make me filthy on the outside — but Christ has made the inside clean!

Is there something you have tried to give up — but can't? It may be something visible, like alcohol, tobacco, drugs — or less obvious, like too much television watching, reading the wrong literature, or listening to the wrong music. Whatever it is, the problem always originates in your thoughts. Even medical authorities have come to agree with Jesus on that point. They can forcibly remove alcohol, tobacco, drugs, or extra calories from a person, but as long as the "psychological addiction" remains, the person will return to his or her old habits at the first opportunity. "Psychological addiction" is just another term for something which our minds and hearts won't let go.

Be honest with yourself and with God. Do you secretly *enjoy* your weakness? Are you trying to give it up, but at the same time allowing yourself to think or daydream about it? Do you imagine the taste of that banana split or the calming effect of the cigarette?

Do you really want to give it up? Test your sincerity. Can you say to God, "Put my thoughts on a screen if you like, so that my wife and children, my neighbors and friends, can know what I think." When a wrong thought presents itself — and it will just to test you — imagine it projected on that screen. Confess it to God and say, "I've surrendered that thought. I won't think it. Absolutely not!"

Deliberately put your thoughts on something else. As Paul advises, ". . . Fix your thoughts on what is true and good and right. Think about things that are pure and lovely, and dwell on the fine, good things in others. Think about all you can praise God for and be glad about." (Phil. 4:8)

When God sees your wholehearted willingness to let go of the thing that shackles you, He will strengthen your faith to carry it through. A man in our church struggled to give up his cigarette habit. One day he realized that God was telling him, "No more delay. I have been patient for a long time, but today is the day I want you to quit." The man was in his car on the way to church, but pulled over and stopped alongside the road. He bowed his head and prayed, "Lord, I want to know if it is really you telling me, because if it is, I know you can heal me of my habit when I surrender it to you." He sat quietly with his head bowed, thinking, "Lord, I sure would like a sign if it is You talking."

Just then a highway patrol car pulled up, and the officer came over to the man's car. There was nothing unusual in that, but the officer asked, "Are you praying, sir?" When the man nodded, the highway patrol man said quietly, "Would you mind if I got in your car and prayed with you?" Was that a coincidence?

God does not give signs to everybody, but He often does when our faith is weak but our heart is willing. Signs are not given to convince us of God's power, but they may be given to encourage us when we have already decided to believe.

If we give ourselves the 'screen test' and decide we don't want to give up our secret thoughts, we can no longer make-believe that our problem is a sin that won't let us go — we know we are the ones who won't let go of the sin. With the truth unmasked, our refusal to surrender becomes a more serious thing. ". . . you are saving up terrible punishment for yourselves because of your stubbornness in refusing to turn from your sin; . . ." (Rom. 2:5)

It was the British author, C.S. Lewis, who said, "God whispers to us in our pleasures, speaks in our conscience, but shouts in our pain; it is His megaphone to rouse a deaf world." If God can't get our attention any other way, He resorts to harder measures than just speaking softly.

Is the Almighty troubling you? Shouting to you through pain? Are you grateful for it? David was. "It is good for me that I have been afflicted; that I might learn thy statutes." (Ps. 119:71 KJV) Is it difficult to understand that God afflicts us because He loves us? The writer to the Hebrews says, ". . . And have you quite forgotten the encouraging words God spoke to you, His child? He said, 'My son, don't be angry when the Lord punishes you. Don't be discouraged when he has to show you where you are wrong. For when He punishes you, it proves that

He loves you. When He whips you it proves you are really His child.' " (Heb. 12:5,6)

I used to think those were hard, unreasonable words. But I have experienced some of God's 'chastenings' in my own life, and have come to realize that God troubles me because He loves me too much to let me continue in my rebellion apart from Him. My heart's desire is to experience a oneness with Jesus Christ. If God has to put me in pain or difficult circumstances to bring me closer, I can only praise and thank Him for the things that hurt enough to get and keep my attention.

Not long ago I received a letter from a couple who had asked us to pray for their son who was awaiting trial for robbery. The boy had left home when he was eighteen because he did not agree with his parents' rules. At first they had grieved and worried, but someone gave them *Prison to Praise,* and they decided to surrender their worries and their son to God, and thank Him for every circumstance He brought into their son's life.

Not long after that, their son came on the scene of a robbery, and was shot and arrested for the crime. He lost an eye in the shooting, but he maintained his innocence and demanded a jury trial. It was while waiting for the trial that he surrendered his life to God.

In the letter his parents told how he had been found innocent and was now home with them, rejoicing that God had spared his life for a special reason. "He is forever saying, 'Thank God I lost the eye' — 'It is better to lose one eye than that my whole body should be lost in hell!' " (See Matt. 5:29)

God does not often resort to such means to get our attention. But if He must in order to save us from total destruction, we have reason to rejoice. Our pain or trial is a demonstration of God's love for us. He wants us to be set free from every little sin that wraps itself around our feet, threatening to trip us up and keep us from oneness with our heavenly Father.

One of the most subtle sins that entangles us is an attitude of criticism. I believe it causes more unhappiness than all the physical diseases put together. It breaks up marriages, chases children away from home, and splits groups. People become physically ill because they have been so wounded in their souls by constant fault-finding. Some withdraw into mental illness; others commit crimes or turn to alcohol, drugs, or overeating, or become social misfits or chronic failures because they have been told over and over again that everything they do is wrong.

Our entire society is marred by the deadly poison of criticism. It permeates homes, classrooms, churches, mass-media, politics, and international affairs.

We all know how a critical remark can spoil our entire day, yet those who make the criticisms usually feel they are right to do it. We criticize, we tell ourselves, only because we want to tell the truth and be helpful!

I have received thousands of letters that illustrate the point. Here is one:

Dear Rev. Carothers:

My husband only came to church when I begged him, and one day I discovered that he was smoking in secret. I told him over and over how wrong it was to smoke, but he wouldn't listen. Then my mother gave me *Prison to Praise*. I decided to try thanking God for my husband's habit instead of complaining about it. That is when I discovered I had a habit of my own. Every day I watched television soap operas for an hour. I wouldn't let anything keep me from seeing 'my' programs! What right did I have to criticize my husband when I was just as 'hooked' myself? I surrendered my habit to God and started spending that hour every day in prayer and thanksgiving for my husband. Within a week he came home to say he had given up smoking and turned himself over to God!"

Most of the letters I get have a happy ending, but I have in my files others that tell of futile attempts to pray and praise — where in the end a husband or a wife or a child left home or remained in the clutches of alcohol or drugs. Often a bitter, critical, or mournful attitude in the letter made it easy to understand why.

Jesus called criticism murder. He also said, ". . . Let the one among you who has never sinned throw the first stone. . . ." (John 8:7 Phillips) Negative, critical, fault-finding words can destroy someone as effectively as throwing stones.

Criticism is dangerous to those who practice it. Jesus said, "Don't criticize people, and you will not be criticized. For you will be judged by the way you criticize others, and the measure you give will be the measure you receive." (Matt. 7:1-2 Phillips)

Other people's sin is likened to a speck of sawdust, and our critical attitude is the plank. The more we talk or think about other people's faults or failures and try to set them straight, the more we become guilty ourselves.

Only by allowing God to remove our plank, do we become fit to help our brother with his little speck. The goal is to get rid of both the plank and the speck — but in that order.

Admitting our critical attitude is the first step, but that isn't easy. Fault-finding is an ingrained habit with most of us. When we look at others, the first thought that pops into our head is usually negative. We tend to think of others as needing God's forgiveness more than we do — a sure sign that a plank of criticism protrudes from our eye. Beyond the circle of our family and closest associates we often hide our critical thoughts behind flattering words to those we don't like. "They speak vanity, every one with his neighbor: with flattering lips and a double heart do they speak." (Ps 12:2, KJV) Try to imagine that everyone you speak to can see what you think about them projected on a screen over your head. That would quickly unmask our critical attitude, wouldn't it!

Nowhere is the damage of criticism as obvious as in millions of homes that have been turned into disaster areas by ugly words and attitudes. We seem to hurt most the ones we claim to love. Every day I hear from people who want to tell me what is wrong with the other members of their family. My answer is, "God wants to heal your family, and He can start with you if you are willing to stop criticizing and start being thankful for your family the way it is."

Our critical attitude must be seen as the horrible sin it really is. We must ask God to forgive us and surrender our thoughts to Him. He can fill us with love for those of whom we have been critical. Then when a fault-finding thought comes into our head we must refuse to hang onto it, and instead, follow Paul's advice, ". . . Dwell on the fine, good things in others." (Phil. 4:8)

Once we start thinking about the good points in others, it is surprising how soon we begin to admire them and appreciate them and thank God for them exactly as they are. Soon their faults won't look half so bad as they once seemed. With our attitude changed, God can reach down and remove any little speck that may still remain in our brother's eye as well.

With our critical thoughts surrendered to God, we must give Him our tongue as well and ask Him to control it. How many times have you said things you wish you hadn't? The tongue has put people in trouble since the beginning of time. ". . . The tongue is a small thing, but what enormous damage it can do. . . . And the tongue is set on fire by hell itself, and can turn our whole lives into a blazing flame of destruction and disaster . . . but no human being can tame the tongue. It is always ready to pour out its deadly poison." (James 3:5,6,8)

Well-meaning parents feel compelled to give their teenage children the same good advice over and over again, even if they know it does no good. Do they also know that in ninety-nine percent of the cases their talking only makes Johnny worse? The disastrous effect of too many words — however well meant — is most apparent in family relationships, but we do the same thing with our friends, on the job, on the telephone, and in the pulpit. Christians who over-talk have turned many people from God.

It is possible to say good and true things and still be wrong in saying them. "Speak not in the ears of a fool: for he will despise the wisdom of thy words." (Prov. 23:9 KJV) Perhaps a fool needs to be told a thing or two, but as long as he won't listen, you are wrong in telling him.

The compulsion to tell others what we think they ought to know does not come from God, but from our attitude of self-righteous criticism, and every word we speak to "set them straight" sows resentment, hurt and discord. Jesus never over-talked. He knew when to speak and when to demonstrate His love in other ways. He told His followers, "I tell you that men will have to answer at the day of judgment for every careless word they utter — for it is your words that will acquit you, and your words that will condemn you!" (Matt. 12:36,37 Phillips) Can you imagine standing face-to-face with God and have an instant replay of every careless and idle word you've ever spoken? It is a sobering thought.

"If anyone can control his tongue, it proves he has perfect control over himself in every other way." (James 3:2) If we let our mouths run off with anything that comes into our heads, our actions are probably just as undisciplined.

Are you a person of few words? If you don't know, maybe you should ask an honest friend. Most of us are unaware that we let our mouths run. But others notice — our talkativeness may hurt them or bore them, and our flood of words may obscure what we really want to say. God gave us the ability to think and speak in the first place so that we could communicate with Him and with others, but most of us have misused this wonderful privilege.

Whether you are a person of few or many words, if you have misused them, God forgives you. He can change our critical or depressing words into loving, encouraging words. Our rambling chatter or helpless stutterings can become meaningful, clear expressions. Let David's prayer become yours: "Let the words of my mouth, and the meditation of my heart, be acceptable in thy sight, O Lord, my strength, and my redeemer." (Ps. 19:14 KJV)

Surrender your tongue to God — ask Him to tame and use it. When the urge to speak comes over you, ask, "God, is what I want to say really necessary?" If we quietly wait on God, He will give us the right words to say — kind, encouraging, uplifting words, speaking directly to people's needs in a way we could never do with our normal intelligence.

Once a lady wrote me an angry letter saying that I should not waste my time writing stupid books. She said she had been foolish enough to try praising God, but it didn't work. Her child had been born mentally retarded, and all the prayers and praising did nothing to change her condition. "So why do you waste your time telling these ridiculous stories?" she wrote.

I could have written back thousands of words trying to explain how she had misunderstood my books. Instead, I asked God if there was something I could say that would help her. In my mind's eye I "saw" a picture of a pregnant woman going shopping, falling down, and hurting herself. I saw her husband angry because she had gone out alone. When the baby was born mentally retarded, the husband placed all the blame on his wife.

The picture was so vivid that I described it in my letter to the lady. She replied immediately. I had told her exactly what had happened, and it convinced her that God really cared and knew all about her situation. It wasn't my intelligence or superior way with words that impressed her, but something God showed me, and I passed it on to her.

Think of what it can do if we let God control our tongues. Then the people we speak to will pick up their ears instead of turning us off. God will be speaking through us, and they will hear Him.

From now on you can be someone who always lifts up people by the way you speak. When they see you coming they will be glad, because they know you always have a kind and loving word. Your husband hurries home, your wife can't wait to see you, your children bring their friends home after school — because your home is a warm and loving place, and you always speak good things about others. Your fellow workers, your friends, or your customers seek you out, because your words brighten their day instead of depressing them.

The oneness Christ promised becomes more and more real as we surrender our hidden sins, our thoughts and our words to Him. The Holy Spirit can continuously be filling these new areas of our lives. With cleansed heart and yielded tongue, praise takes on a richer, deeper meaning. Now we can join David in saying, "I will praise thee with uprightness of heart, when I shall have learned thy righteous judgments." (Ps. 119:7) "Be glad in the Lord, and rejoice, ye righteous: and shout for joy, all ye that are upright in heart." (Ps. 32:11 KJV)

Righteousness and uprightness are conditions for true praise, but we can never achieve them on our own. They are God's generous gift to a repentant heart.

6. What Is Your Strength?

Good things can come between us and God, making true praise impossible. They may not be the same things in my life as in yours, but they can be identified by asking a few questions:

What do you think you *have* to have in order to be happy and live successfully? Most Christians will answer quickly, "Jesus Christ, of course." But is Jesus *all* you need? You may say "Yes," but are you acting as if deep down you believe you need Jesus *plus* something? What about the people you love? Do you ever worry about losing them? What about your job? Are you concerned about having enough money to pay the bills? What about your health, your strength or your talents? Would losing them upset you?

We often are not aware that we rely on something other than God until that something is taken from us. One of the most joyful Christians I ever met is Miriam Peterson. She grew up as an only child, adored by her parents, and married a man who loved her with deep devotion. They had three bright and beautiful children, enjoyed financial security, and a large circle of friends. Neither Miriam nor her husband thought about God. Religion was unimportant until Steve, their teenage son, who had been the apple of his father's eye, suddenly became rebellious. Miriam could not understand what had gone wrong and thought perhaps she had failed as a mother.

For the first time in her life she prayed that God, if He was real, would in some way reveal Himself to her.

Surprisingly, Miriam's husband made the suggestion that they should start attending church. She began to read the Bible and took her first step in faith towards Jesus Christ. Shortly after that, it seemed as if the very fabric of their well-ordered life came apart. Their oldest son, John, started using drugs, and while he was high, beat his girl friend's baby, so that the child later died. John was arrested. Steve was also taking drugs and drifted from one eastern cult to another. Miriam was horrified, and the thought hounded her, "I did not teach my children to love Christ." Driven by guilt, she sought God's forgiveness, and studied her Bible diligently for a better understanding of His Word.

While John was in prison, Miriam's husband died. Steve, who had been arrested for drugs, jumped bail and fled to Europe. Miriam's former friends, shocked that such tragedies could happen to a "good family," rallied around her, but she felt as if she could not endure a moment longer of the nightmare her life had become. Her heart cried out, "Why, God, why?"

Someone gave her *Prison to Praise* and, nearly numbed by fear and anguish, she thought, "What can I lose?" At the end of her rope, she began to thank God for everything that had happened. John had been released from prison, but suffered violent temper tantrums. Psychiatric treatment did not help. One morning he woke his mother to tell her he intended to murder his girl friend and then commit suicide. To demonstrate how strongly he felt, he went through the house knocking over lamps and furniture. Miriam handed him the book *Prison to Praise* and said, "There might be something here that can save both of us."

She came home from work to find John a changed person. He had surrendered himself to God and found forgiveness and peace. Before long, Steve called from Switzerland and told a remarkable story. He had been penniless on a snowy, cold night, when the cook at an inn gave him some food and a place to sleep. Late that night the innkeeper discovered his presence and threw him out in below freezing weather. Steve had few clothes and nowhere to go. Thinking he would be dead before morning, he saw that his entire life had come to nothing. He threw himself down in the snow, and for the first time in his life prayed, "God, if you are real, please help me."

In that moment Steve suddenly knew that Christ was real, and that He had come to save him. With tears of repentance and joy, he asked Jesus to take over his life. Then he got up and started to walk through the snow. Soon he found an abandoned automobile. He climbed inside and spent the night thanking God for saving his life. After calling his mother, he started on his way back to Paris. Working at odd jobs, he saved enough money for the trip home. There he faced up to the charges still pending against him, and was soon completely free.

Miriam is radiant when she tells what God is doing in the lives of her sons, who are both working with young people in our church. But her joy is no less apparent as she recounts the tragic moments God put her through. David wrote, "Make us glad according to the days wherein thou hast afflicted us, and the years wherein we have seen evil." (Ps. 90:15 KJV)

Through those days of pain Miriam discovered the joy and gladness of depending only on God. "I used to depend on my family, and on the friends who surrounded me constantly," she says. "When God removed them all, I learned that I needed only Him to be happy."

Before the trials piled into her life, she thought of herself as a happy, fun-loving person. "But it was only surface deep," she told me. "If anything went wrong, my day was ruined, and I plunged into depression and worry."

With a happy smile, she continued, "My duty is not to worry, but to praise God in everything!"

One day recently she dropped twenty pounds of dogfood on a brand-new shag rug. "I wasn't upset at all," she laughed. "All I

could think to say was, 'Praise the Lord!' — the old me would
have gone into hysterics."

Miriam still has problems with her third child, and once,
during a particular crisis, she worried about it for nearly a
whole day. "But I knew every minute that my worry only
saddened God, who was in charge."

Today Miriam is surrounded by a loving family and friends.
But she is not dependent on them any longer. Jesus Christ is
all she needs. Once we know that — all else can be ours in the
measure God knows we should have it to be truly happy in
Him.

Right now our country and the entire world are going
through perilous economic times. Even the most experienced
observers dare not speak with certainty about what lies ahead.
I believe God is bringing this upon us to give us the opportunity to depend on Him for our financial security. How else would
we learn?

Are the times troubling you? Are you concerned about the
value of your property? Your family's future? If you are, it
indicates that you think you need money to be secure more
than you need God.

A man wrote me to say that he had worked very hard all his
life to make ends meet, but somehow his bills always exceeded
his paycheck. Working overtime did no good, and he lived with
a growing fear that one day he would not be able to keep up
with the demands of his creditors.

Someone gave him a book on praise, and it caused him to
see that there was something wrong with the way he was
trying to cope with his situation. He determined to praise God
for every bill, and sat down to write a check for the most urgent
one. "I looked at the little piece of paper in front of me and said,
"Thank you, God, for this bill. Bless the check and people who
receive it." It occured to him that stamps and envelopes had
cost money, too, so he asked God to bless the people from whom
he had bought them. Then he noticed the lamp on his desk and
said, "God bless the people who send me the electric bill." Next

he asked God to bless the people who held the mortgage on his house, and those who had received the money for the desk and chair in which he was sitting.

"Those who collected my taxes needed blessings, too," he wrote. "On and on I went, and I suddenly realized that always before I had cursed these people for taking my money. Now I felt really grateful for that first check ready to go in the mail. Asking God to bless it had lifted my gloom and my worries."

Within a week the man got a letter back from that first creditor, stating that they had made a mistake on their bill. He did not owe them any money, they owed him! In the letter was his own check back and another one made out for the same amount. Nothing like that had ever happened before. He prayed for wisdom to use the money, and realized that the two checks put together would make a nice dent in an old debt. He had received several letters reminding him what he owed, so he knew his money would not be returned this time. Off went his check with another "Bless them, Lord."

By return mail came a letter from the company asking him to come down to their store so that they could give him a special prize, since he had been the first to respond to their recent letter. He had not received any correspondence from them recently, and thought the invitation was a gimmick to get him to buy something more now that he was paying on his old bill.

Then he remembered how he had gotten the money to pay the bill in the first place, and decided to go to the store after all. A polite secretary explained that they had offered special prizes to anyone who paid on an account a year or more overdue. He had been the first, and they asked permission to take his picture and record the ceremony in the local newspaper to encourage others to pay their bills.

What was the prize? The man nearly fell over when they told him, "Ten times the amount you paid on your bills!"

"Now I had twenty times the amount for which I wrote the first check. I took the new check and went home to ask God to bless it. There were several other bills that needed to be paid, and I asked for wisdom to know how to use the money. The answer shook me. I felt God wanted me to give it away! That would not help my situation at all. I was still deep in debt, but no matter how I prayed, all I could think of was, 'Give it away!' "

Finally the man called his pastor and said he had a gift for the church. When he mentioned the amount, the pastor thanked him for responding so quickly to the need.

"What need?"

"The one I announced in church last Sunday for that exact amount."

The man had not been in church that Sunday, and had not heard about the pastor's plea. Now he was convinced that God was in charge of his money. He continued to ask His blessing on every bill and every check he wrote. In the letter to me he enclosed a substantial donation to our prison ministry, and concluded by saying that God prospered him in everything, so that he was now looking for new ways to invest what God is giving him.

Would God do the same for you if you started to praise Him for your bills? It is quite possible, if one important condition is met in your heart. Praising God became a turning point for this man because it was a demonstration of an inward surrender of his finances. The proof was his willingness to follow God's instructions in handling his money.

God may not make you rich — but you never have to worry about money as long as you realize that every penny comes from God and belongs to Him. Use it as He directs, and your needs will always be met, regardless of the state of the world economy. Paul wrote, ". . . I have learned the secret of facing either plenty or poverty. I am ready for anything through the strength of the one who lives within me." (Phil. 4:12,13 Phillips)

Paul's secret was that he had discovered from where his real strength came — not from money or friends or his own efforts, but from Christ. He *is* our strength.

A prisoner wrote me who had struggled to be a Christian for some time. In spite of his efforts, he slipped into what he called, "a horribly backslidden condition." He gave up prayer and Bible study, and was learning about witchcraft. He finally reached a point where he saw his life without meaning. He wrote, "I hated to admit my own inability to help myself, but it was at that point that Jesus came to lift me up to His strength. Pride had kept me from accepting Him before, but when I reached the bottom I had nothing left of which to be proud. I am glad God brought me down so I could see the truth and His wonderful grace."

From my vantage point as a pastor, I hear from people every day who say things like, "I tried all my life to do the right thing, but failed. When I gave up struggling and accepted whatever God wanted to do with me, something glorious happened. I gave up trying in my own strength and experienced God's strength."

Our own strength, no matter how strong we are, is never enough. It will never be right. And when we learn that we can never be right, never be strong enough, no matter how hard we try, we finally understand that we have to depend on Jesus to do it for us. That glorious discovery sets us free at last from our own self-efforts, and we are free to receive all that God wants to give us.

The stronger and more capable we are, the harder it can be to see our need for God. He may have to bring about circumstances in our lives to destroy our illusion of self-sufficiency.

Tom Silsby was a tall and exceptionally good-looking high school student. His unusually broad shoulders and magnificent physique made him the envy of nearly every boy who knew him. He was a star athlete who won every competition he entered. His parents were Christians, but from his sophomore year, Tom slowly drifted away from his own faith. He was convinced he did not need God. His own strength and skill

made him both feared and admired by other students. By the
time Tom became a senior, he was a heavy week-end drinker
and a bully who enjoyed pushing others around. He made his
money by fixing up old cars and selling them for a high profit,
and his goal in life was to be a big-shot. Already his picture was
featured regularly in the sports pages of the newspapers; Tom
was a star football player, champion wrestler, and swimmer.

Early one morning he was on his way home after an
all-night party. His little VW convertible was going too fast
down the freeway, when Tom nodded behind the wheel, and the
car spun out of control and went over a 300-foot cliff embank-
ment.

At the hospital the cuts on Tom's face and back were
stitched, along with a deep gash in his skull. No bones were
broken, but he was in a deep coma, and tests revealed severe
brain and brain stem damage. A team of surgeons operated,
but held little hope for complete recovery.

In the meantime, Tom's parents and family, their pastors,
and Christians in churches near and far joined in committing
Tom and his future into God's hands. The parents were firm in
their faith that God would heal their son. Tom himself hung
between unconsciousness and semi-consciousness for several
weeks. When he was awake he recognized his parents, but his
memory was gone, and he could only speak a few, halting
words. The doctors felt doubtful that he would ever regain the
full use of his mind or his left side.

Tom spent five weeks in a rehabilitation ward, learning to
sit up by himself, to eat, even to stand for a few minutes, but
his mind was that of a small child. Snatches of memory were
coming back, but everything he had learned before was gone.
Still, the prayers continued. His parents held to their belief
that God was healing Tom, and they rejoiced as they brought
him home.

Now began a long, persistent struggle for Tom to relearn
what he had once known. Encouraged by his parents, he
started exercising, weight-lifting, running, and then swim-

ming. At first he stumbled and fell whenever he tried to run, because one leg was weaker than the other. In the swimming pool he first splashed the water with his hands and giggled like a small child. When he tried to swim, he sank to the bottom and his father had to pull him out.

Slowly Tom was regaining some of his physical abilities, but his mind was still operating on the fifth-grade level, and he had poor recall of the past. His parents told him he could make it if he learned to rely on Christ's strength instead of his own. Tom agreed.

Now began a series of humiliating experiences for the former star athlete. Tom was allowed back on the swimming team, but he had to work hard just to complete the race instead of winning it. In wrestling he was thrown to the floor by guys much smaller than himself. He was accepted back on the football team by his old coach and team mates, who admired his persistence, but everything he had once known about football was forgotten. His old, rough friends laughed at his clumsiness. When he was admitted to junior college he was at the very bottom of his class.

But it was through those humiliating experiences that the presence of Jesus became real to Tom. In his own helplessness he discovered that the strength of Jesus was something reliable. "I've learned to put Jesus first," he says. "And I have learned that just as I need a coach and a team to become a good athlete, I also need a pastor and fellowship to grow in Christ. Athletic games have rules, and often the coach has to explain them over and over before I finally can apply the principle to the game. As Christians we have the Big Coach and the Big Rule Book. Some things in there I don't know how to apply to life, but the Big Coach patiently explains it to me, and I know that one day I will understand more of it."

Tom is doing well in school today, and instead of the clumsy searching for words, he expresses himself clearly. He spends much time working with young people in the church, and is much admired and loved for his quiet, kind disposition. He is very different from the rough bully he once was.

"I almost died," he says, "but God gave me real life. Before, I had everything I thought I wanted. I was big and strong and successful. I got everything I reached out for, and I woke up every morning wondering what I could do to make me enjoy that day more.

I was a winner in the eyes of the world, but it was by losing, that I became a real winner. God took away everything to show me that only He can give me what is really important. I have learned that the secret of life is in receiving from God rather than in trying to take what you can get!"

Tom does not find it difficult to agree with David, who wrote, "Make me to hear joy and gladness; that the bones which thou hast broken may rejoice." (Ps. 51:8 KJV)

When God breaks our bones, it is because He wants us to discover the joy and gladness we find when we rely on His strength.

Shifting from our own strength to God's does not come easy to any of us. We may rely on Him in one area, but not in another — or we trust Him more in some things than in others. Turning ourselves over to Him completely is a life-time process. We think we have done it, and up pops that old ego, still trying to run the show our old way.

It is easier to say, "The Lord is my strength," than to live that way. The last few years our church in Escondido and the Foundation of Praise have grown very quickly. With each new book, the pile of letters from readers mount higher, and phone calls, visits, and requests for personal appearances pour into our offices. I believe that everyone who comes asking for help is sent by Him. So when the number of calls and letters grew larger than I could handle, I began to feel guilty because I couldn't help everybody.

For months I struggled with the growing pressure. My guilt grew worse when we got an unlisted phone number at home, but the calls had kept me up all hours of the night. I cried to

God for more strength, but, instead, my exhaustion grew, and my wife and co-workers began to be concerned for my health. I continually thanked God for every call and letter, while I asked Him to forgive me for not being able to answer them all — yet somehow my guilt was never quite relieved. Finally there was nothing left to do but give up trying to handle it all. I said, "Lord, I am so sorry I can't take care of all the people you send me. You'll have to meet their needs some other way ..."

There was a long silence, then I felt the Lord saying, "I'm glad you finally realize I can get some of these things done without you, Merlin."

"Why, Lord, of course I know you can do things without me ..."

"Then why do you act as if you are personally responsible for helping those people? Don't you know they need Me more than they need Merlin Carothers?"

My own sin suddenly stared me in the face. For years I had been saying that it was Jesus, not Merlin Carothers, who helped the people to whom 'I' ministered. I had prayed, "Lord, use me to your glory, not my own." Yet somewhere, deep in the hidden recesses of my heart, I had been taking some of that glory. I had been operating in some of my own strength. The problem was pride, and my guilt and exhaustion were dead give-aways.

God may be flashing the same warning signals in your face. If you are doing what you think God wants you to do, yet you feel guilty because you aren't doing enough, and you're tired because the workload is growing; ask yourself, "Could God use someone else in my place and do it just as well?" If that nudges your pride just a bit, and you are not absolutely sure God could operate as well without you — watch out!

Confessing my sin, I could finally say, "You are my strength, Lord. Use me only where You want me — and thank You for all the work You are going to do through others."

The guilt and pressure were gone, and others began to respond to the need. Today we have a 24-hour telephone life line manned by volunteers. Over one hundred and fifty deacons and assistant shepherds and shepherdesses do the work of helping and encouraging our own congregation and the many who come to us for assistance. I have seven assistant pastors and an administrator. There are six full-time secretaries in the office and seven hundred volunteer correspondents who answer letters from prisoners all over the United States and several other countries.

Now that millions have read my books, it often happens that people who are desperate call me to say, "If only you will pray for me, I know God will do something." It is always a little frightening to hear people say things like that, because it means they believe I can do something that only God can do. God does not need Merlin Carothers to spread the word about Praise or to pray for people. If I thought He did, I would be in danger of leading thousands of people to depend on me instead of Jesus.

A certain pastor took over a small struggling church, and the members multiplied several times over in just a few months. The pastor was immensely popular, and the church prospered, but after two years the pastor was called away. As quickly as the congregation had grown, it now dwindled, and the church closed its doors. The explanation given was: "Pastor so-and-so had such a wonderful personality — we couldn't find anyone to take his place."

Who had the largest following in that church? The popular pastor or Jesus? Who do people respond to when you are around — Christ in you — or just plain you?

I still struggle with the problem of how to speak at all the places to which I am asked to speak throughout the United States and the world. My schedule has been too heavy, and God has let my health suffer under it. I am getting the message slowly. Thank God He won't let me get away with operating in my own strength — not even a little bit — because that masks my hidden pride. Crying for more strength won't work, nor will all my maneuvering. Steadfastly He will wait until I am ready to surrender it all and say, "Lord, I give up my own strength. I have *no* strength. You are my strength, and I thank you for all the places you will use other speakers than Merlin Carothers."

It isn't easy to say that, because I enjoy speaking. I love to be a part of God's work. But I know it is *His* work, not mine, and it will go on long after I am gone, just as it began long before I got here.

How do we get to the point where God is all our strength? As long as we use our own strength, God cannot use His through us. Only when we surrender our strength will we discover what David meant when he said, "Blessed is the man whose strength is in Thee . . ." (Ps. 84:5 KJV)

Benjamin Franklin said, "The Lord helps those who help themselves." But nothing could be farther from the truth. The Lord helps those who are helpless. But it isn't enough to be helpless; we have to *give up* trying to help ourselves and surrender to God.

Our own strength is only a false illusion; still we cling to it and hate to give it up. If we want God to be our strength, we must be able to say to Him, "I surrender all my own strength to You. From now on I want You to be my *only* strength."

If you say that and then find yourself getting more and more tired — praise God! He is letting you wear out your own strength, and when it is all gone, you will be where you ought to be — dependent on God for everything. At last you can say with David, "The Lord is my strength and my shield; my heart trusted in Him and I am helped: therefore my heart greatly rejoiceth; and with my song will I praise Him." (Ps. 28:7 KJV)

7. Keep Your Eyes Steady!

When your eyes are examined, the doctor holds a card in front of you and says, "Keep your eyes here, but tell me when you see my other hand." Then he brings his hand from behind your head and pretty soon, out of the corner of your eye, you see his hand. You are still looking straight ahead at the card, but you also see that hand.

That is a capacity God has given our physical eyes, and also our spiritual vision. We can be looking at Christ, and at the same time, out of the corner of our eyes, there is something else trying to catch our attention. Now it is up to us. We can focus our full attention on Christ, disregarding the disturbance on the side — or shift our attention over to the other — or do like most of us, hesitate somewhere in between, looking back and forth, and not being able to decide one way or the other.

If you are in the last category, you are what James described: "A double-minded man is unstable in all his ways, let not that man think that he shall receive anything of the Lord." (See James 1:8,7.) No one is more miserable than a double-minded or double-hearted human being. Sometimes you're convinced you believe God, and the next day you don't know for sure.

Jesus said, ". . . When your eye is single, thy whole body also is full of light; but when thine eye is evil, thy body also is full of darkness." (Luke 11:34 KJV) Jesus is saying that to doubt, and to divide our attention between God and something else is evil. Those may seem like hard words, but remember that the first and great commandment Jesus gives us is, "Thou shalt love the Lord thy God with *all* thy heart, and with *all* thy soul, and with *all* thy mind." (Matt. 22:37)

To be double-minded or double-hearted is a miserable condition of uncertainty, and sinful as well. God said of the Israelites, ". . . I was very angry with them, for their hearts were always looking somewhere else instead of up to me . . ." (Heb. 3:10) God had promised the Israelites a beautiful land flowing with milk and honey, if they had only kept looking to Him. But they ruined their chances and lost the Promised Land by looking elsewhere.

What causes double mindedness? What do you see out of the corner of your eye that compels you to look away from Christ? One of the biggest attention getters is our physical body. Since we were born we have responded to what our body tells us about ourselves. We feel hungry, warm, cold, weak, strong, in pain, sleepy, full of lust — and our mind is used to translating these feelings into "facts." We think we are what we feel, and that we must do what our feelings dictate.

When we become Christians, the Holy Spirit enters our body and there is a new voice in our life. The Spirit speaks in our thoughts, usually in direct disagreement with our feelings. Suddenly we have a battle going on inside us.

This is the origin of our double-mindedness. Every born-again Christian starts his new life with a double mind. Our soul is a battleground where Jesus Christ has won the decisive victory, but each of us must "Fight the worthwhile battle of the faith" (I Tim. 6:12 Phillips) till our attention is focused on God with a single mind and a united heart.

Many do not realize their own double-mindedness. They assume that every thought originates in their own head. Once we are alerted to our true condition, we can begin to sort out what we are thinking. We are powerless to stop the thoughts from popping into our heads, but God has given us the power to decide what to do with them once they are there.

". . . We have no particular reason to feel grateful to our sensual nature, or to live life on the level of the instincts. Indeed that way of living leads to certain spiritual death. But if on the other hand, you cut the nerve of your instinctive actions by obeying the Spirit, you are on the way to real living." (Rom. 8:12,13 Phillips)

We cut the nerve of our instinctive action by deciding in favor of God's voice against our feelings and thoughts. We don't have the power to resist the pull of our old instincts, but as we surrender to God and fasten our sight on Christ, His power overcomes our old nature.

In sorting out our thoughts we should recognize that Satan always appeals to our old nature and stirs up our feelings, while the Holy Spirit tells us what God's Word says. We are then faced with the familiar situation from the doctor's office. The Holy Spirit says, "Look this way, here is what God has to say. Keep your eyes focused on Jesus." Now Satan comes up from the rear and whispers, "God doesn't care about your situation. You don't *feel* His presence do you?"

What are you going to do? Will you waver and say, "N-n-no, I don't feel anything. Maybe God left me . . ."? Or will you confess your double-mindedness and decide to believe God's Word no matter what you feel or don't feel?

The Holy Spirit tells us that in Christ we have His perfect peace. (John 14:27) But our circumstances are so miserable that we feel far from peaceful. What can we do about it? Our old nature will blame our circumstances for our lack of peace, but God's Word tells us that if we tell God every detail of our needs in thankful prayer and don't worry, the peace of God that passes human understanding will keep constant guard over our hearts and minds as they rest in Christ Jesus. (Phil. 4:6,7) The promise is that we will have perfect peace as our hearts and minds are focused on Jesus — not on our circumstances.

Isn't it wonderful that we have the freedom in Christ to choose *not* to let the circumstances and our feelings rule our lives? Doesn't that give us reason to shout for joy and praise God?

Whatever your particular weakness, that is where your old feelings will act up, telling you that you are still the same old person. God's Word says that you are a new creature in Christ. (II Cor. 5:17) Who are you going to believe?

Each time we cut the nerve of our instinctive action by obeying the Spirit and surrendering our old feelings to God, our double-mindedness is being replaced with faith. And faith is the quality that enables us to say, "God, I believe You, even if my senses and my feelings tell me the opposite."

The more we waver between two opinions, the less faith we have. We say, "God, if you would just let me *feel* good for a change, or see a miracle with my own eyes, it would be so much easier to believe." We don't have to use faith when we see or feel a miracle. The opportunity to practice faith comes when things go wrong and we feel bad.

The Holy Spirit says, "Always be full of joy in the Lord; . . ." (Phil. 4:4) That sounds impossible, because after all, joy is something we can *feel*, isn't it? But we are commanded to be filled with joy, and God doesn't command something that can't be done. So it must be possible to be joyful always — regardless of circumstances.

We are used to thinking that happy circumstances bring joy, but God wants us to discover the real source. David wrote, "You have let me experience the joys of life and the exquisite pleasures of your own eternal presence." (Ps. 16:11) Under what circumstances do you think David learned to experience real joy and the exquisite pleasure of God's presence? Was it perhaps when he was hiding in a cave, pursued by Saul, who tried to kill him?

Paul and Silas behaved as if they were experiencing the joys of life when they were in a jail cell, their backs bleeding and their feet in stocks, and yet they were singing praises to

God. (Acts 16:22-25) Richard Wurmbrandt, who suffered for years in a communist prison in Eastern Europe, tells that he discovered the joy of God's presence while he was being tortured in his cell. Christian prisoners in Vietnam report the same phenomenon; it was in the darkest dungeon that they discovered real joy in the presence of God. Daily we get letters from prisoners in this country who say that it was in their blackest moments that God's light broke through to them.

We human beings are creatures of comfort, and who do you think encourages us to believe we can best learn to experience God's presence when everything is going exactly the way we want it? In pleasant circumstances we usually focus our attention on things or people we enjoy, not on God. It is when things are difficult that we can learn to look away from the circumstances and discover the deeper joy there is in being with God.

It is in sickness we can best learn that God can heal us. It is in poverty we can discover how He meets our needs. It is in sorrow we can learn that He comforts us. But we won't learn anything if we decide to focus our attention on our problems. We will only get poorer, sicker, and sadder.

Not long ago I heard a father say to a young man who was courting his daughter, "I want you to treat my daughter every moment as if I were right there." If that is what an earthly father wants for his daughter, what do you think our Heavenly Father wants for us? He is with us every moment, and He wants us to act as if we believe it. Your feelings may tell you that you are lonely, but God's Word says He is with you. Which will you believe? If you aren't sure, you need to repent once more of double-mindedness and look to Jesus. Each time you do, your faith will grow and His presence and His joy will become more and more real to you.

When we make up our minds to believe that God uses problems and pain to bring us a deeper joy in His presence, we are able to be truly glad when the problems come. We can choose to surrender our old feelings to God and focus our full attention on Christ in joyful praise.

Some religious cults teach that our body and natural instincts are evil and must be ignored or denied. That is a twisting of what God tells us in His Word. He created our bodies and gave us instincts and feelings. When we surrender it all to Him, it is like a seed that falls into the ground and emerges as a beautiful new plant. Our physical body and our feelings, fully surrendered to God, will take on new life, even while we are still on this earth. We will enjoy a real measure of greater health and vigor, and our feelings will become part of the experience of our new joy in Christ.

When we choose to shift our allegiance from our feelings to the Holy Spirit, our old, demanding nature is put to death. The new you is able to experience the exquisite pleasures of God's presence in a way that involves your physical, emotional and spiritual being.

Next to our bodies, our concept of time causes the biggest stumbling block to faith for many of us. We live in a natural world where events are measured in chronological order, and we project our time-concept to our relationship with an eternal God.

God created time. He uses it, but He is not limited by it. "But you should never lose sight of this fact, dear friends, that time is not the same with the Lord as it is with us — to Him a day may be a thousand years, and a thousand years only a day." (II Pet. 3:8 Phillips)

There is no past or future with God, only an on-going NOW. Jesus told the puzzled Jews, "I tell you in solemn truth, before there was an Abraham, I AM!" (Jn. 8:58 Phillips) If we suddenly lifted the time dimension we are used to, we would see Jesus hanging on the cross for our sins right NOW. We would also see Him risen from the grave right NOW.

To measure God's answer to our prayers by the time it takes for us to *see* results is like trying to measure weight by the calendar. The clock or the calendar is totally unreliable for that purpose, so we might as well shift our attention to something more trustworthy. God's Word says, "And this is the confidence that we have in Him, that, if we ask any thing according to His will, He heareth us: and if we know that He hear us, whatsoever we ask, we know that we have granted us as our *present possessions* the requests made of Him." (I Jn 5:14,15 KJV & Amp)

In God's dimension we already *have* the answer. You may say, "But that isn't *my* understanding of time; it doesn't help me right this minute! If you are a Christian, you have already entered God's dimension of eternity — His eternal NOW. "I have written like this to you who already believe in the name of God's Son so that you may be quite sure that, here and now, you possess eternal life." (I John 5:13 Phillips) It is our double-mindedness that causes us to look out of the corner of our eye at this world's clocks and calendars while we try to muster enough faith to believe that God will answer our prayer some day. That will never work. We have the power to decide which time-plan we want to follow — God's, or our old one.

David discovered how it worked. He wrote, ". . . My times are in Your hands. . . ." (Ps. 31:15) The Holy Spirit tells you that is true for you as well, but the old you, still bound to this physical world and its time-table, will say, "Look, it's been six months now and God hasn't answered my prayer. He probably never will."

We can be a slave of time, or allow God to teach us how to use the time He gives us. Then we'll never have to worry about having too much or too little time. God gives us exactly the time we need to do what He wants us to do. Do you feel too young — or that you're growing old too fast? Are you bored or always hurried? Surrender your time to God. Confess your double-mindedness. He forgives you and gladly takes over the management of your days.

If you are waiting for an answer to prayer, you are looking in the wrong direction, and are letting the passing hours and days weaken your faith. Instead, you can choose to let each passing minute strengthen your faith. Fasten your eyes on Jesus; remind yourself that in God's dimension of time all prayers are answered already. Then be happy for the opportunity to exercise your faith. A weight-lifter holds his weights a little longer each day, and grows stronger muscles. With each second, minute, hour, or day, we hold on to our decision to believe God no matter what earthly clocks may say, our faith grows. We are practicing believing something we haven't seen yet, and as our faith grows, our heart becomes more and more united and our vision becomes more and more single-minded. And we come closer to oneness with the Father.

I used to be extremely irritated when people were late for appointments. I would get headaches and stomach-aches because these people didn't understand — as I understood — how precious time is. They thought nothing of wasting it!

Once I was scheduled to be on a TV program. Another minister was to have the first half of the program, and I was to be interviewed next. I had a lot of important things I wanted to say, and waited with one eye on the clock for the other fellow to finish. But when his time was up, he went right on talking. The interviewer tried, but couldn't stop him. I thought, "Lord, this is a disgrace! He is wasting *my* time. Why don't you shut him up so we can get on with something more important!"

When the man finally quit, there were only a few minutes left. I must confess my prayer was not completely whole-hearted when I said, "Lord, You could have shut up that windbag any time You wanted. Since You didn't, You must have a reason for letting me sit here and wait. Thank You for the whole episode. Forgive me for criticizing the other man — and thank You for what You're going to do with the few minutes we've got left."

There was no time for involved explanations. I launched right into challenging the viewers to thank God for their problems instead of complaining about them, and He would respond in ways that would amaze them. I encouraged parents to praise God for run-away children, wives for missing husbands, the sick to rejoice in their illnesses, and those who had financial difficulties to be glad for their unpaid bills.

Within minutes the network phones started ringing. The response from listeners was so unusual that the interviewer was notified by the station manager to keep the program on the air past the regular schedule. The stories kept coming in as more viewers reported amazing results to their prayers of praise. A mother thanked God for her son who had been missing for six months. In a few minutes there was a knock on her door. Outside stood the son, asking if he could come back home. A wife gave thanks for an alcoholic husband. He interrupted her TV viewing to tell her that for the first time in ten years the thought of alcohol made him ill.

I had thought God's message could be held back by a 'lack of time.' I forgot that He is the owner of all time. He can make the sun go forward or backward (and He has done it in recorded history). If there isn't enough time, He can create more. How ridiculous for me, His child, to be worried when He can take a day and make it into a thousand years.

My attention had not been fixed on Jesus while I waited for "my turn." Instead, I let my old concept of time convince me that God was not in charge of the situation. I had to confess my sin of double-mindedness and thank Him for His endless patience and mercy. But I could have saved myself a nervous stomach if I had kept my mind where I should have.

Our mind is our control center. That is where we register the impulses from our senses and our emotions. That is where our understanding measures new impressions against our feelings and our stored-up knowledge, and we make our decision how to act or respond to a situation.

Satan likes to appeal to our understanding. He puts such clever thoughts in our minds that it makes us proud to think them. He encourages us to rationalize our own behavior and thoughts, and to question anything the Holy Spirit tells us. Always his goal is to divert our attention from God. Once he accomplishes that, he knows we'll slide quickly downhill into the trap he has for us.

I was wondering how best to illustrate this point in a sermon, and thought to myself, "Here I am trying to find out what God wants me to say on the subject — but I'm sure Satan is trying to get my attention, too. What could he be saying?" Right away, the thought came, "I'm probably not working on the right message!" I turned that over in my mind for awhile. It was probably true. I didn't know *what* to say. If it was the right message, God would have given me some ideas, wouldn't he?

I said out loud to myself, "I'm going to trust the Lord to give me the right words . . ." But even as I said it, I was thinking, "I must not be trusting the Lord enough for Him to show me what to say — or I would know something by now . . . besides, even if I could say anything worthwhile on the subject, people probably wouldn't understand me!" I sat there thinking until I became so discouraged I put down the pen and muttered, "There's no use in even trying. If I do my best, it won't be good enough anyway!"

Where was my attention focused? Not on Jesus, but on the thoughts stirred up in my mind by Satan. He will rob us and cheat us and take away all our peace and joy and faith if we let him — but *only* if we let him.

Maybe you don't believe that Satan can do that. You are a rational, intelligent human being and no one can invade your mind, you think. But do you know that Satan's most clever lie is to tell you that he does not even exist, or that he does not speak in your thoughts? We are proud of our understanding, and no one knows that better than the devil. That is why he makes his arguments so reasonable and logical, appealing to our pride in our intellect. God's Word warns us, "Trust in the Lord with all thine heart; and lean not unto thine own understanding." (Prov. 3:5 KJV)

I am so glad for the things God has given me to understand, but if I allow my understanding to keep me from believing what God says, then I am using my understanding in the wrong way. People often come to me with a Bible verse they don't understand, and sometimes I have to tell them I don't understand it either. At one time or another we all say, "I wish I understood why God is doing what He is doing," or, "If I could only understand what that means."

I can focus on the things I don't understand in the Bible and soon be completely confused. How much better it is to focus on what I *do* understand. It is easy for me today to understand that God loves me and wants me to be grateful for everything He does in my life. Just thinking about that makes me rejoice. But I am aware of Satan whispering in my thoughts now and then, "Merlin, don't you think you ought to worry about all the things you *don't* understand? After all, you are a pastor, and people come to you for answers." That sounds pretty sensible, doesn't it, but I know from experience where it will get me.

Now when I come across a difficult passage in the Bible, I look to Jesus and follow the Holy Spirit's advice: "If any of you lack wisdom, let him ask of God — and it shall be given him." Only the Holy Spirit can open our eyes to the things God wants us to understand. If the passage still puzzles me, I can decide to concentrate on what I am certain of: God loves me, and if He wanted me to understand, I would. Therefore I can safely trust the things I don't know to my Heavenly Father, who understands everything.

Our understanding falls into the same category as the rest of our old nature. When we try to use it on our own, it traps us in double-mindedness and confusion. When we surrender it, God will use it to His purpose, and we will discover that He lets us understand things we could never figure out on our own.

Why is it that some people are filled with joy and gladness, while others are gloomy and depressed? So often I have observed two people in identical circumstances. Both have been diagnosed as having terminal cancer. Or both have been fired from their jobs. Or they have lost a close relative in death. Or their wives want divorces. One is miserable, but the other radiates joy. What is it? It is because one has learned to center his attention on Jesus; the other looks at the problem.

Try an experiment. Let one object near you represent Jesus Christ. Pick another object to the left or right to represent everything that you think is wrong with your life. Look at that second object for awhile and think about all the things you wish were happening that aren't. Think of every problem, every difficult person, every pain. Just let your mind dwell on those things for a minute or two. You feel utterly miserable, don't you?

Now look at the object representing Jesus. He loves you. He has overcome every problem you can imagine. He has forgiven every sin of which you are guilty. He put every thing and every person into your life to show you His love. He has come to fill you with joy and peace. Doesn't that make you feel better? Even if you don't *feel* better yet, can you see that things *are* better from this perspective?

Jesus came into this world to tell us that He would do for us the things we can't do for ourselves. We can't erase our problems and our pains by ignoring them, but there is something we *can* do. Maybe right now you feel so weakened by your disease, so depressed by your problem, so misused and misunderstood and abused by people that you feel you can't do anything. God knows how weak and low you are. He knows you can't pick yourself up. But He wants you to do the one thing He has given you the ability to do. Open your eyes and look at Him. ". . . If there is anything worthy of praise, think on and weigh and take account of these things — fix your minds on them." (Phil. 4:8 b. Amp) Think of Jesus. Is He worthy of praise? Let your mind dwell on who He is and what he has done until the darkness around you gives way to light.

If you see someone walking down the street, his face radiant and filled with joy, don't assume he doesn't have any problems. He may have ten times more problems than you ever had. Do you say, "Why can't I be like that? Why am I so miserable and he so happy?" You know the answer. He has learned to fix his attention on Christ. He has learned how to bring Heaven into Hell.

You have the ability to do the same. If a problem comes, you can say, "Praise God, it isn't my problem; it is His. My attention is over here on Jesus, who tells me 'Let not your heart be troubled; ye believe in God, believe also in me' " (Jn 14:1 KJV)

Satan is whispering from the sidelines, reminding you to worry, and telling you that no matter what you do, it will be wrong.

He is a liar. Nothing will be wrong — everything will be right if you decide to keep on looking at Jesus with a single eye and a united heart. Fix your thoughts on Him. Repent of all double-mindedness, and you can say with David, "My heart is fixed, O God; My heart is steadfast and confident! I will sing and make melody . . . I will praise and give thanks . . ." (Ps. 57:7,9 Amp)

8. Authority – Submission

The day I got out of the army after over two years of service in World War II, I actually jumped up and down for joy. It wasn't the joy of the Lord — no, I was just so glad to be out of "that rotten, stinking Army." I hated to be told when to get up and what to wear and what to do and how to do it every minute of the day. I was so glad to get out I declared I would never even turn and look at the Army as long as I lived.

Then one day after I had finished my education in seminary and was ready to serve God, I said, "Here I am, Lord, what do you want me to do?"

"Go back into the Army as a chaplain!"

It took me a long time to swallow that, but I finally decided I must go back in for three years. There were things I liked about the Army, but I couldn't stand to take orders from anybody, and once I was back in, I realized it was worse than I remembered. Now I was an officer and a chaplain, and I still had to get up when they told me, wear what they wanted me to wear, fold my blankets exactly the way they said, and eat what they served me. Sometimes they said, "Get up at four o'clock, fall out at five, march until six-thirty, lay out your full field pack, stand there and wait for inspection." I had to do push ups and crawl through the mud with the troops. It was disgusting and annoying, but now that I was a chaplain I not only had to do it, but act as if *I enjoyed it* in front of the men!

The end of three years came, and I thought, "Praise the Lord, I'm getting out." But the Lord made it very clear, "Merlin, I think you need a little more." So I stayed in another year, then five and six, and finally twenty; and as the time went on, something began to happen inside me. I was learning more about God's love and why He puts us in hard places. The rebellion in me died down, and after a while I actually enjoyed following orders. I had learned a submissiveness of spirit that had never before been a part of me, and God knew that without that submissiveness I would never be able to experience as fully His love and His plan for my life.

There are some things in Christianity that are harder to understand and more difficult to accept than other things. Submission is one of them. When we become Christians, one of the first things we are told about our new life is that, "But as many as received Him, (Christ), to them gave He the power to become the sons of God." (Jn. 1:12 KJV) When I first discovered that verse I thought, "Wonderful, all that power is mine!" Then I found even better news: "And if children, then heirs; heirs of God, and joint-heirs with Christ; . . ." (Rom. 8:17 KJV) Just imagine being joint-heirs with the Son of God, who said, ". . . All power is given unto me in heaven and in earth." (Matt. 28:18)

That's just great! But something puzzled me, and maybe puzzles you. If all that power is yours, how come you can't do anything with it? Jesus had authority over the wind and the weather. He could still a storm, but when did you last still a storm? Jesus had authority over the water. He could decide to walk on it — or go down into it to be baptized. I haven't been able to make that choice for myself yet.

Here is where submission fits into the picture. Our authority in Christ is only valid when we submit to Him, and here is the other side of the same coin — submission isn't real, until we understand our authority as children of God!

If that sounds confusing, it is because we start out with a completely wrong concept of authority and submission. In the process of growing up, some of us have learned how to get our own way always. We have learned to demand and manipulate and take control over people and situations. We call that authority. Others among us grew up learning that we could never have our own way. We were too weak to stand up to those who pushed us around or took advantage of us. We call that submission.

Between those two extremes are the rest of us, who have developed schemes to get our way sometimes, and have felt that we've been forced to give in to people or circumstances the rest of the times. Starting with our parents, brothers and sisters, bullies, we feel we've been squeezed and pressed to our limit. When God says, "Submit!" we don't like it.

In recent years we've seen scores of "liberation" movements pop up. They all teach that we have "rights" as human beings and need to stand up for ourselves. But these movements are all based on the same false concept of authority and submission. They tell us that authority means to take what's "rightfully" yours, and submission means to let everybody walk all over you.

We need to understand that these ideas of authority and submission are counterfeits of the real thing. When we try to apply them in our Christian life it doesn't work.

True authority is a legal and rightful power given us to command or act. It isn't something we claim for ourselves. True submission is the voluntary act of committing ourselves to the will of someone else. It isn't something forced on us.

In the Christian life, authority and submission depend on each other. Neither "works" without the other. Jesus showed us the principle in action. He said, "For I have not spoken of myself; but the Father which sent me, he gave me a commandment, what I should say, and what I should speak." (Jn 12:49 KJV)

Jesus, who had been given the rightful power to command or act, spoke words of authority only when His Father told Him what to say. The Son, who had all authority, voluntarily committed himself to the will of the Father. He said, "I can of mine own self do nothing; . . . I seek not mine own will, but the will of the Father which hath sent me. (Jn. 5:30 KJV)

The most powerful thing that Jesus Christ ever did, was when He broke Satan's hold over this world. Did He do it by exercising all His authority? No, He submitted. The tremendous power behind the crucifixion was the perfect submission of Christ. He could have slain His accusers with a word or by calling ten thousand angels, but then there would have been no redemption for a lost world — no victory over evil. You and I are free today because Jesus submitted to death in our place.

There would have been no power behind that event if Jesus had not held the authority to save Himself. He said, "No one can kill me without my consent — I lay down my life voluntarily. For I have the right and power to lay it down when I want to and also the right and power to take it again. For the Father has given me this right." (Jn 10:18)

The submission God requires from us is always a voluntary act of obedience. When we do it, God responds by releasing His power and His authority into our situation. Involuntary submission releases no such power, and only makes us more miserable.

An army commander wants to be surrounded by men who can submit to orders; not out of fear, because then they would be cowardly soldiers, but gladly, because they trust the judgment of their commander and know that obedience is necessary if their mission is to be successful.

Think of the picture of a well-trained dog. He holds his head up high and his tail is poised. He eagerly obeys the least of his master's commands. There is a beautiful relationship of loyalty and trust between them.

Now think of a dog cowering with his tail between his legs before his cruel master. This dog also obeys, but it is because he fears the whipping he'll get if he doesn't. There is no bond of love and respect between the two, and we know that if the dog got a chance, he would run away.

The dog who eagerly obeys his master because he loves him shows a picture of true submission. God has given us the freedom of choice. Our obedience must be a voluntary thing — but we human beings don't like to submit any more than we like to surrender or repent or forgive. We came into this world screaming and demanding our own way, and submission will always be contrary to our old nature.

When we become Christians, it is hard to surrender that old nature to God. We can only do it a little at a time, because we can't bear to give up all the controls to God at once. When we discover the glorious news that God gives us the right to become His children, we want to shout, "Hooray, I'm free — nobody has any authority over me but God!"

That is right — but what does God tell you to do? He says, "Now I want you to submit — to my Word, to the circumstances in which I have placed you, and to the people with whom I have surrounded you!"

Why do we have to submit? God knows our old nature, and the only way it can be tamed is through obedience. The root of all sin is disobedience and rebellion — and that destroys our relationship with God. Jesus said, "Not every one that saith unto me Lord, Lord, shall enter into the kingdom of heaven; but he that *doeth* the will of my Father which is in heaven." (Matt. 7:21 KJV)

If we refuse to submit to God's will, our Christian life comes to a grinding halt. We can't have oneness with Christ or abide in His love. We will have no peace or joy. "If ye keep my commandments, ye shall abide in my love; . . . these things have I spoken unto you, that my joy might remain in you, and that your joy might be full." (Jn 15:10,11 KJV)

If submission is contrary to our old nature, how do we learn it? First, recognize that the old "submission" — giving in to something you can't control, and resenting it — isn't submission. Ask God to take away the old, rebellious feelings and teach you true submission — the kind that brings oneness with the Father and releases His power and authority into your life.

Jesus submitted willingly because He knew who He was. Here is the key to true submission. We must know who we are. Do you think you are a poor, mistreated human being, pressed by circumstances, and forgotten by God? Then you are in no position to truly submit. You need to know deep down in your heart that you are a child of God — with all the rights and privileges He has given you — and that not for a moment do you have reason to doubt His love. Now you can submit without fear. The only true foundation for submission is to be absolutely sure of our Heavenly Father's love.

A small child is required to obey his parents and has no real choice in the matter. Then comes the moment when he finds out he doesn't *have* to obey. He is strong enough to resist. Have you ever observed a teenager struggling to discover who he is and what his rights and responsibilities are as a person? During the process he often lashes out against all authority, arguing with his parents, and standing up for his "rights."

If the teenager doesn't know, deep down in his heart, that his parents love him, resentment and a sense of rejection can boil into serious, open rebellion. Thousands of young people are caught in that trap today. The teenager or young adult who comes through the crisis into maturity and true submission is the one who knows that he is loved, and that his parents only want the best for him.

As Christians we face a parallel crisis as we struggle to find our true identity in Christ. The way to true maturity leads through submission, but we can't get there unless we know our Heavenly Father really loves us and only wants the best for us. That knowledge is the anchor that keeps us through the storm while our old, stubborn ego battles against the difficult circumstances to which God asks us to submit.

If you doubt His love, stop right now and go back over a few basic truths God tells us in His Word. You are His child if you have decided to believe. You are loved, because God sent Jesus to die for you. Pin some of your favorite scripture verses on your wall where you are reminded of them often. Fasten your thoughts on them. Repeat them out loud to yourself. Are you going to believe who God says you are, or pay attention to your doubts?

When you know who you are, submission is no threat to your true identity, but it spells doom for your old nature, and that is why the old you fights it so hard. At first, even submitting in little things is a battle. Tell God you are willing and confess your feelings of rebellion. As you submit, you will find that God changes you inside. It is a life-long process, but the beginning is the hardest. For each step you take, it will get easier.

In the army, it is the soldier who submits eagerly who is noticed by his superiors and is first promoted from his rank. With each promotion, the soldier finds that the outward demands for submission become less, while his voluntary allegiance and obedience become more and more a part of him. It is the same way in the Christian life. At first we find ourselves pressed by circumstances and difficult people on all sides. But as we submit, and God begins to work that submission into our hearts, we experience a new oneness with Christ. Now we find that true submission takes the sting out of painful circumstances and relationships. We can actually enjoy them, just as I finally learned to enjoy taking orders in the army.

When first we begin to submit, we reluctantly say, "God, I'll accept your will for me, but I would prefer it my own way." We still do most of the deciding and only allow Christ to be a part-time consultant. Next we are able to say, "I admit you seem to know better how to run my life; I'll be glad to follow your directions whenever I get fouled up myself." We give Jesus perhaps half the controls over our life. But when we can say, "Lord, I want to do only your will and none of mine," we are coming closer to the maturity God wants for us.

Paul wrote to the Christians in Colossae, ". . . We want to be able to present each one (of the believers) to God, perfect, because of what Christ has done for each of them." (Col. 1:28) What is Christian perfection? That is when someone looks at you and sees only Christ. There is only one way God can make that transformation in you and me, and that is through our submission.

When we know we are God's children, loved by Him, we also know that He has given us authority over our old, rebellious nature. We can decide to submit voluntarily and gladly to whatever difficult circumstances God has given us. That kind of submission is a powerful thing. It not only transforms us, but releases God's power and authority into our surroundings. The more we submit, the more His power is released.

Suffering is never meant to be the end for God's children. Satan will tell you that submitting to suffering means you'll always have to suffer. The very opposite is true. You may be in a prison cell facing 25 years, or on a hospital bed with painful months ahead of you. Perhaps financial or personal problems are mounting up, threatening to crush you. Satan whispers that you are a victim of circumstances, but he is a liar. You can exercise your authority as a beloved child of God by voluntarily submitting to those circumstances, and thanking God for them. Now the power of evil has been broken. You and your situation are safe in God's hands, and He is in perfect control. You know it is true, because your inner turmoil has been replaced by His peace.

We often quote the verse in the Bible that says we are joint heirs with Christ — but we seldom pay attention to the second part of the statement that we are ". . . joint-heirs with Christ; *if* so be that we suffer with Him, that we may be also glorified together." (Rom. 8:17 KJV)

We are joint heirs with Christ when we joyfully accept suffering with Him. Now can you be glad for every opportunity to submit to a difficulty? You can be sure it will lead to something glorious in your relationship with God.

9. Are You Really Glad?

Is there anyone you would rather be or anything you would rather do than be who you are and do what you do right now? Can you think of any change you would like to see in your circumstances?

If the answer is yes, you haven't learned how to be really glad yet.

I know a woman who was born with only one finger on each hand and one toe on each foot. She believed God had made her that way because He wanted to, and she thought He knew what was best for her, so she was grateful. When she was dating her husband-to-be, he came to her house for dinner and she was on her best behavior to impress him. It so happened that she dropped a dish. Can you imagine the thoughts that rushed into her head? But quickly she quipped, "I would say I am all thumbs, but I don't qualify!" There was no embarrassment, only happy laughter.

Later, when they were married, she became the mother of two children. Both were born with only one finger on each hand and one toe on each foot. From the time they were infants, the children were told that they were very special in God's eyes. When the youngest was four years old, he once said to a saleswoman in a store, "I guess you wonder why we only have one finger on our hands. God made us this way for a reason."

Do you believe God made you the way you are for a reason? And put you where you are because He wants you there? Stop and think about it. If you are like me and everybody else I know, you are surrounded by many kinds of circumstances, and you are reacting to them in one of two ways. If you are unhappy about them, they are getting you down. If you are glad, they are lifting you up. So are you going up or down right now?

As children of God we can have authority over our circumstances. How do we use it? By going up, of course — but what is the way up? Think of yourself standing in the surf with the water up to your armpits — and here comes a big wave. If you don't know much about waves, you may try to run from it, but it will suck you back and throw you down with thundering force. Helplessly you tumble around, until, gasping and fighting for breath, you emerge in shallow water, bruised and dripping like a drowning kitten.

Experienced swimmers know a better way. Calmly they face the threatening wave — and dive directly under the foaming crest. Seconds later they emerge on the surface, turn and float easily on the smooth back of the crested wave all the way back to shore.

For a swimmer, the way to be lifted on top of a wave is to dive under it! For a Christian, the way to be lifted on top of a problem is to submit to it.

Most of us know only too well what it means to go down under problems. We've been tossed around, bruised and hurt by circumstances all our lives. But that is not submission. It is exactly the opposite, and the correct word for it is to succumb, which means to sink down, be overcome.

Submission, on the other hand, is that voluntary act of the child of God who knows that his Father is in charge, and who trusts himself in his Father's hands. Submission releases God's authority to overcome the situation.

When we succumb, our eyes are on the problem and our minds are full of complaints. When we submit, our eyes are on Christ, and our minds are full of praise. As time goes on our succumbing will draw us farther and farther down into misery and grief. In contrast, submission will in time lift us into joy and gladness in Christ, even if the problem remains.

Several nations have developed a poisonous gas for use in warfare. It is completely invisible and odorless and the victims breathe it without knowing it is there. Satan has a deadly "gas" that can flow into our hearts and minds while we don't even know what is happening. It is the attitude of complaining. Some of us are so used to complaining that we think it is our natural right, yet it was complaining and murmuring that caused the Israelites to die in the wilderness. Paul warned the early Christians, "And don't murmur against God and his dealings with you, as some of them did, for that is why God sent his Angel to destroy them." (I Cor. 10:10)

Complaining is a deadly sin because it is an expression of disbelief and distrust. You wouldn't complain if you really thought God was in charge and doing what is best for you. When you complain, you succumb. You are being dragged down by your problem, not lifted up.

But if complaining is like an invisible gas, how do we detect it in ourselves? We may be bravely enduring our pain, even saying, "Praise the Lord for it all." Could there still be an attitude of complaining hiding somewhere in us?

Moses warned the Israelites that God's curse would come upon them: "Because thou servedst not the Lord thy God with joyfulness, and with gladness of heart . . ." (Deut. 28:47 KJV) Here is our complaint-detector. ARE YOU REALLY GLAD, DEEP DOWN IN YOUR HEART? Are you glad you have the problem? Glad you hurt? When you're glad, you're not complaining. When you're glad, it means you are sure you are a child of God. You are sure of His love for you and that He is working everything in your life together for your good in a perfect plan. You have reason to be glad because you know that your problem or your pain is there to do you some good. Gladness is a sign of submission.

When we submit to the point of saying, "I am really glad," our praise becomes pure and wholehearted. The next time you want to say, "Praise the Lord," try saying instead, "Lord, I am so glad you let that happen right now!" If your heart isn't in it, then you are hiding a small complaint or unbelief somewhere. One little complaint will keep you from real submission and real praise in that area of your life.

When my last book, *Walking and Leaping*, was published, I was annoyed to discover several printing errors. I remembered to praise the Lord for the mistakes, but I also wrote a letter to the publisher pointing them out, and I know I wasn't able to be glad they happened. It wasn't till I received an answer from the publisher that I discovered how wrong my reaction had been.

The editor wrote, "You might be interested to hear of a letter we received from a lady who was having trouble with some peach trees in her garden. She was reading your book and came across the most notable printing error: "the *peace* that passes understanding" was spelled, "the *peach* that passes understanding." She read this mistake with great rejoicing, seeing in it evidence that God cared for her peach trees. What could we say? Praise the Lord!"

I had let that little problem annoy me and overcome me, and my words of praise had not brought real joy. The complaint hidden in my heart had been unmasked by my lack of gladness, but I had not heeded the warning.

When we learn to submit so completely that gladness and praise fill our hearts continually, we will be lifted above our problems to a new level of life with Christ. Have you ever had a pair of shoes that always hurts your feet, and then gotten a new pair that fits just perfectly? Didn't it feel good? Exchanging a lifelong habit of complaining for one of gladness and praise is just like that.

Does this mean that we are always to submit to every circumstance, both good and evil? What about our authority as God's children? Don't we get to use it sometimes?

There is only one area where God tells us never to submit and always to use our authority — and that is over our sin. Every trial and pain we face is in some way connected with our old sinful nature. But even in this battle, submission comes before authority. "Submit yourselves therefore to God. Resist the devil, and he will flee from you." (James 4:7 KJV) Step one is always submission — that releases our authority to resist evil. But remember that our authority rests solely on God's power. We fight a losing battle in our own strength.

So if you are faced with a small problem — or big ones piled up until you think you can take no more, the first step is to dive straight into it by submitting yourself to God who has control over it all. Ask yourself the complaint-detecting question: "Am I *really* glad everything is the way it is?" If you aren't glad, now is the time to use your authority. Your complaint is a mask for the sin of unbelief and rebellion. Don't let it pull you down into further misery. Resist it by confessing it to God. Be specific and as honest as you can. Tell God you're sorry for not being glad for the way He is handling your life. When you have honestly repented, you know He has forgiven you. Now you can tell Him that you willingly submit to what He has put into your life. When your submission is complete, it brings God's power into your circumstances and gladness into your heart.

David knew what it was to submit and repent. He wrote, "Hear, O Lord, and have mercy upon me: Lord, be thou my helper. Thou hast turned for me my mourning into dancing: thou hast put off my sackcloth, and girded me with gladness;" (Ps. 30:10-11 KJV)

When we submit to God's will and resist evil, He pours gladness over us. "Thou hast loved righteousness, and hated iniquity; therefore God, even thy God, hath anointed thee with the oil of gladness . . ." (Heb. 1:9 KJV)

The sign of wholehearted submission is gladness. That is why David wrote, "Serve the Lord with gladness: come before his presence with singing." (Ps 100:2 KJV) We can't serve God unless we are submitted to His will — and if we aren't glad, then we aren't submitted.

God wants us to serve Him. He has a wonderful plan for you and for me — but how can He guide us in the right direction if we always want our own way? "He leads the humble in what is right, and the humble He teaches His way." (Ps. 25:9 Amp) The humble are those who have learned to submit with gladness to God's will. There is no better place to learn than in difficult circumstances that rub against our natural inclinations.

We say, "Lord, use me. Send me on a great mission. I'll obey Your least command!" Here is what God says to that kind of request: "I already put you on a mission — right where you are. Show me how obedient you are by being really glad for every detail of your circumstances."

I have known young people who were bored at home and in their job, and so they said, "The Lord has called me to spread the gospel and live on faith." They quit their boring job and moved away from their cranky relatives to a distant community where they expect other Christians to give them a place to sleep and food to eat.

That was no act of submission to God's will. Paul gave new Christians some practical advice: "My brothers, let every one of us continue to live his life with God in the state in which he was when he was called." (I Cor. 7:24 Phillips) Paul himself continued in his trade as a tentmaker and supported himself wherever he went to spread the gospel.

God may have called you to do something different from what you are doing now. But if you don't like where you are, you aren't ready to leave yet. Submission to your present circumstances comes first. God has you where you are for a purpose that can only be accomplished when you are completely submitted. The sign of submission is gladness. When you are glad you are there, God may call you to leave — but not before. If you leave on your own, you are headed for bigger problems than the ones you are faced with today.

The same holds true for every other kind of trial with which you may be faced. God means it for good, but the good can't happen until you submit. When you can say, "Thank you, Lord, for the thing that hurts. I am glad it hurts" — then it may go away. But your gladness has taken the sting from the pain, and you know you'll stay glad even if it doesn't go away. The good has been accomplished. Your submission gave you authority over that trial, and God lifted you up above it where you can ride on it safely to wherever God has planned.

We have been conditioned to think of submission as a sign of weakness, but it is the key to our strength. Each problem and pain is designed to help us grow in that strength. As long as a baby lies flat in his crib, he doesn't need much strength. But when he first stands up, he experiences the forces of gravity pulling him down. To walk and run he needs to develop strength. The stronger he gets, the better he can run and jump, but without the downward pull of gravity he would never develop his muscles in the first place.

The early Christians had to contend against powerful forces; persecutions and trials worse than most of us can comprehend. They were forced to leave their homes, were hunted like animals, tortured, thrown to the lions — survived in caves and catacombs. They had little food, water and comforts as we know them. But it was in these circumstances that God taught His people the true source of their strength and joy. It was there they learned to praise Him with hearts of gladness.

If you are glad and thankful only when things go your way, you are like a baby lying in a crib. You haven't begun to rely on God's strength against the downward pull of your problems yet. So often we first think of getting God's help when a major tragedy comes into our life. Trying to Praise Him for a big problem can be a discouraging experience, because we have a lifetime habit of reacting to every disappointment by complaining.

Like the baby learning to walk, we can best start by
exercising our spiritual muscles on small problems. Each time
we are able to respond the right way we find ourselves lifted up
and ready to face a bigger problem with increasing confidence.
Take something minor, like the wave of irritation you feel
when another driver pulls ahead of you into the last parking
place on the block. Are you going to let that wave pull you
under or lift you up?

Stop right there and take authority over your irritation.
Confess it as a sinful complaint. Tell God you're sorry you
aren't glad, but you are willing to be. Then thank Him for
letting that other driver park ahead of you. He must have a
better parking space waiting. Aren't you glad you didn't get
the one you wanted?

Have you ever complained when you bought something
that turned out to be defective and the store refused to refund
your money? I have, and as long as I was mad that thing
churned inside me and poisoned everything I did and thought
for days. I was being pulled down fast. Remember that you are
a child of God with all the power and authority He gives you.
No one can take advantage of you. If it seems to you that they
are doing it, you are forgetting that God is in complete control
of every store and sales manager in the world. If He allows
them to keep your money or charge you too much, it must be
because you need that experience. You can be glad it happened!

If minor irritations cause you to complain, how will you be
able to stand in a real battle against evil? Everything that
happens to you is brought by God for a good purpose. Submission lifts us above it and releases God's strength and joy. Satan
encourages us to complain, because he knows that the more we
complain, the longer we suffer.

I received a letter from a teenage girl who told me that her
father had recently died. He had been a Christian for only
three months, but the girl was grateful. "My parents were
divorced and I lived with my father," she wrote. "My mother
isn't a Christian yet, but now she has come to live with us. I

know that is why Jesus took my dad home with Him. We are praying for my mom and we know God loves her so much."

That girl did not sink under with grief. She submitted to the circumstances and was glad because she knew God was in charge. The more severe the downward pull is in our lives, the greater is the opportunity for our spiritual muscles to grow. Paul wrote, "I can do all things through Christ which strengtheneth me." (Phil 4:13 KJV) Paul had discovered the truth of that statement through some very difficult circumstances.

Our strength is not our own, it is Christ. We experience it first when we surrender to Him, but it is through our daily submission that His authority and His strength take control in our lives.

Another passage in the Bible tells us that, ". . . The joy of the Lord is your strength." (Neh. 8:10 KJV) It is a joy that can only come through complete submission. When we rely completely on God and say, "I am glad everything is the way it is!" His strength lifts us up and transforms every problem, every pain into joy.

That kind of joy and strength never comes to the proud; only to the humble. The proud person does not know how to submit himself to God and can never experience oneness with Him. "Therefore anyone who humbles himself as this little child, is the greatest in the Kingdom of Heaven," Jesus told his followers. (Matt. 18:4)

The purpose of submission is to reduce our old selves so that Christ can increase in our lives — less of us and more of Him.

I had a letter from a young assistant pastor who told of his joy in praising God for everything. It was the tone of the letter that impressed me. The source of that young man's joy was that he was convinced of his own insignificance and God's greatness. "God has shown me in so many ways what a nothing I really am, and I praise Him because now I understand better how great He is. It is the greatest feeling in the world to know that God loves me. I feel very small and not very wise, but I and all my problems are right in the palm of God's hand. I worry about nothing any more. God has everything under control. Praise Him!"

Are you worried about anything? Do you sometimes stay awake at night fearing a phone call with bad tidings? Are you afraid you will lose your job? Or come down with cancer? So many people live with fears. Why? We only fear those things we have not yet submitted to God.

"Praise the Lord! For all who fear God and trust in him are blessed beyond expression. Yes, happy is the man who delights in doing his commands ... Such a man will not be overthrown by evil circumstances ... He does not fear bad news, nor live in dread of what may happen. For he is settled in his mind that Jehovah will take care of him." (Ps 112:1,6,7) He is settled in his mind.

I am convinced that we will experience some very difficult times ahead — economic hardships, collapse of law and order, shortages of food — frightening things if you haven't learned to depend on God's strength through submission.

Fear pumps adrenalin into the body and gets us moving. It gives us unusual strength to do things we cannot normally do. Think of the effect faith could have on our body if we allowed it to take instant control over us the way we have let fear do in the past — faith that causes us to submit to God without a moment's hesitation. Think of the tremendous power of God released through our submission!

Is it so hard to understand why God wants us to submit to His will? He knows what will happen in our lives when we stop complaining and learn to say, "Lord, I'm really glad!"

10. Who Is Number One?

Do you think it would be easier to be perfect if you weren't surrounded by difficult people? But wait a minute — why do you think those people are there? We often quote a verse that says, "My God will supply all that you need from His glorious resources in Christ Jesus." (Phil. 4:19 Phillips) Did you ever stop to think that God also supplies the people with whom you need to live?

Maybe you say, "But, Lord, I don't need an alcoholic husband — or an unloving wife — or an unreasonable boss — or a runaway, rebellious child!" If that is what you have, that is what God says you need, or He would not give it to you.

We have talked about how God puts us in difficult circumstances to strip us of our old nature and teach us joyful submission to His will. Nothing teaches us submission as effectively as having to live with difficult people. Often God brings someone into our lives who just irks us to death, because we need that person. That person brings out the worst in us — and we need to see that in ourselves in order to get rid of it. Our stubborn, self-willed ego, bristling, says, "I don't want to do what anybody tells me to do — I won't take that kind of nonsense from anybody!!" Do you recognize that ugly thing inside rearing up, always wanting to have the last word? It is called the flesh, the old nature, and only submission can bring it under control.

Paul gave some specific guidelines for the Christian life:
1. ". . . be filled instead with the Holy Spirit . . .
2. Always give thanks for everything to our God and Father in the name of our Lord Jesus Christ.
3. Honor Christ by submitting to each other.
   (Eph. 5:18,20,21)

Step number three is the hardest for us to accept — but without it, the other two won't work. Submission to other people is an absolutely necessary part of the Christian growth process. God, who knows us better than we do, gives us opportunities to be in submission to certain people just so that we can become what He wants us to be.

Even Jesus learned submission through experience. As a young boy He had more wisdom and understanding than anyone else in the whole world, and I am sure He was aware of it. When He was twelve, His parents brought Him to the temple in Jerusalem. They returned home, but Jesus remained in deep discussion with the learned Temple teachers, who marveled at His understanding. When the parents discovered that their boy was left behind, they worried and came looking for Him. When they found Him, He was told to come home immediately.

We read that he went home with them to Nazareth and was obedient to them. (See Luke 2:41-52) Think of it, the perfect Son of God lived in total submission to his earthly parents, although He was much wiser than they. He kept His mouth shut and did what He was told. He listened and learned. What did He learn? "And even though Jesus was God's Son, He had to learn from experience what it was like to obey . . ." (Heb. 5:8)

Jesus was thirty years old when He began His ministry. The power behind His authority was His perfect submission to His Heavenly Father and to the circumstances and people among whom His Father put Him.

If you are young and want to have the joy of the Lord — obey your parents! Maybe they are always picking on you.

Maybe they don't trust you. Maybe they don't understand your religion and want you to stop talking about Jesus and stay home from church. You may say, "I'm going to obey God, not man," and go to church anyway. You are making a mistake. God's first instruction to you is: "Children, obey your parents; this is the right thing to do because God has placed them in authority over you." (Eph. 6:1) You will be closer to God when you stay home from church in obedience to your parents than if you go there against their will.

Try being submissive for at least one week — then if you can do it, try another week — and another — and a month — and a year. Can you do it joyfully? Maybe you say, "All I can do is just do it!" That is fine for a starter, but in the meantime look inside yourself and see why you can't do it gladly.

Can you believe that God gave you the parents you have because you need them? If He had wanted it differently, He could have put you in another family. If you are living with foster parents or adoptive parents, the same holds true. God placed them in authority over you because you need it. Can you thank God for them? Are you really glad they are the way they are? If you aren't glad, then you are complaining, and remember, complaining is a serious sin. God will forgive you and give you a new love for your parents when you ask Him for it.

If you love them, submission is easy because love is ". . . never haughty or selfish or rude. Love does not demand its own way. It is not irritable or touchy . . ." (I Cor. 13:5) Does that describe the way you feel and act toward your parents?

A young man wrote me, "My parents are unsaved, and my heart's desire is that they come to know Jesus. I try to be a good Christian, but every time I say or do something against my parents' will, they blame it on Jesus. I get so discouraged and depressed."

The most powerful way to demonstrate Christianity to your parents is to obey them in love. Remember that you are in a three-way relationship. As you submit first to God, He will help you submit to your parents in such a way that they can see Christ and His love in you.

God has placed parents in authority over children, but authority will be false and destructive unless we learn to combine it with true submission. The first step is to submit to God's will and recognize that He has given us exactly the children we need. If they are bright or slow, talented or clumsy, obedient or unruly, they are what we need — and we are what they need. God matched us up with infinite care, whether our children are of our flesh and blood or came to us some other way.

There is chaos and constant friction in homes across our land because we as parents have not learned to use our proper authority and submission. We always want the very best for our children, and we tend to blame ourselves when they do wrong. In our frustration we often give up all attempts to discipline or become too harsh. The Bible tells us there is a better way: "And now a word to you parents. Don't keep on scolding and nagging your children, making them angry and resentful. Rather, bring them up with the loving discipline the Lord himself approves, with suggestions and godly advice." (Eph. 6:4)

Don't be too harsh, and don't let them go without loving discipline. That task is impossible unless we submit to God and ask Him to meet our children's needs through us. He alone knows their needs — it may be a spanking, or a fishing trip with Dad. If we haven't understood our dependency on God before, we have a chance to discover it when our children are growing up!

For most of us the problems surface when our children are teenagers. Parents come to me who cannot understand why their once loving and affectionate children have become distant, rebellious and even hateful. At this point it is easy for parents to give in to a sense of guilt. We are afraid we have failed completely.

From God's perspective, things look different. Our family crisis is a wonderful opportunity for us to learn together. Giving thanks for the problem is the first step.

A common failing among us parents is that we think of our children as belonging to us — we cling to them and try to mold their lives. We need to submit our children to God and realize that their relationship with Him is more important than their relationship with us. Can we thank Him for being in charge of them? Can we thank Him for everything they do and say?

A mother told me how her teenage daughter would get mad and swear at her, yelling, "I hate you!" The mother would yell back, telling her to shut up, but the daily screaming sessions only got longer and louder. At this point the mother came to our church and began learning how to praise God in every situation.

One evening her daughter exploded with a stream of curses, but the mother remained calm and responded with, "Praise the Lord!" The daughter got madder when she couldn't stir up her mother and accused her of drinking. Still the mother kept smiling and saying, "Thank you, God, for all this."

Enraged, the daughter closed herself in her room for the evening. The next morning she came to breakfast a new creature, smiling and sweet. That was three years ago, her mother told me. They haven't had a single argument since.

God's power came through the mother's submission and changed the daughter. But what if God required that you be firm with your teenager? Even then your firmness must be based on submission, asking God to give you the right words to speak in love.

If your eighteen year-old says, "Thanks for the advice, but I choose not to obey," the decision is his. Can you be grateful? Can you submit him to God and rest in the knowledge that the disciplining is now up to his Heavenly Father?

A Christian couple dedicated their daughter to God and raised her in church. When she reached sixteen, she fell in love and ran away. With her boyfriend, she drifted across the country, calling home only to tell her parents that she was happy and did not want their interference.

The parents grieved for three years. Then in a Bible study group they discussed the verse, "And we know that all things work together for good to them that love God, to them who are the called according to His purpose." (Rom. 8:28 KJV) The leader interpreted this to mean they ought to thank God for every circumstance in their lives. His words upset the mother, who thought God did not intend them to be thankful that their daughter was living in sin.

A few weeks later a friend gave them *Prison to Praise*. They read it, but didn't think it applied to them. Next they read *Power in Praise* and studied carefully the scriptures referred to in the book. It finally convinced them that God wanted them to trust Him enough to praise Him, believing that their daughter was doing what she was doing because God allowed it. He was going to use that situation for something good.

Once they submitted to the situation, they found a new peace and joy in their own lives. They were trusting God in a new way, with new authority and power to help others.

At this time their daughter and her boyfriend were living in a dilapidated shack in another state. The girl was searching through some boxes left by the tenants of another shack, when she found a cardboard fan advertising a local funeral parlor. There was a picture of Jesus the Shepherd, holding a lamb. Suddenly the girl found herself thinking, "God loves me like Jesus loves that little lamb." The thought did not go away, and a couple of days later she found a crumpled page torn from a Bible. Hungrily she read the familiar words and realized that she longed to find her way back to God. She called her father and asked him to pray that she would know what to do. His response was, "Honey, you know you can find Jesus right where you are if you only talk to Him."

That week she called home several times and finally told her parents, "I have given my life to God. I want to do His will." She asked her father if she should leave her boyfriend and come home, but her father said, "I'll be glad to send you a plane ticket, but you must make the decision to come when you feel it is the right thing to do."

The daughter loved the man with whom she was living, but finally decided that it was wrong to stay with him. She flew home to a reunion with her parents and filled her days with Bible studies and prayer. Her submission to God's will was so thorough that she matured rapidly in her Christian life.

A few months later her old boyfriend came looking for her. She was not home, but a Christian friend was there. He greeted the young man warmly and asked if he knew Christ.

"No," the fellow shook his head. "I've never been to church, but I know my girl loved me and wouldn't leave unless something important came up. I would like to pray to her God and see if I can find what she has found."

A couple of hours later he accepted Christ as his Savior. He had no job and no material possessions, but stayed with the Christian friend of the family, and soon was an enthusiastic dedicated Christian. He wanted to do God's will, and was willing to give up hope of ever getting his girl back if that was God's plan.

About this time God arranged the circumstances to bring these two back together again. Their wedding was one of the happiest the church had ever seen, and they are active together in Christian work today.

The story has a happy ending, but I know parents of runaway children who cannot submit their children to God, and who cannot resist trying to control the young people when they find them. For lack of submission there is still a painful, broken relationship.

Being a wife or a husband gives us another wonderful opportunity to submit. Aren't you glad your husband is exactly the way he is? Do you appreciate that God picked your wife especially to fill your need? A woman in our church told how she first tried to praise God for her husband, hoping God would change him. But nothing happened. Then she started listening to the sermons on how to submit to what God wants for us. She began looking at her own attitudes and asked God to change her instead. As she was changed, so was her husband.

Submitting to our spouses means first of all that we are really glad they are exactly the way they are. If they are difficult to live with, it is because we need that. There is no better way to get rid of the rough edges of our own stubborn ego. Aren't you glad for an opportunity to be changed into a more loving, kind, and patient person?

True submission is a powerful thing. That is why Peter wrote, "In like manner you married women, be submissive to your own husbands . . . So that even if any do not obey the Word of God, they may be won over *not by discussion* but by the godly lives of their wives." (I Pet. 3:1 Amp)

Not long ago our office received the following note: "My husband was an alcoholic for 35 years, and I was a self-righteous goodie-two-shoes who probably drove him to it. Then God showed me in the Bible that if I let Him put me in my right place in the marriage, He would be responsible for my husband's place in His kingdom. I knelt by my husband's bed while he was drunk, and asked him to forgive me for all the times I had usurped his authority, and promised to be a submissive wife from now on.

Guess what? God took charge immediately. My husband lay in that bed for three days without moving. Then he got up and has not been drunk since. He accepted Christ and His Holy Spirit. Praise God! He is so wonderful."

There are wives who have lived for years under the domination of a demanding husband. They have learned an outward adaption to keep peace in the house, but that is not a true submission. If you are a suffering wife, examine your attitude. Self-pity hides a complaint, and complaining is sin. Can you be thankful your husband is the way he is? Or do you wish he were different?

Submission isn't real until you *enjoy adapting yourself* to your husband. When that happens, you will discover that God has transformed you inside. You will know a greater joy and peace, and God's authority and power will be at work around you as well.

Marriage is a three-way relationship. Wife, whom do you think of as number one? It should be Jesus, with your husband a close second. If you think of yourself first, wanting attention, wanting to be loved more, you are not practicing love — because love does not seek self-satisfaction, but seeks to please the beloved.

Husband, whom do you think of as number one? It should be Jesus, with your wife a close second. A husband is placed in authority over his wife, but nowhere in the Bible is he told to enforce his authority. "And you husbands, show the same kind of love to your wives as Christ showed to the church when He died for her," (Eph. 5:25)

In many modern marriages husbands have left the decision making to their wives. If that is what you are doing, you are neglecting her true needs. God has appointed you as her head, to guide and direct her with the love of Christ, Who is your Head. If she doesn't want your advice — are you glad? That gives you an opportunity to depend on God and submit your wife to Him. If you let God put you in your right place as head of your wife, you can trust Him to be in charge of her submission as well. Your job is to concentrate on being glad she is the way she is, and to love her.

Wives and husbands have a way of bringing out the innermost rebellion in each other. That gives us wonderful opportunities again and again to see ourselves as we really are and to turn our sins over to God. We can't get rid of them as long as they remain hidden, so aren't you glad God gave you a wife or a husband who really knows how to get to you?

Perhaps the hardest thing to take from anybody is criticism. I was frequently hurt by people who found fault with me, and my natural reaction was to retaliate in kind. Then I began to understand that God allowed me to hear those words because

I needed them. If you are willing to *do* what God tells you to do, are you also willing to *hear* what He wants you to hear?

Jesus bore criticism and humiliation and never returned an ugly word. Sometimes what is said about us is true. David wrote, "Let the righteous smite me; it shall be a kindness: and let him reprove me; it shall be an excellent oil, which shall not break my head: . . ." (Ps. 141:5 KJV)

When someone finds fault with us, our first reaction should be to thank God. Be really glad. Then let the searchlight of the Holy Spirit show us if there is truth in the words. If there is, we need to confess.

If we are criticized unjustly, there is also reason to rejoice. This is a wonderful opportunity to demonstrate God's power in submission. If we answer in ugly words, the evil circle continues. If we respond in love, the circle is broken. The love of Christ takes the sting out of the words and brings promise of healing to the bitter and hurt soul of your accuser.

One day I was playing golf at Lawrence Welk's golf course with my friend, Roy Wyman. It was a beautiful day, and we walked leisurely on the green grass shaded by large trees. At the last hole we heard angry shouts behind us. A red-faced man shook his fist at us: "Don't you think of anyone but yourself?" he shouted, "There are people waiting to play after you!"

We had been so relaxed that we completely forgot to hurry with the game. For an instant I felt a flicker of the old Merlin, wanting to justify myself. Years ago I would have shaken my golf club and told the man to shut up! Instead, I felt a wave of compassion for the poor man, and was genuinely sorry that we had caused him pain. With a smile I apologized and watched as the purple color left his face. He muttered a word or two and left. Once his critical words would have ruined my afternoon. Now I felt peace and joy as I realized what a transformation God had brought in me.

Somehow we feel justified in not submitting to what we think is wrong. If our boss is critical of our religion, we feel we have "a right" to "stand up for Jesus" against company rules.

But what does the Bible say? "Servants, you must respect your masters and do whatever they tell you — not only if they are kind and reasonable, but even if they are tough and cruel." (I Pet. 2:18)

If your boss tells you to keep your mouth shut about Jesus during working hours — you should keep your mouth shut and be glad! Your boss couldn't talk to you like that unless you needed it. The most powerful Christian witness on the job is your joyful submission to whatever the boss asks of you. When you've learned what you need to learn, you'll be so glad your boss is the way he is that you don't care if he ever changes. You can praise God for him, and God's power and authority will radiate through that shop or office.

Is there a limit to your submission? Never in the inward attitude, but there may come a day when God says, "That's enough, now I want you to speak with my authority." If the boss says, "Go kill a man," you will have to say, "Sorry, Boss, can't do it." If he says, "Go get drunk!" you say, "Sorry Boss, can't do that either." But if he says, "Shut up and go back to work, you can say, "Yes, sir!"

The government may be wrong, but if we rebel against it, we are disobeying God. "Obey the government, for God is the one who has put it there. There is no government anywhere that God has not placed in power." (Rom. 13:1) That means communists or fascists or crooked officials. If you think the rules and regulations are getting too harsh; the taxes too high; the speed limit too low; they are that way because we need to learn submission. Are you grateful for the highway patrolman who stops you when you are speeding? Are you grateful for the IRS?

There may come a day when your government says, "Round up six million Jews and get rid of them!" That's when God will tell you to exercise His authority, and you can answer, "Sorry, government, I can't do that." Or they may say, "Deny your faith or you'll lose your freedom." And you say, "Sorry, government, you'll just have to put me in jail!" Or they may even kill you. That has happened to many Christians through the years, and they counted it a joyous privilege to die for Christ. Would you?

Most of us have a long way to go in the school of submission before we get that far. We can't even submit to each other in the church! All the different denominations are a result of Christians not being able to submit to one another.

Why do you think God puts difficult people together in the church? He does it so that we can learn to love each other. And our love is not real until we can submit. Are there cantankerous elders in your church? A stuffed-shirt pastor who tells everybody what to do? A gossip in the pew? A sour Sunday school teacher? Isn't the church as spiritual as you want it to be? If you leave before His spirit leads you, you'll miss a wonderful opportunity to learn submission. God can change those people, and there is a good chance He will, when you've learned to be really glad they are what they are.

Paul must have been a very proud man when he persecuted the Christians before his own conversion. He was proud of his superior education and wisdom; proud of his heritage and position. It took many difficult and humiliating experiences to teach Paul submission and true praise. But he learned. When Paul spoke with authority, his inward submission was obvious. He wrote, "Now . . . I have a command, not just a suggestion. And it is not a command from me, for this is what the Lord himself has said . . ." (I Cor. 7:10) Paul is saying, "I'm not putting my own authority over you; it comes from God." Later he wrote, "Here I want to add some suggestions of my own. These are not direct commands from the Lord, but they seem right to me! . . ." (I Cor. 7:12) He is careful not to command when God had not given him specific authority.

When Paul wrote his letter to Philemon who was an elder in the church at Colossae, he put aside his authority and submitted to the other man. The letter concerns Philemon's runaway slave, Onesimus, who became a Christian under Paul's ministry in Rome. Paul sends him back to his master with a letter: ". . . I could demand it of you in the name of Christ because it is the right thing for you to do, but I love you and prefer just to ask you . . . My plea is that you show kindness to my child Onesimus, whom I won to the Lord . . . I really wanted to keep him here . . . and you would have been helping me through him, but I didn't want to do it without your consent. I didn't want you to be kind because you had to but because you wanted to." (Philemon, verses 8-10,13,14)

Paul had authority to demand obedience of Philemon, but he knew that Philemon's submission would lose its power and purpose unless it was voluntary. So Paul himself submits to Philemon, saying that he will accept whatever the other man chooses to do. He also gives Philemon the opportunity to do the same to his slave, Onesimus, who voluntarily returns to submit to his former master. Can you see how that kind of authority and submission sets everybody free?

True authority never seeks to exalt itself or force others. It seeks only the greatest good for those over whom it has been placed. Jesus called himself a servant, and to demonstrate it he knelt before his disciples and washed their feet. If you have been placed in authority over someone at home, in church, at work, in government, do you think of yourself as serving them? Do you seek their greatest good, wanting their submission to be mature and voluntary?

If there is conflict — are you glad? If someone is lazy, careless, disrespectful, argumentative — are you grateful? Do you know that God allows them to be like that to teach you true authority? Do you think of Jesus as number one and your difficult subordinate as a close number two? Can you see yourself kneeling before him, washing his feet? If you can't, there is something lacking in your submission, and your authority isn't what God wants it to be. Are you glad you discovered it? Now you can confess it and be forgiven and ask God to remove any obstacle to true submission from your heart.

You can't separate authority from submission. Once you really understand it, no one can take advantage of you and you won't take advantage of others. You are learning to submit with joy to God's will whether He asks you to take authority or to be a doormat. If He wants you to be a doormat, be the happiest doormat ever, because you are learning to be what God wants you to be, and your praise will flow from a heart filled with the joy of Christ. Jesus said, ". . . Well done, thou good and faithful servant: . . . enter thou into the joy of thy lord." (Matt. 25:21 KJV) You are seeing Heaven flow into Hell.

11. In Love With God

My grandmother was one of the happiest people I ever knew. When she was dying, both of her legs had turned black with gangrene, making even the room stink. People came to sympathize, but left filled with astonishment at the joy coming from Grandmother's lips. The only thing she could think of was that she would soon be with her beloved Jesus. From a human standpoint, Grandmother's circumstances were horrible, but for years her attention had been so focused on Christ that joy was the theme of her life.

My father was like her. He worked in a steel mill in Pennsylvania as a laborer. When I was a young man, seven years after my Father's death, I got a job in the same mill. I had a small office near the steel furnaces where Dad had worked. An elderly Roman Catholic Italian worker often came to see me, always removing his hat before speaking, "If you ever become a Christian, Merlin, become a Christian like your father."

"What do you mean?" I felt awkward.

"Your father was always happy. He went along the steel furnaces and when he found someone who was tired or discouraged he talked to him, then stepped off to the side. We could see him raise his hands and knew he was thanking God."

The stories always embarrassed me, just as I had been embarrassed as a boy when I sat on the front row in church with my father. He would sometimes explode with joy in that staid Methodist church, jump to his feet and say, "Praise the Lord!" I wanted to hide under my seat, but Mother was proud of him, for she had prayed for many years that Jesus would become real to him.

Dad was only thirty-six years old when he died, but I remember the happiness that was so typical of his life, as he sat up in bed and said, "Look, they are here to take me!" Then he leaned back against his pillow and was gone.

It took many years before I began to understand the secret of grandmother's and father's happiness. They were certain of God's love. They knew Him and trusted Him and saw every circumstance as a gift from His hand — even pain and death.

It has long been the desire of my heart to be able to praise God like that. One day recently I was thinking about it, and felt a nudge inside: "Come up higher, Merlin." The thought was repeated several times, and I wondered what it meant. All I could think of was high mountains and airplanes. Perhaps I needed to do more hiking and flying!

A small squirrel ran straight up a tree in front of me, and my heart gave an involuntary leap. What if the squirrel caught hold of a piece of loose bark and tumbled to his death? As I watched, he ran even higher, to the very top of the tree, and out on a tiny limb that bent and swayed under his weight. It was fearful just to watch, but as the squirrel moved gracefully back and forth high up against the blue sky, I suddenly perceived that he was having a wonderful time. What seemed like a dangerous height to me was his natural environment. He was more at home in the tree tops than on the ground.

I felt that little nudge again: "Come up higher, Merlin, up here with Me where you belong. You'll have a wonderful time!" We human beings are as frightened of spiritual heights as we are of physical heights. We don't want to fall, and so we think we are safer on the ground, even if we belong up higher. God says, "I created you for fellowship with me. I want you up here in the clean and pure air of Christian maturity, not down where the pollution of filth and degradation will discourage and pull you down."

"Lord," I thought. "I want to come up higher, but how do I get there?"

My mind went to the story of Jesus meeting the woman at the well in Samaria. He told her that the water in the well could only quench her thirst for a little while, but He had water to give that would become like a well springing up inside her, flowing continuously with eternal life. The woman said she would like some of that water, and then she asked a question that seemed unrelated to the topic: "Where are we supposed to worship God; on a mountain in Samaria, or in Jerusalem?"

Jesus answered her, "You (Samaritans) do not know what you are worshipping — you worship what you do not comprehend . . . A time will come, however, indeed it is already here, when the true (genuine) worshippers will worship the Father in spirit and in truth (reality); for the Father is seeking just such people as these as His worshippers." (Jn. 4:22,23 Amp)

"But, Lord," I thought. "I already know about that well of living water — it is the Holy Spirit inside me — and I know something about worshipping you in Spirit and in Truth . . ."

"To worship in Spirit and in Truth is a continuous thing, like the well of living water never running dry — are you doing that?"

"No, Lord . . ."

"Do you want to come up higher?"

"Yes, Lord . . ." There was a long silence, and I thought how often we come to church, sit down, sing songs, say, "Praise the Lord," and we are not worshipping in Spirit and in Truth. As we begin to learn to praise Him, we see answered prayers, and our praise makes us feel good and satisfied for a time — then discouragement sets in and we are thirsty again.

The question formed itself in my mind, "What makes the well inside me flow continuously?"

"The more you love Me, the more it flows . . ."

"But I do love You . . ."

There was silence, and my eyes fell on the words in my Bible: "You worship what you do not comprehend." The meaning was suddenly clear. When our worship is empty, it is because we don't understand or comprehend enough about God, and we can't love what we don't know. Often I have heard people say, "How can I really love God? I don't see Him, I know He is almighty and great — how can a small human being actually love something that big and vague?"

Most of us will have to admit that to love God is a difficult concept at times, but then to love Him is not something that we human beings can do on our own. "We love him, because he first loved us." (I John 4:19 KJV) It is when God's love reaches us that we can respond by loving Him. Once we have accepted the love He offers us through Christ, we are told by Jesus Himself, ". . . Thou shalt love the Lord thy God with all thy heart, and with all thy soul, and with all thy mind. This is the first and great commandment." (Matt. 22:37,38 KJV)

So loving God is not just something desirable for us to do; it is a command. We must come to God and say, "How do I learn to love you?" Jesus tells us how to proceed: ". . . If a man love me, He will keep my word;. . ." (John 14:23 KJV)

Love is a verb, an action word, and we love God by doing what He tells us to do. When He says, "Express your love in praising Me for everything," we start doing it because He says we should, whether we feel like it or not.

The more we obey Him, the better we get to know Him, and the more we will want to love Him and obey Him some more. Jesus said, "The one who obeys Me is the one who loves Me; and because he loves Me, my Father will love him; and I will too, and I will reveal myself to him." (Jn 14:21)

Where do you think Jesus will reveal Himself? — in the very circumstances where before we could see only suffering.

Sandra, a young housewife in her late twenties, had suffered with terrible migraine headaches since she was a teenager. The headaches would come without warning, virtually crippling her for the 24 to 48 hours they lasted. Her vision would blur, she would have a fever, and no medical or therapeutical remedies seemed to help.

When she became a Christian, she cried to God for relief, but the pain did not diminish. At times she thought that since she was now assured eternal life with Christ, she would be better off dead than suffering such agony.

One day she was given my book *Walking and Leaping*. The idea of thanking God for everything was new to her, and she wasn't sure she agreed with it. A few days later she was at a party when the headache struck again. She confided in a friend and explained that she would have to hurry home before her vision blurred so that she could no longer drive.

"Have you ever thought of thanking God for your headaches?"

"Of course not!" Sandra was visibly shaken. "I thank Him for good things, but how can I blame Him for something as horrible as this pain? It would not be right."

"Then do you mind if I thank Him for you?" the friend asked. "You see, I believe God is more powerful than your pain, and He could take it away if He wanted. Since He hasn't taken it away, doesn't it make sense that He must want you to have it for a good reason? So why not thank Him for it and see what happens?"

Sandra listened as her friend quoted several scriptures emphasizing that we should thank God for all things. Then she nodded resolutely. "I know God is more powerful than my pain," she said. "I've always wondered why He allowed me to have these headaches. But if He says I should thank Him, then I promise to try it — even if it kills me." She grimaced and her face showed the increasing pain. "God must know better than I do what's good for me, and I want to obey Him . . ."

During the next 24 hours Sandra made an important discovery. When she directed her thoughts to God and thanked Him for her agony, it became more bearable. When she let her attention focus on the pain itself, it became worse. "So You *are* in control of my pain, aren't You, God?" she whispered into the darkness of the night. "I thank You for showing me that You are really here and care about my headache."

That night, for the first time since the headaches had begun, she did not get out of bed to try to find a remedy for her pain. She did not apply ice packs or take cold showers or swallow any pain pills. Instead, she told God, "Now that I know you are in control, I know You know best what I can take. You won't make it harder than I can bear. Thank You."

The next morning her husband saw her fever blisters and said, "Honey, you must have had a bad night. Why didn't you wake me as usual?"

"It was bad, but it was all right," she smiled. "God was there, and He was in charge of my pain. I know I can take anything He gives me."

Several weeks later some member of Sandra's family came to our church and asked special prayer for her. They felt assured that God heard and healed her, and returned home with the good news to a surprised Sandra, "You will never have another of those pains."

Two weeks later the headache struck again, as blinding as ever, but Sandra confided happily to her friend, "So God didn't want me to get healed yet, but I actually consider myself lucky to have those pains. God is using them to show me how much He loves me. My husband was disappointed that I didn't get healed, but I told him, 'Don't worry, Just let me lie still and enjoy what God wants to teach me this time.'" Her voice bubbled with happiness. "I am getting to know God in a completely new way. All those hours when I have the pain, God is right there with me. I talk to Him like I never do when I'm running around with my daily activities. I am quiet, and His presence becomes so real. He makes me feel very loved and very special."

Sandra's voice faltered, "To think of the years I spent feeling sorry for myself. Why, the very thing I complained about has turned out to be one of the biggest blessings of my life."

She had prayed that her mother would find a personal relationship with Jesus, and said, "Since I started thanking God for my pain, Mother has become very curious about Christianity. She watched me all those years nearly going out of my mind with the headaches. Now she sees that something real has happened to me. Wouldn't it be wonderful if God could use my pains to show Mother His love?"

Sandra believes that God may take her pains away some day. "But He won't do it as long as He has something wonderful to teach me through them, and I'm glad!"

Sandra discovered what Paul meant when he wrote, "Therefore, I take pleasure in infirmities, in reproaches, in necessities, in persecutions, in distresses for Christ's sake: for when I am weak, then am I strong." (II Cor. 12:10 KJV)

Paul took pleasure in problems and pain. He didn't endure them, he enjoyed them. You may not understand why your problems or your pain are there, but of one thing you may be sure — if you enjoy them, they will reveal to you the hidden treasures of God's love.

I was in Alaska when someone pointed out a hill where a man named Ed Lung sat, broke and discouraged, during the Gold Rush Days of 1897. Ed was one of the first to arrive in Alaska when gold was discovered, but somehow he was always a day late to any site where gold was found. One day he sat on a hill, nearly weeping, and decided he might as well go back home to Tacoma, Washington, empty-handed and broke. A few weeks later another man put a pick into that same spot and discovered the famous Gold Hill that produced a billion dollars worth of the precious metal.

Are you sitting discouraged and dejected over the very problem that may be the source of your greatest joy if you will obey God and thank Him for it?

God wants you to trust Him and love Him enough to obey Him. Have you ever been to dinner at someone's house and they served something you had never before seen? You didn't know whether you should take a small spoonful just to be polite, or fill your plate. Your wife, sitting next to you, whispered, "Honey, I know what it is — you will love it!" Without hesitation you would take a big serving, because you know that your wife knows exactly what you like best.

If you can trust your wife like that, can't you trust God when certain circumstances come into your life, and He leans over to whisper, "I know what that is — you love it!"

To reject what God gives us is to disobey Him, and it means we don't love Him. To say we love Him when we disobey Him is a contradiction. It doesn't work. Jesus said, "If ye keep my commandments, ye shall abide in my love;. . ." (Jn. 15:10 KJV)

If you've been disobedient, you need to confess it and say, "Lord, I'm sorry I don't care enough about you to do what you want. Please forgive me and help me to love you more."

When you tell God that, you are saying that you want to come up higher, and He only asks two things of you: That you show your love by obeying Him to the best of your ability — and that you declare your love for Him in worship and praise.

Why does God need people to tell Him how great He is? He doesn't need it, but we need to do it. God knows His greatness, but we are still learning about it. When we praise Him for all He has done for us, it does something inside us and we see more of His greatness than we did before. The Holy Spirit within us joins in our praises, and we are lifted up higher and higher.

Tell God daily that you want to love Him more, and confess when you find yourself complaining. We can't love God enough as long as we're living in our old bodies, but God rejoices to see us do the best we can. That is all He asks, and He loves us just as we are. Try making a list of all the reasons you have to love God. You'll find it growing day by day. Thank Him for each item. Say it loud; sing about your blessings. Share them with others.

Paul advised the Christians in Ephesus: "Talk with each other much about the Lord, quoting psalms and hymns and singing sacred songs, making music in your hearts to the Lord." (Eph. 5:19) As you make it your regular practice, you will find yourself lifted high above your depressions and moods, and your love of God will grow and grow.

A young woman named Gloria complained a great deal about her housework, and her husband accused her of being sloppy and careless. It was true that her house never looked very neat. One day she heard about praising God for everything, and realized that her complaining was a serious sin. She told God she was sorry and promised to do her best to be obedient in the future. She began by thanking Him for the things she disliked the most; the greasy stove top, the cluttered refrigerator, the dirty floors. As she went about the house, she suddenly realized that God had given her all those things. He would not give her anything unless it was very special and precious, and He wanted her to love the very things she had never liked.

It was an exciting discovery for Gloria. "I began to see that God loved my house and my things. Each chair, each rug, each picture, each pot, and each dish suddenly looked different. How I had neglected them before! I asked God to forgive me for not loving the things He had given me enough to take care of them. Whenever I found a neglected corner, I said, 'You poor corner. God loves you and I love you, and I won't neglect you any more.'" She laughed as she shared her story. "I'm falling in love with my house, and I even love me! I hated my own carelessness and sloppiness, but God forgives every mistake I make, and all He asks is that I do my best. He only wants me to love Him as much as I can, and each day I love Him a little more."

Housework was no longer dull. Gloria's brown eyes shone with excitement. "This new love of mine is more solid than an emotion. It isn't affected by how I feel from one day to the next. When I think of how God loves me, I just *have* to love everything He gives me. I even love the dirty footprints my children leave on the living room rug and the greasy smears from their hands on the walls. I say, 'Thank You, Lord, for those dirt marks. Thank You for my children, help me to love them even more.' And I feel the love swell inside me, and I am the luckiest person in the world with so much to love."

Her husband no longer complains about a messy house. The rooms are neat, flowers bloom in pots and Gloria's kitchen usually smells of good cooking. She has discovered what Paul meant when he talked about taking pleasure in necessities. So often it is the little things we *have* to do — like getting up in the morning, doing dishes, washing the car, shopping for groceries or patching a hole in the roof — that gets us to complain. But God assigned each of our chores with special care, and we are told, "And whatever work you may have to do, do everything in the name of the Lord Jesus, thanking God the Father through Him." (Col. 3:17 Phillips) Each of the things we *have* to do should be a declaration of love to God — and His love will lift us even higher.

Is there someone you really adore? Perhaps your wife or your husband, or your first grandchild? Just looking at them makes you want to melt. You love to be near them. You praise them continuously, and you think of things to do to make them happy. You love them, not for what they do for you, but for what they are. This is the kind of relationship God has given my wife, Mary, and me. We have never had an argument, a cross word, or even the slightest desire that the other person would change in any way. We marvel continually that God would choose to give us such perfect, undeserved, unending harmony.

She does give me one problem, however. She occasionally wakes me during the night with her gentle laughter. She is asleep, murmuring, "Thank You, Jesus," and then another soft, happy laugh. Her happiness does also give us another minor problem. After Mary had given her testimony during one of our city-wide crusades, I asked the audience who had been thinking, "She surely is a lot younger than Merlin." About ninety percent of the audience raised their hands. I told them I knew the Lord would forgive them and shared that she is the mother of a twenty-four year old boy. The Oh's and Ah's showed they could hardly believe she was more than twenty-four years old herself. Happiness and love make some people look many years younger than they are.

When our love for God reaches a certain point, we begin to adore Him. Our hearts overflow with unspeakable praise, and we say, "Father, I don't want you to do anything for me. I just want to be near you and love you. I don't need another blessing to quench my spiritual thirst. I am satisfied because you love me, Lord, and I love everything you give me."

David wrote, "Bless — affectionately, gratefully praise — the Lord, O my soul, and all that is (deepest) within me, bless His holy name!" (Ps. 103:1 Amp) When all that is deepest within us affectionately and gratefully says, "God, I really love you!", the well within begins to flow uninterrupted. Your Christian life doesn't go up and down any more, it just goes higher. You don't need to ask anyone to pray that you will feel good, because the well inside keeps flowing.

Your joy doesn't come through being healed, wonderful as that may be. It doesn't come through having your prayers answered, wonderful as that may be. It comes from being in love with God.

One of the most joyful people I have ever met came to our church on a bed. Esther Lee was blind, paralyzed, and could only move her thumb on one hand. Her bones were so brittle that they would break if her limbs were moved.

When I spoke to her over the phone earlier, her voice rang with confident happiness, like someone abundantly blessed with every good thing. I knew she had been in bed for many years with rheumatoid arthritis. Not long ago her doctors had given her up and told her husband to prepare her for heaven. A friend had brought *Prison to Praise* and read it out loud to her three times. With nothing to lose, she had determined to try praising God for her pain instead of blaming Him. It became the turning point in her life.

She kept up the praise while calamities befell her household; a bankrupt business, her husband's heart attack, the children's sicknesses. Through it all she began to glimpse the love of God in a new way. "He showed me what a snivelling, miserable, complaining and bitter creature I had been all my life, and as I cried for forgiveness, His love came down to heal my sin-sick soul and fill me with joy and peace."

Her voice was weakened by her condition, but she kept exclaiming out loud, "God, I praise you, God, I love you," until her voice grew stronger. She had never had an ear for music, but as she praised God, melodies and words came to her mind. She began to sing, and her voice developed a quality it had never had before. Others were blessed by her singing and persuaded her to make a recording, named "Where Glory Began."

A phone was installed by her bed. It could be operated by her one thumb, so that she could talk to people from all over the United States who began calling her to be encouraged in *their faith!*

To come to our church, she traveled all the way from her home in Palm Springs to Escondido in a U-Haul trailer wide enough to carry her bed. The day was hot and the closed-in trailer felt like a tin oven. The trip had to have been torturing. Esther Lee had waited two years for an opportunity to visit us, and believed that she would be healed the minute she entered the church.

What happened instead made a greater impression on those present, I believe, than if she had leaped from her bed. She thanked God in such heartfelt praise that we knew she was rejoicing. Lying on her bed at the front of the church, she spoke to the congregation for the next hour of the blessings God had given her. She led in singing and praising with a voice bubbling with laughter.

Her physical condition was such that those who saw her would be tempted to feel pity and sorrow. Instead, we were moved to laughter and tears as we glimpsed, beyond the weak and wasted body on the bed, a beautiful relationship with God. She was blind and immobile, yet she was teaching us about the glorious power in praise. She spoke of finding life in surrender, and finding the amazing, intimate love of God through pain and sufferings more severe than most of us could imagine.

Love shone in her face as she led us in singing praises to our Heavenly Father — a love not dependent on what He does for us, but on what He has already done in Christ. It was a love stronger than the greatest physical infirmity — a love that sees God through blind eyes. I thought of David's Psalm: "Let the saints be joyful in glory; let them sing aloud upon their beds." (Ps. 149:5 KJV)

Are you singing praises to God? In pain, in problems, in difficult circumstances, can you sing aloud, "I love You, God; I thank You, God; I praise You, God!"

Or are you discouraged, waiting for God to come from somewhere outside to comfort you? Listen and you will hear him say, "Come up a little higher, learn to love me . . ." If you don't love Him enough, love Him as much as you can. You love Him a little, don't you? He forgives you for not loving Him more, and He will help you as you begin saying, "I love You as much as I can, Lord, help me to love You more."

Paul wrote, "And the Lord direct your hearts into the love of God; . . ." (II Thess. 3:5 KJV) Jesus Himself will direct our hearts when we sincerely desire to love God. As you obey His directions, you will discover a comfort that doesn't come from a change in your outward circumstances. Something happens inside you when you begin to love God more. A well of living water starts flowing continuously, until you worship God in Spirit and in Truth. Your problems are designed to help you do it. When that well flows within you, it no longer matters whether your problems stay with you or go away. What matters is that you are in love with God.

It is that love Paul speaks of "The ultimate aim of the Christian ministry, after all, is to produce the love which springs from a pure heart, a good conscience and a genuine faith." (I Tim. 1:5 Phillips) When you love like that, you will praise God till the day you die. During the last day of his life, Charles Wesley was heard whispering the words of the hymn, "I'll praise my Maker while I live." As he grew weaker, he could only say, "I'll praise, I'll praise." He repeated the words till his last breath was gone.

The Bible is full of passages reminding us of the greatness of our Heavenly Father. Reading them aloud helps us express our love for Him. One of my favorites is Psalm 103. It gives me wonderful reason to say, "God, I really love You!"

> "Bless — affectionately, gratefully praise — the Lord, O my
> soul,
> and all that is (deepest) within me, bless His holy name!
> He ransoms me from Hell.
> He surrounds me with lovingkindness and tender mercies.
> He fills my life with good things!
> My youth is renewed like the eagle's!
> He gives justice to all who are treated unfairly.
> He revealed His will and nature to Moses and the people of
> Israel.
> He is merciful and tender toward those who don't deserve it;
> He is slow to get angry and full of kindness and love.
> He never bears a grudge, nor remains angry forever.
> He has not punished us as we deserve for all our sins,
> for His mercy toward those who fear and honor
> Him is as great as the height of the heavens above
> the earth.
> He has removed our sins as far away from us as the east is
> from the west.   (Amp and Living)

He has brought His Heaven into what was once
my Hell.

EPILOGUE

Many thousands of readers have accepted Jesus as their Savior while they read the praise books. I pray that you too have received something from the Lord.

Since I wrote *Prison to Praise*, twenty-one years ago, my conviction has steadily grown stronger that a dynamic force is released in our lives when we praise the Lord for everything.

Once we have accepted Christ as our Savior, the Holy Spirit begins to work in our hearts. If you want His work in you to accomplish God's purpose, I **strongly recommend** four things:

I. Earnestly study God's Word every day. Powerful forces will strive to convince you that you do not need to do so. The Bible says of itself that it is "God's breath." Without that heavenly breath we can soon become lukewarm Christians.

II. Pray regularly - Jesus did. He rose before daylight to talk with God. He asked His disciples why they couldn't pray **at least** one hour. Never let yourself be deceived into thinking that you are too busy or that prayer doesn't work. Pray fervently, and God will reveal Himself to you in new and exciting ways.

III. Turn your back on evil of all kinds. Evil has an insidious way of making itself appear to be acceptable, if we fellowship with it. For example, many television programs and movies are designed to make evil look attractive or even good. Before you watch any program decide if this is God's will for you. Be sure to spend more time each day in prayer and Bible study than you do in entertainment!

IV. Witness for Him daily! God forgave us of our sins and gave us the free gift of eternal life. In return He asks us to tell others about His Son. Many Christians spend much time in learning how to be a stronger Christian, but never learn that one of our greatest sources of strength is to bring other people to Christ! Don't miss out on this blessing!

What's On Your Mind?

MERLIN R. CAROTHERS

KINGSWAY PUBLICATIONS
EASTBOURNE

Preface

Imagine a motion-picture screen above your head. Now visualize on that screen the thoughts that have come to your mind in recent weeks. Would you be ashamed for everyone you know to see your thoughts? If so, you urgently need to read and understand, *What's On Your Mind?* I wish I had known these truths when I was a young man.

I will share with you what I have learned, and I pray that God will take these words and use them to spare *you* needless suffering.

I'm writing this book because I need to read it, because God is burning it into my own heart - constraining me to make it available to others.

PLEASE CONSIDER THE FOLLOWING QUESTIONS:

WHICH ARE MORE IMPORTANT TO GOD?

1. Our actions
2. Our thoughts and desires

Wait until you have read this book before answering.

INTRODUCTION

I was sure it could never happen.

I was positive it couldn't happen.

I knew, without a doubt, it was impossible for it to happen.

IT HAPPENED!

My desires changed. I no longer *wanted* to think immoral thoughts.

A miracle? No, a discovery!

For the first time in my life I would be pleased for my wife to know everything in my thoughts. It would not embarrass me for my daughters to know all the thoughts of my heart. I could look at any woman, even the most beautiful, and feel free to reveal to her everything that was in my mind.

God had sent me on a journey that would change the most secret parts of my thoughts and desires.

CONTENTS

Chapter 1

A Minister Falls

The minister sat across from me, tears streaming down his face as if he had lost everything in the world that was important to him. And indeed he was very close to losing everything that he had taken a lifetime to build. A lifetime of sacrifice, hard work and helping others was about to be shattered. This is the story he told me.

His secretary had made an appointment for him to counsel the most attractive lady in their congregation. He was pleased that she was coming. Wherever she went, men always stopped to give her admiring glances that nearly always turned into prolonged stares. It was obvious that she was aware of the attention and that she thoroughly enjoyed it. But as far as the pastor knew, she was not interested in a close relationship with any man.

The pastor explained that when the woman came into his office he experienced a sense of physical pleasure. He had always considered himself happily married and had carefully protected himself from ever doing anything that would taint his image as a "Man of God." He and his wife were raising several children in what he considered an exceptionally happy home. Members of the congregation often referred to them as the "ideal family."

The woman's problem was quite unusual. She lived with a continual feeling of guilt because of her constant desire to have sex with different men. Her appetite for immorality haunted her day and night. She explained a few details of her lurid past, but assured him that since becoming a Christian several years earlier, she had been able to control her passions - until now.

The crisis point in the counseling session came when she told him that more than anything in all the world she wanted to have a physical relationship with him, her pastor. Instead of cutting her off at this point, he sat and listened as she explained in detail everything that she would like to do with him.

The pastor told me that it required all the strength he could muster to usher the woman out of his office.

For several weeks all he could do was to think about this woman. He repeatedly told himself that if she were scheduled to see him again, he would make sure that his wife was present. But she came back to the church without an appointment and the secretary brought her into his office.

During this visit the woman became even more specific about all the things she wanted to do with the pastor. He explained to her that these were very wrong desires and that she needed to find a man that could be a good husband and meet her needs. But then she used the weapon that confuses most men - she began to weep. Trying to comfort her, he went to her side and placed his hand on her shoulder. With that she rose and embraced him. From that point on things deteriorated. The outcome was that the woman became pregnant and was now demanding that he divorce his wife and marry her.

It was obvious to me that this pastor was sincerely repentant and would do *anything* to get his life back in order. But the big question was, *what* could he do? The woman insisted that if he didn't marry her she would announce to the congregation that he was the father of her unborn child.

I wanted to know what had led the pastor into the situation

he now faced. After a life-time of trying to be a model husband, father and servant of God, what had caused this tragic error? Was he an evil man? Everything about him indicated that he was a man of integrity. Twelve years earlier he had come to this church when the congregation consisted of less than fifty people. He had inspired them to increase the membership to over two thousand, and had led them through two successful building programs. He and his family lived in a beautiful home and had new cars every three years. The children attended a Christian school. All this was provided by the congregation. Now he was about to lose it all - perhaps even his family and his reputation.

What had his spiritual life been like? As I questioned him, I found him sincere and consistent in his devotion to God. His weekly sermons had been used of God to win people to Christ. He was dedicated to teaching his people and he led them to seek the fruits of the Holy Spirit. What was wrong?

Since the present problem had developed because of an immoral relationship, I asked if he had ever before been unfaithful to his wife. He assured me that this was the first time since he entered the ministry that he had done anything of which he was ashamed. I picked up on his use of the word "done," so I asked him why he had used it. "Because, before now, I have never done anything other than think normal thoughts about other women." There it was. All he had been doing was "thinking" about other women. After about thirty years of "only thinking," his thoughts had blossomed into an act. Was the culminating action the result of the beautiful woman coming into his office? Hardly! His action came because of years of *thinking*. How do I know this? Because this is exactly what the Bible says in Matthew 15:19-20, *Out of the heart proceed evil THOUGHTS...adulteries, fornications...These are the things which defile a man.* The above account is not unusual. Though the details might be different, similar heartbreaking scenes unfold regularly throughout the Christian community.

I asked the pastor to explain what he thought the Bible says about lustful thoughts. His answer showed that he was thoroughly aware of the Biblical warnings against adultery, but wasn't familiar with any emphasis on our thoughts. I was surprised to learn how little this minister knew about God's requirements for pure and holy thinking. Perhaps I shouldn't say I was surprised, for I had been learning how little the average Christian knows about the importance of what we have on our minds. Do Christians *want* to know what God requires? It is simpler to accept the fact that we aren't perfect and to get on with going to church and doing the things that we know how to do.

Since the pastor had asked my advice, I suggested that he resign, move to a distant place and rebuild his life. He said he had reached this conclusion, but was reluctant to leave the security of his church. The ministry was his entire life, and being a pastor was the only thing he knew. He agreed that for all concerned this was the best solution.

Months later I learned that this man had confessed his failure to his wife and that she had forgiven him. He confessed to his church, knowing the members could receive it better from him than anyone else. Did they forgive him? Probably some did and some didn't. It is very difficult for average laymen to see their pastor pushed off his pedestal. He is *supposed to be perfect*. Everyone knows he isn't, but at least he is supposed to give that impression.

This man now has a new occupation and is doing his best to provide for his family and for the other woman and child. He still grieves when he thinks about what he did and of the people he hurt.

I've asked the Spirit to reveal whether seeds of immorality may lie within me, waiting for an opportunity to blossom. If they are there, they will come forth! I ask you to examine your own heart under the microscope of God's Word. Do you have secret desires, hidden longings or concealed passions that are not

4

morally pure? If so, you probably never intend for them to be activated. But any thought connected with illicit sex is like a monster waiting to take over. It can be kept hidden for many years, but at the right moment it emerges. This evil force is often willing to wait for the right moment to manifest itself. It wants to damage the greatest number of people possible. Does this frighten you?

Let me assure you that I'm not talking about evil spirits *possessing* Christians. But there exists in this world an evil force whose desire is to destroy everything God wants to build. That force, Satan, is far more clever than the average Christian believes. Satan leads *his* people to live in open rebellion against God, but he is content to work secretly in the inward parts of Christians. His strategy is to entice us to want things that God has forbidden. Once the desire is created, Satan keeps fortifying that desire. He repeatedly brings it to our attention until it outweighs our desire to be obedient to God.

The pastor wanted to be obedient to God, but he had also been indulging in a dream world - the world of his imagination. He had frequently fantasized about sex with other women. He enjoyed this world of the imagination, but never expected to *do* anything about it. I doubt if he would ever have gone out looking for a woman with whom to commit adultery. As always, Satan had to arrange a situation that would fit this man's personality. And Satan knows each of us better than we know ourselves! He has had many thousands of years to observe mankind.

Most of us know people who have committed immoral acts. We have no reason to judge them, for God has strictly warned us against setting ourselves up as judges. What we *can* do is learn from their experiences. By diligently studying the Bible regarding *thoughts* and *imagination*, we give the Holy Spirit the opportunity He seeks to cleanse our hearts.

At the close of a speaking engagement, a woman came up to me and asked for the opportunity to obtain my advice. I suggested that we sit on the front row while she shared with me. But she said her situation was so personal that we needed a more private place. An usher brought the pastor, who said we could use his office. There the woman poured out the details of the situation that was pushing her toward suicide.

This attractive and cultured lady had been a part of that church her entire life. Her father had helped to build the original church some fifty years earlier. And most of her friends and relatives were in the congregation. She was part of nearly everything that went on in the church and loved it.

The home life she described was close to ideal. Her husband provided a beautiful home, a new car and any clothes she wanted. Their children were healthy and attending good schools. She had the freedom to come and go as she liked and was probably envied by most women who knew her.

But (and in nearly all of our lives there is a "but") her husband was not a very warm person. He seldom showed her any affection. When she saw a man acting lovingly toward his wife, she was filled with longing. She repeatedly told herself that she would gladly exchange everything she had if she were only married to a man who would meet her physical and emotional needs. When she saw a man who looked and acted as if he were the kind of man who could make her happy, she day dreamed about what it would be like to be married to him. The idea of experiencing passion with such a man excited and stimulated her imagination. She knew that she would *never* do anything to disrupt her home, but she continued in her fantasy. She studied different men and wondered what it would be like to have them hold her. What could be wrong with that? After all, her *actions* were always above reproach.

One evening she and her husband went to dinner at the home of their friends. During the evening the host was especially attentive to his wife. The wife seemed disinterested in her husband. The woman told me, "I couldn't help but think what a waste it was to have such a loving husband lavishing attention on a woman who didn't even care."

From that evening on she began centering her dream world on that husband. After months of *only thinking*, she had an occasion to speak with him privately. She told him how much she admired his loving attention to his wife. He responded by telling her how much he longed for a woman who wanted him. Their discussion led to the conclusion that the two of them should have been married. This led to a warm embrace and eventually into many secret meetings.

For months they lived in agony. They couldn't stand the torment of having the person they loved living with someone else. They hated the thought of divorce, with all its ugly complications, but the man was pressing her to make a break with her husband. She understood her husband well enough to know he would *never* let her have the children. If he discovered what had been going on, he would use every resource to make sure he obtained permanent custody. She felt that losing her children might soon destroy the love she had for the other man.

The problem seemed to have only one solution. She would end her life in some way that appeared to be accidental and the whole mess would be over.

Did God look down from heaven and say to this woman, "You are living in an adulterous dream world, therefore I am going to punish you for your disobedience?" No, I believe God longed that she recognize her world of imagination as leading into something she could not control. I believe the Holy Spirit tried to get her attention many times, but she persisted in doing what *she wanted to do*.

I wish there were a happy conclusion to this story, but there wasn't. I did the best I could, but I wasn't successful. Several months later I learned from the pastor that she had been involved in a fatal "accident" in her car.

God's laws are not designed to destroy our fun. They are designed to *protect* us. Only He knows the forces that are working against us. There is a real spirit world that has arrayed itself against God. God has made it very clear in His Word that these evil forces are powerful and that they can manipulate many things here on this earth. He repeatedly urges us to become more like His Son if we want to be protected from the painful things that evil can work in us.

The line of people across the front of the church was made up of people who were obviously in need of special prayer. Some were on crutches. One young lady was in a wheelchair. A number of people had walked to the altar in obvious pain.

When I finished speaking, I invited those who needed prayer to come to the front. About fifty people came. Among them was a young man who stood out as someone you wouldn't expect to see in a prayer line. He was well over six feet tall, broad-shouldered, strikingly handsome and a picture of health. I wondered what physical problem he might have.

As I prayed for the people, one by one, I noticed that the young man kept to the rear of those who had come forward. He stayed back until everyone had been prayed for and then asked if he could speak to me privately. I guided him to a quiet part of the sanctuary and, as we sat down, I asked, "What is your problem?"

The young man's composure fell apart as he tried to tell me. He had wanted to be a doctor all his life. In high school he had taken every course that would help him reach his goal. He was now in pre-medical school and was near the top of his class. Everything looked as if he were going to see his dream fulfilled.

But a few weeks earlier he had noticed symptoms in his body that worried him. Medical examinations and tests con-

8

firmed his fears - he had an incurable type of venereal disease! He hadn't been able to find out for sure whether he would be permitted to enter medical school, but the doctors who examined him, doubted that he would. At this point his problem was that he couldn't concentrate on his studies. He knew his grades were sliding and his emotions were running wild.

As he poured out his heart, I saw a picture of an ideal young man. He had attended church all his life and received Christ as his Savior before he went to high school. He had never been involved with smoking, alcohol or drugs, was active in sports and had never been in any kind of trouble. But now....

He had only one affair with a young lady in his life. They attended the same church, and he had believed that he loved her. She either hadn't known she had a venereal disease or had failed to tell him. He was trying to forgive her, but he was obviously quite bitter.

We prayed, and I did my best to help him release the burden of his sickness to the Lord. His faith seemed quite weak, so I did my best to believe for him. Before we parted, I asked him what caused his present situation. His answer made it clear that he felt the cause was his failure to observe God's laws. He said he never should have had sexual relations with the young lady.

I didn't want to add to this young man's suffering, but I asked him to tell me what his thought life had been prior to his experience with this girl. He admitted that for many years he had *wanted* to have sex with many attractive girls, but had refrained since he believed it wouldn't be right. But from his point of view, the desires he had lived with were only "natural."

It wasn't part of God's plan for this young man to have his dreams shattered. But if *anyone* follows the natural order of "the flesh," trouble will usually result. It may not be as obvious as in this case, but Satan is always careful to make the situation fit his purposes. He wouldn't want *everyone* to contract an incurable venereal disease, for then nearly everyone would be more careful. He prefers to leave it as it is, so people will always be able to believe, "It would never happen to me!"

It is *never* safe to step into Satan's territory. He goes about seeking whom he may devour. He selects his own time to accomplish his own purposes. We never know what he will do. I've had men tell me that they lived with immoral thoughts and desires for twenty-five years before they yielded to immoral acts. Time is irrelevant to Satan. If you believe that he is a reality, and that he has spiritual power, it will profit you greatly to stay out of his territory! He, too, has a plan for you and it very likely will be fulfilled if you allow any part of your life to be under his control. He is especially interested in what's on your *mind*. Ephesians 6:12 says, *We wrestle not against flesh and blood, but against principalities, against powers, against the rulers of the darkness of this world, against spiritual wickedness in high places*.

During my twenty years in the Army, I was always blessed with excellent Commanding Officers. I would classify each one of them as a "good man." They tried to do their best and had a sincere interest in helping those who served under their leadership.

I became close friends with a number of my CO's, but there was one that I remember as being a dear friend. He was a Christian, active in all our chapel activities, friendly with everyone, and one of his goals was to become a Four-Star General. He had every potential for reaching this goal. I suppose that nearly every Regular Army officer wants to become a high-ranking General Officer, but this man had an above average zeal to succeed.

When I was in my commander's office, we would occasionally be interrupted by his secretary. She was, to say the least, a beautiful young lady. After she would leave, my boss would say things like, "Don't look at her too long, Chappie. She will get under your skin!" Or, "I have to keep my eyes off her or I will

10

lose my convictions." It was clear that he had a *strong* attraction for this lady, but it was also clear that he had no intention of doing anything wrong.

At our staff meetings, other officers would jokingly say such things as, "Colonel, how do you keep your hands off *that secretary* of yours?"

He would laugh, but come back with. "That lady is married and so am I. I wouldn't even come close to touching her."

On one occasion he told me he had known several officers who lost their careers because of illicit relationships with women. He said that he didn't intend to become one of the casualties. I *know* he meant it.

But - and that one word can be the prelude to a multitude of tragedies - my friend, the Commander, looked at this beautiful secretary once too often. His pent-up, inner desire eventually got the best of him, and he reached out to enjoy her. He was handsome, strong and successful, and the young lady was apparently attracted to him as well. He was never able to tell me exactly what happened, but he held his face in his hands as he asked me to pray for him so he would know how to handle the "mess" he had gotten into.

My friend resigned from the service. His dream of becoming a General Officer was destroyed. The young lady's life was severely damaged. The Army lost a superior leader. As his spiritual leader, I felt that I had failed.

That experience caused me to begin digging deeper into Scripture. I became angry with the forces that destroy good men and women, and I wanted to find ways to combat those forces. There had to be a way to defeat this "Fifth Column" activity in the hearts and lives of God's people. I was determined to find some means to help them overcome the temptation to commit adultery. My search took many years.

I spent much of my time as a chaplain and pastor trying to help myself and others fight the temptations that Satan thrusts at us. He has learned what works best, so he keeps using the same tactics. I thought that it would help if I kept reminding my congregations of the dangers we faced. I encouraged men to: go to the right places, read the right things, associate with the right people, pray much, etc. But I wasn't getting to the heart of the problem!

My friend, the Colonel, had a desire in his heart for that beautiful secretary. All Satan needed was time to bring that desire to the surface. I ache now as I realize how I might have helped my friend, if only I had known then what I know now. I hurt deeply when I think of the thousands of young men I might have kept from getting into hopeless situations. As a spiritual leader, I failed to present the whole truth - the entire will of God - because I didn't know what it was.

I know *now* that we must have morally clean desires. We must give up the inner, unholy longings that can be used to destroy us. And with God's help I want to use whatever abilities I have to teach men and women what *we can do*.

I pray that you will share with others the insights in this book. I especially urge you to share them with your children. Instead of worrying about the immoral influences they will have to face, patiently and prayerfully teach them what the Bible says on *thoughts* and *imaginations*. Train them to have the right kind of *desires*. It can be done!

Do everything you can to train the children in your Sunday School and church to seek pure thoughts. The traditional method of telling young people what to avoid has great merit, but it will not give them the strength they need to face the world in which they live.

After we have received Christ as our Savior, what should happen next? During a long period in my life I was taught, and believed, that we could receive an instantaneous, transforming experience that would free us from all sin. That sounded glorious to me, but I painfully observed that many who taught and believed in this experience were as prone to commit sins as were other Christians.

I now see in the Bible God's call for every Christian to move forward into becoming more like Jesus - a call for us to strive to become holy, even as He is holy. I realize that some people cringe at the very word "holy" as if it were a term too sacred to use when referring to humans. But God has urged us to be holy, so we should squarely face that word and permit it to work in us.

God does not present this potential growth as something extremely difficult. God doesn't - but *Satan does*! He convinces Christians that holiness of any kind is so far above their reach that they might as well not even think about it. His tactics are clever, and he plays on our natural weaknesses. After all, how could we ever hope to make even a dent when there is so much that needs improving in all of us?

Once we accept this philosophy from Satan, we are content to relax and drift with the flow. If you have been "drifting," you should note that the Bible clearly states God's will for every Christian. He wants us to "strive" to enter into His will. Jesus taught us in Luke 13:24, *Strive to enter in at the strait gate: for many, I say unto you, will seek to enter in, and shall not be able.*

To strive, in the Biblical sense, is not painful once we have made up our minds. It is the making up of our minds that can be *horribly* painful. It's somewhat like learning to run in a race. Who wants to go to all the work required to compete in a foot-race? But once we decide to train, and really work at winning, running can become a real joy. The non-runner might think, "Ugh. Who would want to put all that energy into running?"

If striving to become more like Jesus seems like a real drag, I promise you that it's *far* from that! It's the most thrilling thing

13

you can *ever* do!

Jesus came to the world to help us become what God wants us to be. We have the privilege, the honor, the joy of letting His Spirit help us!

Jesus has no interest in condemning us! He only wants to bring us into fellowship with God. If you have felt condemned or worthless, it certainly wasn't He who gave you these feelings. Jesus is like a gigantic cheering section, urging us on to win. He said, *I am come that ye might have life and that ye might have it more abundantly* (John 10:10). That is what Christian perfection is all about. It isn't giving up fun things so we can sit around and look holy. It's entering into the *excitement* of communication with God! It's learning what God had in mind for the human race when He created us.

Please don't think of this book as an effort on my part to point out all the things that are wrong with you. You probably already know what's wrong. What I want to do is share how you can be delivered from wrong thoughts, so you can enter into the abundant life Jesus talked about. When He was talking to God, Jesus said, *I say these things while I am still in the world, so that My joy may be made full and complete and perfect in them - that they may experience My delight fulfilled in them, that My enjoyment may be perfected in their souls, that they may have My gladness within them filling their hearts* (John 17:13 AMP).

This book and Bible commentaries are far different from anything you have ever read. You could listen to one thousand sermons and read one thousand Christian volumes and never hear one word about the central theme of this book.

As you ponder what you read, you may ask yourself why you haven't heard this message before. If the subject is as important as my comments indicate, why hasn't it been clearly proclaimed from every pulpit in the world?

If you examine the history of the Jews and Christians, you

14

will observe that we have repeatedly ignored subjects that are of great interest to God.

The Jews had been held as slaves for four hundred years. You can believe they wanted to possess the land God had promised them. When they were on their way from their captivity in Egypt to the Promised Land, they ignored God's will for forty years. He wanted them to trust Him and not to complain. They disregarded His instructions and complained at every opportunity.

What happened? Did the earth open up and swallow them? No, they marched painfully onward, year after year. God didn't force His chosen people to stop complaining, but neither did He help them reach the Promised Land.

It is estimated that from one to three million people left Egypt, enroute to the Promised Land. Of the adults who began the journey, only two, Joshua and Caleb, ever entered into the land God had promised them. How tragic! But this is a clear lesson to you and me. The crowd *can* miss God's will. Keep that clearly in mind as you read this book. If you have been marching along with the crowd, I urge you to read the Scriptures and the comments, and you will realize that God has much to say on a subject that has been ignored for at least forty years. The Spirit is saying, "Listen carefully to what God has said!"

You and I want to enter the "land of rest" that is so clearly promised in the New Testament. Even today, few seem to enter. Why? I believe this book will answer that question for you.

Chapter 2

Incredible Power to Imagine

Your mind is like a computer. Every thought that flows through it, and every image that you create, is indelibly inscribed on the cells of your brain.

Recall some of your thoughts and created images. Then imagine them on a motion picture screen. Would you be willing, and pleased, for that film to be shown to every Sunday School class in our land? No? Why not?

God has called us to holiness in all our thoughts. This must be our goal even when we feel too human to begin. This may seem an impossible task, but anything less falls short of what He has asked. Few Christians seem to know what it is that God has told us in His written Word about holy thoughts.

IMAGINATION! WHAT IS IT?

It is "The act of creating mental images of what has never been actually experienced." (Webster)

May I reveal something that you probably never realized? Not something bad, but something good - something about you that is *so* good that God considers it one of your most valuable assets. It's so good that if you are misusing it, you probably will want to make some important changes in your life. It is your power to IMAGINE.

Have you ever considered your *incredible* power to imagine? Think of a beautiful lake with the sun shimmering on the water, trees and flowers along the shore. Can you picture it? Picture a garden filled with flowers of every color of the rainbow. Can you imagine it? Think of a giant tree reaching up into the sky and of a skyscraper stretching up to the clouds; create in your mind a beautiful woman or a handsome man. Can you do this?

You may never have painted a picture, or planted a beautiful garden or built a building, yet you can create a picture in your mind. Have you ever pondered your power to do this? Or why you can? Has it dawned on you that this ability is God's special gift to you - you who are created in His own image? He set you apart, a jewel in the midst of all His other creations.

You may never have considered yourself of great value, but consider this one talent alone - your ability to imagine! Let your mind wander for a few minutes and see what you can create...see how endless your power is! Your mind is awesome in its ability. This may be the first moment in your life that you realize how incredible your imagination really is.

God values our power to imagine *far more* than any of us do. He knows why He created this power in us, and how He intended us to use it. Our creative ability is a mark of *His image* in us.

Jesus showed the control that God originally intended us to have. He saw the sea and a fish with a *gold* coin in its mouth. When Peter caught the fish, sure enough, there was the gold. Jesus created it. Jesus saw pots of water becoming wine, and the water became wine. He saw bread as multiplied, and it was multiplied. He said He never did anything until He first *saw* the Father doing it (John 5:19).

Throughout history, men and women who have reported miraculous answers to prayer have repeatedly said, "I saw it before it happened." What did they mean, they "saw" it?

Katherine Kuhlman frequently said things such as, "I see a person with cancer of the stomach. It is now being healed." How did she "see" it?

We "see" things all the time. Think of "white" and what do you see? Think of black, red and sunsets. As you think, you "see." But only when our power to "see" gets united with God's power to create, do we see miracles. And they happen because that is what God originally intended.

Our imaginative power received a destructive blow when man sinned against his Creator. However, in the eyes of God, our imagination is *still* a holy gift. He knows its power, even if we don't. The Bible contains many references to God's attitude toward our imagination. I've learned that He wants to help us be free of every thought that brings distress or anxiety! This potential is easily within the grasp of *everyone* reading this book. It isn't a mystical exercise that would take years to accomplish. It's a simple gift of the Holy Spirit to *any* Christian who will receive it. You do not have to be a spiritual giant or an accomplished Bible student. All you need is a sincere desire to please God.

If you carefully examine each Scripture and comment that I've included here, you will find that every part of your life - spiritual, emotional and physical - will be strengthened. No matter how strong or how weak you now are, you have in your hands a tool that will enable you to make gigantic strides forward.

I cannot over emphasize the need to keep our imaginations under the leadership of the Holy Spirit. There is an anti-Christian movement here in the United States that centers its emphasis on the imagination. Its students are trained in the art of manipulating the imagination to the point of controlling every emotion. The trainee decides what person he wants to be and then uses images to create that person. The organization especially stresses the need to be free of moral laws, religious training and social restraints. Their code says: "Forget God, people, family, friends. Be yourself. Get what you want. Learn to isolate yourself from every outside influence."

Their devotees become totally committed to selfish living. And their training isolates them from any arguments or rebuttal from friends or family.

When I realized that imagination was extremely important in God's eyes, I began to search the Scriptures to see if this could be confirmed in the written Word. I found far more recorded information than I expected. The following are a few of the many references.

> 1. *God saw that the wickedness of man was great in the earth and that every IMAGINATION of the THOUGHTS of his heart was only evil continually* (Genesis 6:5).

The result? God destroyed the world with a flood. Man's *corrupted imagination* caused the face of the entire earth to be changed!

> 2. *The IMAGINATION of man's heart is evil from his youth* (Genesis 8:21).

This occurred after the flood ended. Noah was able to re-establish his family on dry ground. He built an altar and made a sacrifice. God was pleased, but then it was almost as if He sighed as He looked at mankind.

> 3. *Now nothing will be restrained from them which they have IMAGINED to do...Let us go down, and there confound their language, that they may not understand one another's speech* (Genesis 11:6-7).

The next tragedy to strike the human race was the confusion of the spoken language. Men were building the Tower of Babel.

The pool of world knowledge was suddenly divided. After thousands of years, it is still very difficult for people of one language to communicate their thoughts and feelings to another.

When God took such drastic action, He was saying that man's imagination had the capacity to accomplish things he was *no longer* permitted to do.

In the beginning, man's boundaries were unlimited. Whatever he could imagine, he could do. Later God found it necessary to say: *Many evils and troubles are befallen them...for I know their IMAGINATION* (Deuteronomy 31:21). Although our ability and power to imagine is a sacred gift, we have long misused it.

4. *These six things doth the Lord hate: yea, seven are an abomination unto him* (Proverbs 6:16). Among this list of only seven things is: *A heart that deviseth wicked IMAGINATIONS* (Proverbs 6:18).

As history unfolded, God's attitude toward man's misuse of his imagination hardened.

5. *They say unto everyone that walketh after the IMAGINATION of his own heart; No evil shall come upon you* (Jeremiah 23:17).

Frequently God spoke through the prophets to express His hatred of the misuse of imagination.

The gentle voice of our conscience may say, "You ought not to use your imagination to picture things that God has forbidden." But the evil force that corrupts says, "But you enjoy this! What harm can it do? Surely God doesn't care what you imagine. He wouldn't be *that* severe."

God asked: *Can any hide himself in secret places that I shall not see him?* saith the Lord. *Do not I fill heaven and earth?* (Jeremiah 23:24).

The carnal mind always suggests, "God isn't paying any attention to what you are thinking, and even if He does, He understands that you are merely a weak human being. After all, He made you like you are, didn't He?" This delusion entices us to forget that God made mankind in His own image. God invested Himself in man through His Son, Jesus, and proclaimed that the weakest Christian is greater than all the angels. God's *not interested* in what we think or imagine? That is the most ridiculous thought Satan could give, yet Christians regularly accept it and imagine immoral thoughts.

Being human, we naturally ask, "Why does God *hate* an evil imagination? How do our secret thoughts hurt anyone?"

Our ability to imagine is connected with our original creation, for God said, *Let us make man in our IMAGE.* God used *His Power* to create an image, and we were the result. From that point on, our power to imagine was of vital concern to God. We had part of His power invested in us.

Most scientific advancements have involved man's imagination. Men "see" things before they do them. Inventors repeatedly tell of "seeing" a machine in their imagination long before they know how to build it. Inventors awaken in the middle of the night and write out solutions to problems they have "seen" in a dream. Men see solutions in the form of pictures, and then work for years to materialize their visions. Men picture buildings in their minds and then set about making them a reality. There is something intriguing and mystifying about our ability to imagine things known and unknown. To God, that ability is sacred. He does not want it misused. And that is exactly why evil forces have an *intense* desire to see that ability misused. Our minds are the battleground; our imaginations are the trophy to be won.

If we use our imaginative power to visualize anything that represents lust or impurity, we are in *direct conflict* with God's will. Men enjoy using the power of imagination to create a multitude of images that God has forbidden. For example, when a man sees a woman who is attractive to him, he can disrobe her in his mind, bit by bit, until she is completely undressed. He then can use his imagination to feel what it would be like to touch her

22

body. He can continue this mental activity until he has experienced every possible sexual act. He has taken God's special, holy gift and consumed it upon the altar of lust.

How do I know men do these things? First, I should confess that I engaged in such desecration of God's gift for much of my life. I continued doing this even after I became a Christian.

I have counseled with men by the hundreds on this subject, and invariably they confessed to having done the same thing most of their lives.

Married or single women are also capable of wrong thoughts, but they are usually tempted to use their imaginations in a different way. They see or think of a certain man and begin to picture life with him as their husband. They imagine his filling all their emotional and physical needs. "*He* would listen to me, *he* would talk to me, *he* would understand me." The man is coveted - mentally possessed - whether or not he is married to another woman. For a few moments he belongs to her, and again God's precious gift of imagination has been used in direct violation of His will.

Jesus taught us that there are sins so attractive and habit-forming that even if a man came back from the dead and warned us, we would not give them up!

No sin fits this category more clearly than that of immoral thinking.

Jesus explained, in a new way, a message God presented throughout the Old Testament. He said: *Whosoever looketh on a woman to lust after her hath committed adultery with her already in his heart* (Matthew 5:28).

These are not the words of a wild-eyed radical. They need to be seriously considered by every Christian, yet I believe they have been glossed over. Men and women have thought that it would be impossible to eliminate lust in their hearts, therefore Jesus must have been saying that *everyone* has lust, so no one should find fault with anyone else. I accepted this theory for most of my life, for it seemed an excellent way to handle my own moral dilemma. But now I know that Jesus is calling us to eradicate adultery from our hearts. This is what He says, and this is exactly what He means. The entire Bible is calling us to purity of heart and mind.

Chapter 3

Where Thoughts Originate

Satan did not try to *force* Eve into disobeying God. He simply maneuvered her into *thinking* about it. He suggested the benefits she should consider.

Eve thought about them and then looked at the forbidden fruit with new interest. It looked good - but it had always looked good. The fruit hadn't changed. Only Eve's *thoughts* had changed. Satan's strategy worked then . . . and it is still working now!

Evil forces have skillfully and carefully conditioned the human race to believe that we are not responsible for our thoughts. Educators, "wise men" and teachers have indirectly taught that man is responsible only for what he does with thoughts that "come to him." Few have tried to explain where these thoughts originate. If a man can have that one flash, that one lustful moment, he is then willing to accept the teaching of Jesus and to cut off his immoral thoughts. Men have supported one another in this theology so they can continue to enjoy this brief disobedience to God.

The teaching comes in many different packages. "You can't help what you think. After the thought comes to you, then reject it. God will only hold you accountable if you dwell on wrong thoughts. He knows we can't keep from having such thoughts, but He requires that we cut them off as soon as we can." These efforts are attempts to excuse us for directly and willfully disobeying God. Thoughts of adultery come from no place other than a man's heart. We cannot blame the opposite sex, pictures, movies or our circumstances.

If I indulge in the sin of immoral thinking, should I expect God to give me a sign, to show me I am displeasing Him? The answer to this question is in Luke, chapter 16, where Jesus tells the story of the rich man and of Lazarus. The rich man died and was in torment. He saw Lazarus and Abraham in the luxury of heaven, and begged Abraham for help. But Abraham had to tell him that the gulf between them was too great to cross.

The rich man plead with Abraham to get word to his five brothers, who were still alive, so they wouldn't come to the same place. Abraham's answer is: *If they hear not Moses and the prophets, neither will they be persuaded, though one rose from the dead* (Luke 16:31).

The point is this: the prophets of the Old Testament and the New Testament have spoken. They have told us that God wants our hearts, minds and imaginations to be morally pure. We can expect no further messages or miracles to persuade us. God has spoken. We have heard.

If an immoral thought is free to work in our minds for one brief second, is that wrong? In our passion for self-justification, we might declare that fallen man could not keep such one second thoughts out of his mind. But consider that one second from *God's* perspective. How long is a second to Him? The Bible says one period of time can be as one thousand years to Him! At that ratio an immoral thought that seems one second to us could be over an hour to God!

Of course, time is not the issue at all. God requires clean, pure, holy thoughts, and our objective must be to become what *He wants*, no matter how violently our fallen natures may resist. And you can be sure they *will* resist! If you have spent many years enjoying flash, one second immoral thoughts, you will not easily give up this pleasure.

I've often heard expressions like, "If a bird lands on your head, you don't have to let it make a nest there." The point is that when a thought comes we don't have to retain it and mull over it. This is true. It is wrong to have an evil thought and then keep meditating on it. The more we think about it, the worse it becomes, and the greater our guilt becomes.

But why have the thought in the first place?

At this point, I can hear the cries of those who will say, "No one can control the thoughts that flash into his mind. He can only refuse to meditate on them."

Since little has been written on the subject of continuing in lustful thoughts after they come to us, perhaps I would be wise simply to write about that aspect of our thought-life. If I did this, I would not be faithful to what I believe the Holy Spirit is telling me, nor would I be honestly reporting what the Bible says.

The following are a few of the Scriptures which make it clear that Christians are responsible for thoughts that come to their minds for *any* length of time.

> 1. *Search me, O God and know my heart: try me, and know my THOUGHTS, and see if there be any wicked way in me* (Psalm 139:23-24).

The implication is that David had reached a new spiritual plateau in his walk with God. Once, his thoughts had led him into adultery and then to murder. Now he is inviting God to let him know if *any* of his thoughts are wicked.

> 2. *When I was a child I spoke as a child, I understood as a child, I thought as a child: but when I became a man; I put away childish things* (I Corinthians 13:11).

Paul is talking about spiritual progress. That is what this book is about. Let us renounce the idea that Christians cannot

27

control what they think. If we accept that approach, we will never be victorious in Christ. Such a philosophy insists that, if a thought comes to you for one second, you aren't responsible. But what happens eventually? You know what happens! It stays for two seconds, then three. Year after year the pattern is reinforced. It's time for us to learn how to cut off evil *before* it begins, and then reap the rich rewards of a mind cleansed by the power of His Word.

> 3. *And Jesus knowing their THOUGHTS*
> *said, wherefore THINK ye evil in your*
> *hearts?* (Matthew 9:4).

The scribes hear Jesus forgiving people of their sins, and the thought comes to their minds, "this is blasphemy." They don't accuse Him. They simply "think." Jesus then asks them why they are *thinking* evil. He clearly is holding them responsible for their thoughts. I strongly recommend that you accept the fact that Jesus will one day hold you and me accountable for *our* thoughts - every one of them.

> 4. *For to be carnally MINDED is death; but*
> *to be spiritually MINDED is life and peace*
> (Romans 8:6).

It would be foolish for us to think, I have carnal thoughts but I am not "carnal." Peace of mind comes only to those who learn to have "spiritual" thoughts.

> 5. *Let this MIND be in you, which was also*
> *in Christ Jesus* (Philippians 2:5).

Do you believe Jesus' mind was *perfectly* pure? He was "equal with God!" God calls us to have the mind of Christ. Later in this chapter, Paul exhorts: *Work out your own salvation with fear and trembling...That ye may be blameless and harmless, the sons of God, without rebuke, in the midst of a crooked and perverse generation* (Philippians 2: 12, 15). Moral decay is sweeping over our nation to a degree that is almost unbelievable. Lust and immorality are portrayed as acceptable. If

28

Christians do not cling to purity of thought we will be swept into the chaos of corruption.

We have a source of assistance, as emphasized in Joshua 1:8: *This book of the law shall not depart out of thy mouth; but thou shalt meditate therein day and night, that thou mayest observe to do according to all that is written therein: for then thou shalt make thy way prosperous, and then thou shalt have good success.* (Want to be prosperous and have good success?) And also, *Wherewithal shall a young man cleanse his way? By taking heed thereto according to thy word...Thy word have I hid in mine heart, that I might not sin against thee (*Psalm 119:9, 11).

> 6. *Unto the pure all things are pure: but unto them that are defiled and unbelieving is nothing pure; but even their MIND and conscience is defiled* (Titus 1:15).

Paul is not saying that if the pure in heart see a murder, they will think it is pure. He *is* saying that if we are defiled in our minds we can look at anything and make it impure. If our thoughts are defiled, our mind and conscience become defiled. We can then repeat the evil thoughts, time after time, without any strong sense of guilt.

> 7. *If a Levite come...with all the desire of his MIND...then he shall minister in the name of the Lord* (Deuteronomy 18:6).

Have you known that God wants *all* the "desires of your mind" if you want to serve Him?

> 8. *I know the things that come into your MIND, every one of them...ye have not walked in my statutes, neither executed my judgments, but have done after the manners of the heathen that are round about you* (Ezekiel 11:5, 12).

There is no more glaring illustration of God's people following the ways of the heathen than if we think adulterous thoughts.

Let's move on to another illustration. My doctor placed me on a strict diet that allowed me to eat nothing but meat and vegetables. Meditate on this for a moment, and you will realize how *many* foods are not meat or vegetables.

My mind was craving a certain food that was not on my diet. I would wake up thinking about it. A dozen times a day the thought would come, "I sure would enjoy some of that to eat." The food itself was not bad. The desire to eat wasn't bad. The problem was that I was being tormented by the *thought*. The Holy Spirit spoke to me: "Merlin, you have listened to me and allowed me to help you defeat the power of immoral thinking. Now I will teach you something new. You do not have to think about wanting that food."

My reaction was, "I must be hearing my own desires." (I have learned that this can happen to any one of us very easily!)

The voice insisted that I *was* receiving an important lesson and that I should listen.

My answer was, "But I can't help it!"

GOD HAS GIVEN YOU AUTHORITY OVER YOUR THOUGHTS. YOU CAN DECIDE WHAT YOU WANT TO THINK.

This was quite a revelation to me - perhaps one of the biggest in my entire life.

A little later, I realized the same thought was coming back to me - the desire for *that food*. I tried what the Spirit had told me, and to my absolute amazement it worked! I could think of the food and then literally cut off the thought of wanting it! This was an exciting moment, for I was experiencing something that to me was completely new.

I confess that my faith wasn't too strong at that point. I wondered how long I could use this ability to control what I was thinking about the food. But as the same experience came to me many times that day, and each time I was successful in cutting off my *desire* for it, I realized what a blessing the Holy Spirit had given me. I'm not saying that being able to shut off the desire for a food is such a big thing. The point is that God wants to restore in us the power to "control the thoughts that flow through our minds." I believe that when He created mankind, men and women had total control over what they thought. Through the "fall," we lost that ability, and now the Holy Spirit wants to help us "renew our minds." It is exciting to realize the potential God has given us in many areas of our lives!

I do not mean that I now have instant control over *every* thought. It's a matter of learning and growing. I learn something new every day. Yesterday, a carpenter examined a shower in our home and told me it had been leaking through the drain and under the floor - probably for many years. As he took up the linoleum, he discovered that the floor, and possibly the material under the floor, had rotted away. He recommended that the entire shower be taken out, replaced and a new floor put in. When he told me the estimated cost, my first thought was, "Oh, what a waste." I really wasn't too happy about it. Eventually I would have realized that God would make it work for my good, but for a few minutes I was burdened by the whole thing.

Then the Holy Spirit witnessed to me, "You don't have to accept that unhappy thought." The moment I rejected the thought it was gone!

There was a time, as a Christian, that I had many lustful thoughts. I honestly thought I could not help myself. I knew that I did not actually want to commit adultery, but I *did want* to imagine and think about it. As the Holy Spirit dealt with me, He urged me to pray that the thoughts of my mind might be cleansed. It wasn't easy! I was indulging in a practice that had started in my mind when I was a young boy. These thoughts became part of me. They seemed to control me, rather than my controlling them. I don't mean I thought lustful thoughts all the time, but in certain situations these thoughts would explode into my conscious mind.

During the years that immoral thoughts flowed through my mind, I always felt guilty, but I was never too worried. I guess what kept me from being too concerned were conversations I had with other Christian men. I came to the conclusion, and still believe, that a vast majority have the same difficulty.

What is written here may cause some wails of agony within the Christian community, but many Christians will rejoice that these hidden matters are being brought to light. Those who have felt a burden in their hearts for many years, will *now* realize that their secret thoughts are being condemned by God. As the Holy Spirit helps them to renew their minds, they will experience new victory in Christ. Christians will be set free and then with new enthusiasm go on to win others to Christ.

Often, men and women have an inner sense of unworthiness. They may think it's because of some weakness beyond their control. Frequently, the problem lies in their immoral thought-life. This saps and drains away spiritual life, until they are powerless to help themselves and others. But by cleansing our thoughts, we open the door to many things the Holy Spirit wants to do in our lives.

Keep your mind open to the Scriptures in this book. If you have been guilty of thoughts such as, "I wish that man were my husband," think carefully about the Scripture, *Thou shalt not covet*. The commandment means we are not to *want* someone else's husband or wife. God would never have outlawed covetousness if He didn't know He had given us control over our thoughts.

If a husband is mentally committing adultery with a famous actress, how can his wife ever live up to his expectations?

If a wife visualizes herself a beautiful actress and is hostile to the plain "Joe" she is married to, what chance does the marriage have? This wife needs to look in the mirror and ask, "What does he see when he comes home?"

If a wife saturates herself in daily soap operas that are loaded with glamorized, illicit sex, she is creating in her mind a desire for immorality. Soon the mental desire will become a desire of her heart. Without realizing what is happening, she will take on the desires of the characters she is watching. Why not? She is watching what she *wants* to see.

If a wife learns to fantasize her emotional life by reading many romantic novels, she may not be able to adapt to real life. Novels often depict a wife in a beautiful romantic setting. The heroine is encircled with opportunities to be glamorous, beautiful, popular, witty and desirable. The reader may spend her days washing diapers, cleaning the same house and coping with the same problems day after day. But her mind becomes steeped in an imaginary world until eventually the desire of her heart is to escape her real world. Her marriage may develop serious problems since no man can compete with men who are the product of someone's imagination.

If you become convinced that the Bible demands strict moral thoughts, will you conform?

If you have a strong desire to conform to Biblical standards, will you?

The answer to both questions is, *maybe*.

The mind is amazingly deceptive. It can find unlimited ways of excusing whatever it wants to do. It can say, "Yes, the Bible demands purity of thought, but I'm not perfect. Who is?" Or, "Yes, I have a strong desire to do everything the Bible requires of me, but in this case I can't. My mind is not controllable."

Conveniently, the mind has side-stepped the issue. It has excused its actions so it can continue to do what it enjoys.

The truth is, we think what we want to think. The Bible makes us personally responsible for *every* thought we have. We are not computers, programmed to respond to forces beyond our control. We were created by God, in His image, as free moral agents. This is precisely why God says, *Every one of us shall give account of himself to God* (Romans 14:12).

The alcoholic continues to drink because he wants to. He may be aware that his body is suffering from the effects of alcohol, but he finds some way to excuse his acts.

The person misusing drugs may know his body and mind are being destroyed, but he thinks, I can't help myself.

The Christian who thinks immoral thoughts usually knows he is damaging his spirit. He feels guilty and wouldn't want anyone to know, but he thinks, I can't help myself.

Are you aware how often immoral thoughts involve the mental disrobing of the body? This takes us back to man's original sin. What was the first thought that came to Adam and Eve after they had sinned? They realized they were naked!

Rebellion against God opened a new consciousness. The unclothing of the body is still rebellion against God, if it is done in ways He has forbidden. Satan has always used the human body as a way to foster rebellion, and thus to damage the human spirit. He uses countless methods to convince us that even if we wound and hurt our spirits by immoral thoughts, we are not responsible.

Man has never been clever enough to disobey God and not eventually suffer the consequences. So often men think, I've thought wrong thoughts often, and nothing drastic happened. God is patient, kind and longsuffering, but He cannot violate His own Word: *Whatsoever a man soweth that shall he also reap* (Galatians 6:7).

Have you already observed that your natural mind does not want to be controlled by God? The Bible puts it this way, *The carnal mind is enmity against God* (Romans 8:7).

It's a little heavy to realize that our mind is God's enemy. There are many illustrations of this. You may have observed some of them working in your own life:

     1. God says we are to: *Rejoice in Him always*
       (Philippians 3:1).

Our mind says, "I will rejoice when I feel like it."

    2. God says: *Whatever we eat or drink should be done to glorify Him* (I Corinthians 10:31).

The mind says, "If I like it or want it, I'll eat it." What a tremendous change would take place in many people's eating habits if their diets were controlled by that which would give glory to God!

    3. God says: *If we think another person has done wrong, we should first go to that person and discuss their acts with them.*

The mind says, "Quick, find someone and tell them what you have just heard."

    4. God says to: *Honor those who have rule over us.*

The mind says, "I'll honor them if they are in my political party, and if I like them and if I agree with what they do."

    5. God says to: *Thank Him for everything* (Ephesians 5:20).

The mind says, "I'll thank Him for whatever I like, and complain about whatever I don't like."

    6. God says: *Fear not*!

The mind causes most people to be afraid, dozens of times a day, about things that never happen. But the mind says, "Well, they *might* happen."

    7. God says: *He will work everything for our good* (Romans 8:28).

In the same chapter He lists some things He will use for our good: Tribulation, distress, persecution, famine, nakedness, peril, sword (atomic bombs?), death, life, angels, principalities, powers, things present (which would include everything), things to come (eliminating the need to be afraid), height, depth, any other creatures (things).

The mind says, "I don't believe it."

8. God says: *Love others - even your enemies*.

The mind says, "I will love those I like."

9. God says: *Don't covet*.

The mind says, "Ridiculous. How can I keep from wanting something that I want?"

Chapter 4

Our Most Consuming Temptation

In 1971, I completed twenty years of service in the military. I was ready to retire. What a sweet word that was to my ears. In every way I was ready to retire. It had been a long and rugged twenty years - perhaps far more so than the average civilian realizes. During those years, I had seen hundreds of men dying - on battlefields around the world. I was one of the favored few. I survived. Others who "survived" with me were without legs, blind, deaf or armless. Some had multiple losses. I had survived, and I was ready to retire.

I looked back over my past and realized why I felt so tired. World War II had been a traumatic experience. Many of my closest friends had died as we, the members of the famed 82nd Airborne Division, fought our way through Europe. When I was discharged from the Army in 1946, I wanted nothing more to do with the Army.

By 1953, the Lord convinced me that He had other plans. At His direction, I went back into the Army as a chaplain. For just three years - I thought! Three years were extended as the Holy Spirit convinced me my work wasn't completed. Then came Korea, where I saw more death. In the Dominican Republic I had the painful assignment of helping to load into planes, dead soldiers from the 82nd Airborne Division. Their bodies were to be sent back to their families. Then came a grueling, exhausting year in Vietnam. In ninety-seven degree temperature and ninety-seven percent humidity, I watched hundreds of soldiers pay a colossal price for our country's mistakes.

By 1971, I had completed *Prison to Praise*. Everything I knew about anything was written, and I was ready to retire. And retire I did. But the Holy Spirit kept prodding me, and from within came *Power in Praise*. Now surely I was finished and could retire.

But then letters arrived from all over the world. My books were helping people, but they had many questions. The Holy Spirit urged me to answer their questions as best I could. Prisoners all over the United States were given copies of my first two books, and they were writing things like, "Are you a real person? Are your books true or just stories?" I had to answer them. They were living, hurting people. Out of all these letters came a new book, *Answers to Praise*. I was certain that this would end my writing career. But, like *Prison to Praise* and *Power in Praise, Answers to Praise* rose to the Ten Best-Selling Christian Book list. More letters poured in from many places. No time for retirement; too many people were asking for help; too many churches were inviting me to come and share the message of praise.

Then came a call to build a church in Southern California. "But Lord, I've already built dozens of churches all over the world."

Go do it, was all I heard. As told in *Walking and Leaping*, my work in that church ended, and I expected to retire. But over seven hundred people left that church and urged me to begin another new church. No retirement, and two more books had to be written.

After this church was established and a building purchased, the Lord led me to resign. Now I was ready to retire. This was it. No more churches to build and maybe no more books to write.

But now another book is being born. I believe God is using my previous experiences to help us learn the importance of what is on our minds.

Many Christian men have told me that when they first accepted Christ, their minds were made clean. They could look at beautiful women and every thought was pure.

Days, weeks, or perhaps months later, when an impure thought entered, they held on to it for just a second or two. The thought stirred old memories, and the old wants began to reassert themselves. For a time, these occasional immoral thoughts brought strong feelings of guilt; gradually the conscious guilt declined. These men eventually decided that even Christian men cannot be expected to be pure in heart. They were not aware that the guilt feelings were still there, working their way deeper and deeper into their hearts.

During my time in the military, I was at the side of many Christian men who believed they were dying. When I asked them what they would like me to pray for, in nearly every case, they asked me to pray that they would be forgiven for past sins. When I asked what specific sins they wanted to confess to God, their first thoughts were frequently about the men they had been forced to kill in their roles as soldiers. Their next requests were usually about immoral acts or thoughts.

The point is, we can hide our guilt over impure thoughts even from ourselves, but in times of great danger, problems, stress or death, what is hidden in the heart will surface.

Women report similar experiences. After receiving Christ, their lives are more content. Jesus meets their needs. Later, old desires begin to surface. They remember, see, or meet men who "really could meet their needs."

Sometimes when men and women seek a new relationship with the Holy Spirit, their expectations are even higher, and their guilt even greater, when immoral thoughts creep back into their minds.

39

Inevitably, we have to face the reality that God has given us the responsibility of cleansing the thoughts of our hearts. The Holy Spirit and God's Word are available to help us, but each person must decide for himself what he will think, and what he will imagine. Being created in God's image requires that we be responsible for our thoughts.

Why do men and women think immoral thoughts?

Because they want to!

They want to because they enjoy it.

These thoughts bring physical pleasure to the body.

The sensations are pleasant and gratifying.

The mind becomes programmed to renew this pleasure at the slightest provocation. In time, the mind needs no stimulus - it can create its own. Self-gratification becomes habitual and seemingly uncontrollable. But man is always responsible for his thoughts, because he is made in God's image. God has said, *As he THINKETH in his heart, so is he* (Proverbs 23:7).

There is a remedy! *The Word of God is quick and powerful and sharper than any two-edged sword...and is able to discern the thoughts and intents of the heart* (Hebrews 4:12). If any man wants to continue enjoying immoral thinking, he must keep his mind off the Scripture verses that are in this book. They are "powerful and able to pierce" the wall we build around our hearts. Once that wall is in place, we are able to think, "What I'm doing isn't really wrong."

Thousands of men have told me that their most consuming and overpowering temptation is immoral thinking. Many men declare that this problem gives them a sense of guilt that torments them dozens of times every day. They assert that the temptation toward immorality is stronger than all other temptations put together. Christian men frequently say that their wives have little idea how traumatic the conflict is between their need to be morally pure and the seductive influence of adulterous thoughts. Men would be even more concerned if they realized that when the mind is permitted the freedom of immoral thinking, it will eventually find ways to excuse immoral acts!

Some women report a different type of problem - a longing that causes them to want a different man - one who would meet their emotional needs.

Is there a solution? Yes, there is!

Men and women must first realize the seriousness of the problem. All too often immoral thinking is considered uncontrollable. A man excuses his thoughts with the rationalization that he is merely doing what every other man does. But once we understand what Scripture says on the subject, realize how important our minds are to God and permit His Words to penetrate our hearts, we can be set free.

*In the beginning God created...*And God said, *Let us make man in our image...male and female created He them*. We are a part of God. He invested His image in us. I had read this verse hundreds of times, and I confess that it hadn't made too much of an impression on me.

Earlier in my Christian walk I received a beautiful gift from God. He emptied my mind of all lustful thoughts. I expected that cleansing to be permanent - and it could have been. I neglected one important thing. I didn't keep renewing my mind with the spiritual resources God had provided in His Word. Gradually, and without my making a conscious decision to disobey God, the old thoughts began creeping back into my mind.

One day my immoral thoughts disturbed me. I had been disturbed often, but on this particular day my heart was especially heavy. From somewhere deep within I was crying out, "Oh God, please help me. I know my bad thoughts are in disobedience to You, but I can't seem to help myself. I think things about women, and I'm deeply ashamed. I don't want to do this." I really *wanted* to give up this sin.

I didn't hear God speak to me audibly, but I sensed His asking me, *Do you really want to be helped? If I help you, then you will be far more accountable for what you do in the future.*

I was able to make a decision, and I cried out, "Oh please, God, help me."

He said to me, *The answer is in My Word.*

"I know Lord, but where?"

Look!

I began to look. What better place to look than at the very beginning of His Word? There it was: *In the beginning God created.* When we look at the opposite sex, we are looking at a part of God - His creation! When it dawned on me what the Spirit was revealing, I was so frightened I began to shake. I had been looking at God's creation and lusting for an adulterous relationship with what was a part of Him. For a while, I found it difficult to breathe. The Word of God was piercing my heart, and it was quick and powerful. Although I had known for many years what the Word said, it had only now begun to reveal the thoughts of my heart.

The secret of learning how to have a clean mind requires two things:

1. Learn what the Bible says about the mind.
2. Let God's Words move from our minds down into our hearts. To me the heart means the center of the person I am. That "center" has to be convinced before I will make any important changes in my life.

When I meditated on the significance of what I had learned, I gradually understood the drastic pronouncement Jesus had made: *If thine eye offend thee, pluck it out: it is better for thee to enter the kingdom of God with one eye, than having two eyes to be cast into hell fire* (Mark 9:47). In the book of Matthew, Jesus went as far as to say that even wanting adultery was an act of adultery in God's eyes. *Whosoever looketh on a woman to lust after her hath committed adultery with her already in his heart* (Matthew 5:28).

As I've shared my new understanding of what Jesus said, many have told me it was so powerful that they were shocked into making a commitment to abandon immoral thoughts.

When a man or woman accepts Jesus as Savior, they are told: *We will come into Him, and make our abode with Him* (John 14:23). If a man looks on a woman who has God living in her, and has adulterous thoughts, he is wanting to commit adultery with God's Temple! Understanding this helps me see why the Bible has so much to say about adultery, immorality and evil thoughts. Satan wants man to lust after God!

If a man wants to be delivered from immoral thinking, he has abundant resources. The Bible has so much to say about God's will in this matter, that if we meditate on these Scriptures, our resolve will be greatly strengthened.

It is increasingly evident to me that Christian men do not realize the importance that God places on both morality in actions and purity in thoughts. My discussions with men verify that few have an adequate understanding of how much the Bible has to say about this subject. I have therefore, felt impelled by the Spirit to put these scriptural references into a convenient, handy form that men can easily read. If a man has a slight interest in being morally clean, these verses can set him free. But they must be received into the "heart" and meditated upon regularly. If a man refuses to keep his attention on the resources that God has given, he will probably be lured back into the darkness and hopelessness of immorality. If he meditates on these words frequently, I believe the Holy Spirit will provide all the strength he needs to flee this sin which God has spoken against so strongly. He said, *Now are ye clean through the Word which I have spoken unto you* (John 15:3).

Our minds are comparable to a radio. We pick up a message that says, for example, "I want a hot fudge sundae." Exactly what is it that "wants" and where does the thought originate? Does the body need this for health? Will it improve the body's ability to enjoy tomorrow? Probably not.

What process does the mind go through to reach the conclusion, "I want?" Previous experiences that brought pleasure? Anticipation?

If we understand the process that leads us to want something, then we may be able to control what we will want in the future.

If we say, "I want a hot fudge sundae," that is an honest expression of our desire. How can we change that desire?

If our doctor says, "You may have diabetes," that gives us some incentive to change what we want to eat. One person could hear this from his doctor and immediately be inspired to change his diet to exclude all refined sugar. Another person wouldn't even consider changing.

If our doctor says, "You have diabetes and need to change your eating habits," we have quite a strong reason to change our desires, perhaps even to the point where we do not want a hot fudge sundae. But, strange as it may seem, some persons would continue eating whatever they wanted.

If our doctor says, "You have a severe case of diabetes and refined sugar could put you into shock," a person with reasonable intelligence should give careful thought to his future diet!

There is a comparable mental process in other decisions we make. A mind that says, "I want to have immoral thoughts" can be changed. What might change it?

A Scripture verse that says immoral thoughts are wrong? Maybe.

Several verses that say God does not want thoughts to be impure? A better chance of getting our attention.

Dozens of Scripture verses that clearly say immoral thoughts and desires are forbidden by God and that He may bring severe suffering on those who disobey? This should get and hold the attention of a reasonable person.

Receiving Christ as Savior is much more than accepting Him with our minds. It must be a decision of our hearts. The decision must be so permanent and binding on the individual that it becomes more than a mental assent that Christ is divine, or that He is The Savior. The decision is a complete surrender of self to Jesus as Lord.

Accepting the Holy Spirit as Lord of our thinking habits is more than a mental decision. It must be a complete surrender of our hearts. This decision commits us to a permanent stand against immoral thoughts. Once this complete commitment is made, the Holy Spirit then moves to help us do whatever we cannot do for ourselves.

When you gave your life to Christ, wasn't it a complete commitment to believe in Him as Savior - forever? Your total commitment made your conversion real. You didn't promise not to fall. God didn't ask you to do that. But you did promise to believe Jesus as Savior, without any reservations, now and forever.

When we commit our minds to holy thoughts, we are submitting our minds to the Holy Spirit's control. This opens the way for a life of service to God and closes the door to the untold suffering that comes when we are disobedient to Him.

You may wonder, "What happens if I make a commitment to God to think only clean thoughts, and then slip back into my old thoughts?" The answer is found in the very encouraging promise: *If we confess our sins, He is faithful and just to forgive us our sins* (I John 1:9). John also assures us that when Jesus sets us free, we are free indeed! And who wants to leave freedom to return to bondage?

Chapter 5

When Will There be
a Spiritual Revival?

Have you ever been around a person who gave you confidence, who made you feel that the situation was under control? Some people seem born leaders. Others follow without questioning.

If a human being has the potential to create confidence, how much greater is the Holy Spirit's capability! But the Holy Spirit is not pushy. He wants us to accept His leadership. Then He wants to lead us into thinking holy thoughts no matter how far we are now from reaching that goal.

When the Roman Centurion expressed his faith in Jesus, He responded as recorded in Matthew 8:10: *I have not found so great faith, no not in Israel.*

The Centurion believed Jesus could heal, but that wasn't why Jesus praised him so highly. Many people believed He could heal. This Roman officer understood something about Jesus that no one else had! What was it?

This soldier compared Jesus' authority over sickness to his own authority over servants. He, the Centurion, could tell his servants to do something, and they did it. He had absolute authority over their lives. If they should dare to refuse his command, he could order them to be immediately executed. This is real authority!

The Centurion was saying that he knew Jesus had authority over sickness. Though illness seemed to have great power, he knew Jesus was more powerful than the forces that caused sickness.

We know that evil forces are inciting immorality throughout the world. The results are devastating. It would be impossible to measure the pain and suffering caused by immorality. Consider venereal disease with all the ramifications: blindness, heart disease, birth defects that stay with a child for a lifetime, emotional agony, suicide and divorce. The list is endless. Consider prostitution with all its tragedies: white slavery that causes thousands of innocent young girls to disappear every year, crime associated with pimps, graft, beatings, threats and blackmail. Consider divorces caused by immorality: children deprived of a wholesome home, poverty, emotional collapse.

Consider the rapid increase of suicide among young people. They are presented the delusion that immorality will satisfy all their wants. They try it and discover that, instead of improving their lives, it results in a feeling of futility. If illicit sex, which is supposed to be the most desirable thing in life, turns out to be unfulfilling, what then is there to live for? Nothing, some say, and so there is another suicidal sacrifice to the god of this world.

Today, how many followers of Jesus realize that He has authority over immoral thinking? Contrary to the opinions of a multitude of Christians, we do not have to live under the authority of lust and immoral desires! We can and should be free! Jesus provides that freedom. Freedom from immoral thinking is far more important than physical healing. Lust is a sin of the heart. Jesus said: *Out of the heart proceed evil thoughts* (Matthew 15:19). Many authorities believe that a bad diet causes much physical illness. But the more dangerous sickness - immorality of thought - comes from the heart.

You may have observed the present emphasis on healing of the physical body. Sermons by the thousands are preached, telling people how they can be healed. Books are written by the hundreds on this subject. Many are helped by these ministries, and all of this has a part in pointing people to Christ as Savior. But how many sermons and books deal with holy thoughts and desires? It seems that this subject is ignored because it is considered either unimportant or impossible. Since it isn't unimportant from a Biblical perspective, it must then be considered impossible. Or, perhaps it is considered too unpopular a subject with which to deal. Most of us are not likely to get excited over any effort to uncover our hidden thoughts!

Great emphasis is now being placed on abortions, but abortion is a by-product of immoral thinking! Man must first have something in his heart, before he puts it into action. The Bible repeatedly emphasizes that our first concern should be the spiritual condition of our hearts.

Many Christians reach a plateau in their spiritual lives and seem able to go no further. They pray, study the Bible, attend church regularly, tithe, memorize Bible promises, and keep trying to grow in faith. But they stay at the same level year after year. Any resemblance to your situation?

Eventually, all Christians must come to realize that God is not foolish! He has filled the Bible with many generous promises of all the things He will do for His children. But He was wise enough to build perfect controls into His Word. We can obtain only limited answers to our prayers until we learn to keep His Word! Many Christians put a lifetime of effort into trying to "release faith" to get God's promises, while they are refusing to keep His Word. Impossible! We can't use miracle-working faith if we refuse to follow God's directions. It doesn't matter how enthusiastically someone tells us that we can receive everything from God simply by claiming His promises. It simply isn't true - that you may have already discovered. Every promise of God is conditioned on our

49

obedience. Jesus clearly said that He received everything He prayed for because He always did God's will. I'm thankful there are some things God will give us even when we are disobedient. But He will not give us, for example, power to work miracles until we know how to use that power wisely.

The following Scriptures emphasize this point.

> 1. *If ye abide in me, and my words abide in you, ye shall ask what ye will, and it shall be done unto you* (John 15:7).

Being in Christ's will is clearly a requirement for receiving from God.

> 2. *And whatsoever we ask, we receive of Him because we keep His commandments and do those things that are pleasing in His sight* (I John 3:22).

Pure desires are pleasing in God's sight!

> 3. *Ye ask, and receive not, because ye ask amiss, that ye may consume it upon your lusts. Ye adulterers and adulteresses* (James 4:3-4).

Didn't Jesus make it clear that adultery in the heart was as destructive as the act of adultery? Doesn't this verse make it clear that God will not give us blessings that will be enjoyed in the midst of our lusts?

> 4. *Purify your hearts, ye double minded* (James 4:8).

Note that He doesn't say, "Ask Me to purify you," but rather, "You purify." This means we are capable, and we cannot expect miraculous answers to prayers until we do purify our hearts.

God makes this so clear, yet people vainly seek an easier way. They go to hear anyone who will tell them it is easy to receive health and wealth if they will only believe. It is easy to receive from God, but only if we come to Him while we are doing what we can to purify the desires of our hearts. Of course we will never be perfect, but our goal must be obedience to Him. His goals for us are clarified in:

1. *Sanctify yourselves therefore, and be ye holy* (Leviticus 20:7).
2. *We should be holy and without blame before Him* (Ephesians 1:4).
3. *Let us cleanse ourselves from all filthiness of the flesh and spirit, perfecting holiness in the fear of God* (II Corinthians 7:1).
4. *Follow ... holiness, without which no man shall see the Lord* (Hebrews 12:14).

You have heard the adage, "Half a glass of water is seen as either half-full or half-empty." You can see these verses and this book as a pronouncement that you are half-empty, or you can see them as a great blessing. You are learning how you can be full!

If our spiritual lives are in a rut, and we are trying - method after method - prayer after prayer - year after year - there is only one way that will work - seeking holiness of heart, mind, soul and imagination. God will honor every step we take toward becoming what He wants us to be.

Many books have been written and many sermons preached exhorting us not to: commit adultery, steal, hurt others, drink alcohol, etc. We have also been frequently told to: go to church, help others, care for our families, study the Bible, etc. These are good things, but if we never do wrong and always do good, we will still be a long way from the holiness described in the Bible.

In this generation, little has been written or taught about our need to be pure in heart, thought and imagination. The Bible is filled with God's exhortations to be pure in our desires and thoughts. It is in these areas that we win the real victories.

To concentrate our energies on what men do, is like sending all our fire-fighting equipment outside the city to put out brush fires, when the heart of the city itself is burning down!

The hearts of Christians are being corrupted by the world in which we live. Men and women are being sucked into the filth of lustful, adulterous, covetous thinking, and the only warning Christians are receiving, is not to do any of the physical acts! Of course we are not supposed to do the acts, but we shouldn't be indulging in the thoughts either.

IMMORAL THINKING DRAINS AWAY THE SPIRITUAL POWER WE SHOULD HAVE. Satan knows this, and he uses his most skillful tactics to keep our inner decay from being called exactly what it is - disobedience to God.

How do I know there is spiritual decay in Christians' hearts? Everywhere I have spoken on this subject, the audience has confirmed what I'm telling you. Immorality in the minds of Christians is rampant! Holiness of desire, as taught by Jesus and His disciples, is almost unknown. Spiritual leaders are often caught in the same web as we are, and are therefore unable to say anything about the dangerous condition. How do I know this? I'm not just making a statement of what I think may be true. I'm reporting what men and women in positions of leadership have been telling me for many years!

Many men are predicting an outpouring of the Holy Spirit upon our nation in the future. I wish that I could unite with others in these enthusiastic expectations, but I am unable to do so.

My understanding of Scripture leads me to believe that God will pour out His Spirit upon us as His Spirit controls us. My conviction is that here in the United States we are moving further away from obedience.

In writing this prediction, I know I am going against the mainstream of what is being said and written. The United States will not have a great revival until there are changes in the hearts of Christians. Now, there is moral decay that will prevent our country, and much of the world, from entering into the good things God has prepared for us.

But there is no need for discouragement! The Holy Spirit is ready to minister His fullness to each one of us as we are ready. If we are willing for Him to control the desires of our hearts, He is willing to work God's perfect will in our lives. We do not have to center our attention on what other people are doing or not doing.

As individual Christians are changed into the likeness of Christ, we will see the moving of the Holy Spirit throughout our land. This makes the future contingent on our spiritual progress rather than God's set time when He will sovereignly pour out His Spirit. When I examine the history of God's dealings with the human race, I see the Lord doing His part as man acts in obedience to His Word. The Bible promises a special work of the Holy Spirit in the latter days, but the Word also says there will be a purifying of hearts in believers.

If the Body of Christ in our country does not seek holiness of heart, there will be further decay, and the freedom of religion we now enjoy will be gone. This has happened in nation after nation since the beginning of time, and we have no reason to expect anything different. God turned His back on disobedient Israel time after time. They came under slavery for as long as four hundred years! The same thing could happen to our nation.

Do I see signs of increasing decay in the hearts of Christians? I do. Moral and spiritual filth is being accepted into homes - through television - that fifty years ago would have caused Christians to react as Jesus did when He saw the temple being desecrated. We are being conditioned to accept anything. God will not tolerate this indefinitely.

This book is my effort to come against the forces that are striving to pollute our thoughts and desires. Noah warned the people of his day that God was angry. If Noah were alive today he would say, "God is angry that men's and women's desires are impure." I don't have his gift of prophecy, so I can't say what is going to happen, but exactly what is going to happen isn't relevant. It's sufficient to know that God wants His people to strive to be holy in thought, desire and heart and to do everything we can to obey Him.

If the message of this book ministers to you, please use every means available to bring it to the attention of other Christians. Being an author is only a small part of getting any message distributed. You, the reader, can be used by God to change hundreds of people by your efforts to share this message with them.

Exactly who needs this message?

WIVES

Ladies need to understand that men can be as easily tempted to think immoral thoughts as ladies are tempted to eat excessively. And just as frequently! In some cases, far more frequently. If you find it easy to damage your body by overeating, meditate on how easy it may be for your husband to give in to the temptation of immoral thoughts.

I have been greatly saddened by the many marriages that are ending in divorce as a result of wives becoming overweight. You ladies may react, "That should never be!" Yes, you would be right, it shouldn't be, but it is. Couples who have been together for five, ten and twenty-five years are separated, and the wives are expressing great shock that such a thing could ever happen. I know that on this point I am stepping where angels fear to tread, but please, wives, listen to me. If you allow your love of eating to control your life, you are inviting your husband to fasten his attention on another woman. He should not do this, but I should give you the facts as they are, so you can then decide what it is that you want most. Once your husband has given his heart to someone else, there may be absolutely nothing you can do.

HUSBANDS

Men need to understand that ladies need tenderness and understanding. If they don't find these in their husbands, they are tempted to look for them in other men. They can be tempted just as frequently as men are tempted to think immoral thoughts. In some cases, perhaps more frequently. If you find it easy to damage your eternal spirit by thinking immoral thoughts, think how easy it may be for your wife to give in to the temptation of longing for someone else to meet her emotional needs.

You need to be aware that your attitude toward your wife can encourage her to center her attention on another man. Many men have contacted me after their wives have filed for divorce, and they were overwhelmed that such a thing could happen. When I studied their problems, it often became clear that the husband failed to provide his wife with the attention, kindness and love she craved. When the husband didn't provide what she needed, she was tempted to look at other men. Of course, she should not have done this, but I should give you the facts as they are, so you can then decide what it is that you want most.

UNMARRIED PERSONS

If you believe you should not commit the act of adultery (sex with a married person), or fornication (sex with someone who isn't married), and yet you indulge in lustful thoughts, the odds are that you will not be able to be true to what you believe. The odds are better than nine-to-one that you will eventually slip into some immoral act. The pattern of those who have gone before you has established this tragic record. And the world's environment promises an ever increasing moral decay.

What is the solution? Accept God's guidelines for His children. Let His Spirit help you to have holy desires. Possible? Yes it is! You can have your mind renewed in the image of Christ. The desire to please God will become stronger than the desire to please your nature.

If, during your period of courtship, you depend on your ability to fight against your desires, you will more than likely become one more example of the nine-to-one odds. But if you seek holy desires, you will become an example of what happens when we accept God's will.

Please believe I am suggesting something that is possible. The world has presented sexual desire as being *so* strong that no one can control what he desires. Even many Christians have become convinced that if their desires aren't immoral, there must be something wrong with them!

As you seek God's will through His written Word, His Spirit will actually help you to change your desires! You can face your intended wife or husband, let them look into your eyes, and know they will see the mind of Christ in you.

If you accept God's will in this crucial matter, He will protect you from a multitude of sorrows. If you reject His will, you open yourself to problems as numerous as the grains of sand on the sea shore!

I am not exhorting you to pray for a miracle. I'm informing you of a potential that God has already provided through Jesus. Consider this:

1. God created man with holy desires. Man and woman wanted to please God. When man sinned, his desires came under the authority of evil forces.
2. Jesus became the second Adam and lived a pure, holy, perfect life. He broke the chains and made it possible for you and me to change our desires! Believe that, and you are on the way toward purifying what's on your mind!

And on your way keep in mind:

1. Men have been conditioned to believe that their immoral thoughts are caused by women.

56

2. Women have been conditioned to believe
   that their immoral thoughts are caused by
   men.

Adam said, "The woman...gave me of the tree."

Eve said, "The serpent beguiled me."

Other people can lead us into many things, but they can only lead us where we agree to go. The ultimate responsibility for everything we do rests on no one but ourselves.

The human mind will go to any length to reject guilt. Its objective is to disregard the law of the Creator without suffering the uncomfortable feelings of guilt. You can perhaps verify this from your own experiences. If you have engaged in immoral thinking, you probably have found some way to excuse yourself. The mind says, "I am guilty but...or I am not guilty because..."

Chapter 6

That Perfect Affair

Things on planet earth are not usually the way we would like them to be.

We would like to:

Eat what we want and never gain weight

Plant a garden and not get weeds

Give young people good advice and see them follow it

Enjoy living but never get old

Spend money and still have it

Clean the house and have it stay that way

Cook a meal that everyone in the family likes

Change the world for better without having to do anything to make it change.

The world needs to be changed. People need to be changed. We can get ourselves into a position where we know changes need to be made but we don't feel we can do anything. How do we get ourselves into such situations? By trying to mix the wrong things.

A business that had once been quite successful, was failing. The owner hired a cost analyst to study the company's methods and personnel and tell him what was wrong.

The analyst's report was short and simple. "Your relatives."

The owner had hired relatives and then felt he couldn't discipline or fire them. They were destroying the company. Even when he knew what the problem was he couldn't bring himself to do what had to be done.

The business man tried to mix his desire to help his family with what would make his business successful. It didn't work. The business failed. The owner lost everything, and his relatives no longer had jobs.

If we try to mix our commitment to Christ with our desire to think immoral thoughts, we have a combination that will not work. God invites us into His family, but He requires that we strive to become like His Son. He always knows in what direction we are moving. Remember the Prodigal Son? When he wanted to leave home, his father helped him. The father gave his son freedom.

God gives us freedom to choose which direction we will take. There is much that needs to be done in this world, but we have the freedom to select what we will do or even to do nothing.

Satanic forces are on the attack. They are committed to the destruction of every Christian element in American life.

Adolph Hitler said he was going to rule Europe. Few paid any attention, much less believed he could accomplish such an impossible task. He believed in himself and eventually ruled most of Europe. The people of other nations enabled Hitler to accomplish his goal - by doing nothing!

Atheistic forces say they are going to strip America of every evidence of Christianity. Will we allow the Holy Spirit to spark a desire in our hearts to be involved in moral issues? That spark was ignited in Jesus when He saw money-changers cheating the people in the Temple. He didn't call for prayer - He moved. The Bible says He was moved with "indignation."

What provokes us to indignation? It usually is something about which we feel deeply. It stirs our emotions. Our hearts tell us we must act. Jesus knew this! That is why He urged us to be pure in heart. If we want to please God, and still indulge in immoral thoughts, we are backed into a corner, just like the business man who couldn't deal with his relatives.

We can see that there are moral problems all around us, but if we have lustful thoughts, we can't rouse ourselves into action. The results can be tragic.

A father longs to spare his sons and daughters the disasters associated with immorality. He wants to tell them to keep their minds free from every thought that might draw them into impure acts. He may love his children so much that he would gladly give his life to protect them. But what if the father lives with lustful thoughts? How can he give his children the information they need if he knows he himself is harboring adulterous thoughts? He can't! And he doesn't. The father doesn't teach his son to think pure thoughts, and that son doesn't teach his sons. Soon the message is lost, and no one remembers that God wants us to be pure in heart.

I see a battle plan for the Body of Christ. We can:
1. Learn God's will for our thoughts.
2. Change our minds to fit His will.
3. Teach our families.
4. Introduce others to the Word of God.
5. Move against evil forces.
6. Elect government officials who will fight for legislation that reflects God's laws.
7. Support those in government who uphold moral principles.

Most of us do not like the idea of being at war. But we are at war. There is no way out. We are either under attack by evil, or attacking evil - advancing or retreating.

There was a time when evil was hidden on the back streets of our nation. Now it flourishes under ten-foot neon signs. It was once confined to sleazy theaters; now television channels it into the living rooms of millions of Americans.

Let's take the situation as it is and make it work for good. We can! You may have been in a church service where all the lights were turned out and one candle was lit. That one small light could be seen by everyone. Then other candles were lit from that one and the light spread throughout the meeting place.

You and I have the thrill of being a light. Jesus said: *You shine as lights in the midst of a crooked generation.* We have the joy of saying to the world, *Jesus has changed my mind. He will change yours too if you will let Him.* By sharing the light with the next person, that light will spread in the midst of darkness. But we need always to remember what Jesus said: *If the light that is in you be darkness, how great is that darkness.*

I propose that our lights burn brightly. A star may appear the size of a candle's flame yet actually be a million times larger than earth! It looks small because it's so far away. We are not limited in what we can do by our apparent size! We have all the resources of heaven available to help us!

In the book of Revelation Jesus told the church at Ephesus that He would take the "candle" from their midst *if they were not obedient to God.* We can be obedient. All we need is that spark in our hearts to make whatever changes need to be made.

Consider the atom - too small to be seen. It can move a mountain when its power is released. God sent the Holy Spirit to release power in us. But the Holy Spirit is *holy.* He will only work in a heart that is willing to be used.

You and I have the capacity to bring change into our world. God makes available to each of us more power than we could ever use! The secret is in permitting the Spirit of holiness to work in us.

If your heart longs to be used by God, let Him purify whatever is on your mind.

Jesus said, *If a kingdom be divided against itself, that kingdom cannot stand* (Mark 3:24). Our lives - our kingdoms - are threatened. Our potential losses include our: marriages, homes, children, employment, friends, health and anything else we value.

How do we get into a position where one part of our personality is divided against the other? Here is an illustration of what can happen.

Our legs respond to our brains and carry our bodies from point A to point B.

Introduce alcohol to the brain.

The mind says, "I want to go from A to B."

The brain says, "Okay, lets go."

But the "house" has been divided. It isn't capable of fulfilling its function as a unit. Without the brain's help, the legs are unable to move the body.

Our minds may want to protect our marriages, homes and families, and to preserve our obedience to God. But if the heart deserts the mind we have a divided kingdom.

You may intend to protect the security of your present lifestyle and eventually to improve it. You do not plan to do anything that is impure or foolish.

During the years that you engaged in impure thoughts, but never followed through on them, your heart increased its desire for an exciting sexual encounter. Your mind successfully held that down.

Then one day you meet a person and something is triggered inside you. *That person* is different and possesses some magical quality that is exactly what you have always wanted. The attraction is so intense that you might easily be convinced that this person was created by God for *you*. You couldn't want them so much if God hadn't given you this intense desire.

If you are fortunate, the other person responds to your advances with, "You must be crazy!"

If you are unfortunate they say, "I feel exactly as you do. We need to get together soon."

All of that magic and harmony and desire promises lasting

excitement and fulfillment.

The mind may hesitate and think, "What if my husband finds out? My home would be destroyed." Or, "What if her husband finds out? He might kill me."

But the heart will not listen. It has an intense desire to be with *that* person. It refuses to consider fleeing the temptation. Reason and common sense go out the window, and the inner desires rule.

If the temptation is consummated, how long will the magic last? The desires say, "Forever! This is the most real thing that has ever happened to me."

But wait! Jesus said a kingdom divided against itself will fall. If you know that something is wrong and you want it anyhow, the divided kingdom is set up, and the fall will come. Jesus' prediction has been fulfilled tens of thousands of times. Probably millions of people have felt *their* situation was different. Their illicit affairs were too pure to end in tragedy. But the odds are overwhelming. If we get involved in something we know is wrong, our "fall" will come. One wrong step prepares the way for another...and another.

There is only one solution. The desires of our hearts must be changed. We must do whatever is necessary to intensify our desire to please God. He alone knows what will give us lasting pleasure and happiness. We must meditate on His Word regarding thoughts, desires and imaginations. We must keep informing our hearts that pleasing our Creator is our reason for being alive. If we do this, our inner resolve to please God more than self will continue to grow. The kingdom is united in desires, thoughts, goals and ambitions and will remain so until Jesus comes!

Evaluate yourself and ask this question, "Can I commit myself to having the mind of Christ?" You may say to yourself,

"That's a good goal to consider, but I might as well forget it. Some people might be able to have a clean mind, but that's beyond my ability."

Remember two important things:

1. God has said that all His children can, *do all things through Christ which strengtheneth me* (Philippians 4:13).

Nothing in your situation makes you ineligible to claim this promise.

2. God recognizes our weaknesses, but He never gives up on us.

He didn't give up on David. He appointed him King over the strongest nation in the world. David had everything, but his heart desired more. That desire made him a thief and a murderer. If anyone ever gave God a reason to disown a man, it was David. When David repented, God forgave him. Later, David wrote the Psalms that have helped people for three thousand years. This means that failures do not exclude us from being used of God. He wants us to be successful in our desire to have a pure mind and He will rejoice that we, like David, have the courage to try!

We have a great God. No case is too hard for Him. He doesn't just heal the sick. He also raises the dead! That shows He doesn't look for the easy way to demonstrate His power.

Chapter 7

My Dream

My dream was filled with confusion. I knew I had received orders to go back into the Army, but I couldn't find the orders and couldn't remember where I was to report for duty. I was distressed that I couldn't even remember my reporting date.

In the dream there was a crisis when I couldn't find my army clothes. My fatigues and boots were gone. I was going from place to place searching for my uniforms so I could go somewhere, sometime.

When I awakened, it was time to get up, but my shoulder muscles were tight. My face was tense. My hands were pushing down on the bed.

I thought, what a ridiculous dream!

Then I realized that the dream was so intense I must have been expected to learn something. I meditated on all the details, but I couldn't think of one redeeming quality that would make the dream worthwhile.

My mind drifted to several important decisions that I needed to make that day. Each decision could determine the success or failure of important activities. I was straining to decide what I should do.

In the midst of my efforts I was interrupted by a voice within. "That is what your dream was all about."

"What?"

"You are doing now exactly what you were doing in the dream."

"How could that be? In the dream everything centered on completely irrelevant nonsense. Now I'm thinking about things that are important."

"You have only one thing to do today."

By this time I knew there was something the Holy Spirit wanted to teach me.

"Yes, Lord, but what is it I'm supposed to do? There are all these different decisions I must make. What should I do first?"

"Please Me. That is the only thing you have to do."

Then complete silence. I had my orders for the day - for the week - for years to come. The reality of it filled my mind. Pleasing God was what I had to do! Everything else was secondary. My concern over the decisions I needed to make was as unnecessary as locating my army clothes in the dream.

All that day the message from God filled my mind. My mission, my work, my whole duty was to please God. Each time I felt tension in my shoulder muscles or face, I remembered the dream, and peace flowed through my mind. God was working to change my understanding of what was important to Him. I wanted to be used by God to change the world - He wanted to change me.

Romans 8:29: *...to be conformed to the image of His Son.* This is what God wanted to do in me. His Son knew what His purpose was on this earth. Redeem the human race? Heal the sick? Provide salvation? Be crucified and resurrected? He did all these things, but they weren't His only mission. His total mission was to please God.

If I picture Jesus as only a man, just like any other man, I would see Him as powerless. If I picture Jesus as so separated from mankind that He has nothing in common with us, how can I use Him as my example?

I see Jesus as One I can look to as a perfect model. He was pure, but He permitted Himself to suffer every temptation that we do.

He was tempted to have wrong thoughts, but He never had them! Some may react unfavorably to the idea that Jesus was tempted to think immoral thoughts. But He was tempted in all points as we are. The difference is in His reaction! He was tempted to be discouraged, but was never discouraged. We can read *conformed to the image of His Son* and know that there is a comparison between the temptations He endured and our own. When we remember our own failures we may think, I could never be sinless in my desires so why should I try? But He endured the same temptations so He *could be* our example!

Satan released maximum temptation on Jesus at one point in His life. Satan became so desperate that he offered to release all the influence he had over every part of this world. He was determined! "Just fall down and worship me once, Jesus, for only one second, and everything I have will be yours."

Since Satan went this far, what previous offers must he have given Jesus? Whatever they were, nothing succeeded. Jesus remained our perfect example.

The point is, no matter what temptations Jesus faced, His mind remained pure.

You and I can be changed once we perceive an image of ourselves made into His likeness. He was human enough to serve as our example, yet divine enough to be a perfect sacrifice. His death and resurrection released the power that we need to follow Him.

I do not believe that the moment a man accepts Jesus as Savior he is expected to be immediately pure in heart! It doesn't happen that way. Neither do I believe that God assigns an angel to clobber a new Christian if he or she slips into a pattern of wrong thinking.

69

Before we became Christians, our minds were filled with wrong thoughts. Our memories and inclinations reflected our less-than-perfect natures. At our new birth, by the grace of God, we may have been instantly delivered of some bad habits, but others clung to our coat-tails waiting for an opportunity to control our future.

I've experienced and observed God's great patience. He loves, forgives and cares for us. He longs for us to mature and lay aside things that hold us back.

Why doesn't He make us instantly free of all temptations? This little dot of time in eternity is our brief opportunity to learn how to be obedient to God when everything around us says, "Disobey!"

When we are received into God's family, we may be as weak as a newborn eagle. We have great potential, but as we develop, we need considerable understanding and care.

The skeptic might think a new Christian is a fraud if he sees in him anything less than perfection. Those who know nothing about an eaglet might think he should know how to fly - but he doesn't.

When a man or woman has been a Christian for months or even years, he still has many faults, and may be considered a hypocrite by the skeptic. An eagle can be mature enough to have wings capable of lifting him to the heavens, but that doesn't mean he can fly! A novice might say, "Shove him out of the nest and he will learn to fly before he hits the ground." But he won't! Eagles don't learn to fly that way. Push him out of the nest too soon and he will fall like a rock and land on his head.

Day after day the mother eagle perches on the edge of the nest and patiently flaps her wings. The young eagle watches and eventually imitates his instructor. Flap, flap. "Hey, this is fun, but why are we doing it?"

By and by the long wings develop muscles. At the right time the giant mother nudges the fearful offspring out into the world.

70

The mother flaps her wings like she has done so often before, and the babe follows her example. Together they now reach up into the sky.

The new Christian may want to "fly," but he often doesn't want to go to all the work it takes to develop spiritual muscles.

God knows our potential, and He keeps reminding us of whom we are. We feel it when the Spirit within says, "Those thoughts you are having aren't right. You need to change."

"But I can't change!"

"Yes you can. Look around you. See the world I have created. It is glorious. Behold the heavens. They tell you of My glory. Look at a flower - it reflects My love for beauty. I made you for purity and goodness. You can do it!"

Paul wrote: *We are taking every thought captive to the obedience of Christ* (II Corinthians 10:5 NAS). He was giving us an up-to-date report on what the early church was learning.

The Greeks of Corinth lived pretty much as slaves under the Roman Empire. They understood steel and swords and soldiers controlling everything. Paul is describing a new brand of captive - one held by the love of Jesus. In verse one he said, *I beseech you by the meekness and gentleness of Christ.*

The Christians of Corinth faced no easy task in their efforts to have the mind of Christ. It was customary in Corinth to offer public prayers asking the gods to multiply their prostitutes! The religious leaders bound themselves, by vows, to increase the number of such women, for this occupation was considered spiritually uplifting. To people with this background Paul was presenting his challenge for purity in every thought!

Releasing our minds to Christ's control must be a voluntary act. He will not accept authority over our thoughts unless this is what *we* want. Jesus is not pressuring us to make our thoughts like His! Rather, He is saying, *You were polluted by thoughts that enslaved you. I say that you can be free.*

71

Like the baby eagle, we need to stretch our wings and feel what it's like to be created in God's image. We were made for lofty heights, where the air is fresh and clean. He gives us His Spirit to convince us that we are worthy of reaching for the goal of holiness in heart and mind.

We may not soar into realms of perfection while we are still here in this flesh, but we can at least begin to flap our wings and declare our freedom in Christ. We do not have to be bound by the beggarly thoughts of impure desires! God has declared that we have the capacity to be changed into the image of His Son!

Like the baby eagle, you and I received our new lives way up in high places. We were born for heavenly adventures. The spirit within us longs for everything that is holy. Haven't you felt that longing many times?

Our flesh wants to stay down in the baser environment. It relishes the earth-bound desires that seem so enjoyable, but have proven to be so futile.

We are free to fly. Jesus is our example. He said we could follow Him. When we first try, it seems impossible. Our minds may say, "I can't. I'm too human." We *are* woefully human, but because of Jesus we can change. He provides the way.

What's on *your* mind? Does it need to change? If so, begin to move out and up. Leave the impure thoughts behind. We are spiritual beings. We are born to attain spiritual heights.

And now to the ultimate solution:

GOD'S WRITTEN WORD

ATTENTION!

You may have decided that you agree with my message but are not too interested in studying additional Scriptures.

CAUTION!

I believe the Holy Spirit has given me extra help in understanding the following references. My comments are brief but crucial.

BE ALERT!

Many men and women have read this far, agreed with what they read and *intended* to have pure thoughts for the remainder of their lives. But later they contacted me with heart breaking stories of broken homes, illegitimate children and shattered dreams. Therefore I beg you to pay close attention to the following pages.

Be alert to the tendency to merely scan these Scriptures. If what I have written thus far has pointed out spiritual needs in your life, please believe that you need to *study* carefully chapter eight.

Perhaps you may not initially understand the need for including so many Scriptures in this chapter. But please believe me! Stories about other people's lives are interesting, but they do not have the power to change our hearts. The human tendency for immoral thoughts is so strong that only God's Word can change us.

Saturate your mind with the Bible verses in this book, read them daily. Carry them on cards in your pocket. Tape them on your dashboard, bathroom mirror, other places where you will see them throughout the day. If you do this, you can maintain a mind that is free. With a clean mind, the door is wide open for you to enter into a multitude of blessings from God.

Chapter 8

The Ultimate Solution

There are those who teach that all we have to do is believe the promises in the Bible and we can have anything we want. God's promises are true, but if we disregard His will, we cannot convince Him to give us the things we want. His promises are based upon our obedience. This is made quite emphatic in:

1. *If I regard iniquity in my heart, the Lord will not hear me* (Psalm 66:18).

2. *You have ignored all my counsel... When distress and anguish come upon you...Then shall they call upon me, but I will not answer; they shall seek me early, but they shall not find me* (Proverbs 1:25,27,28 RSV).

We will do well to be obedient. None of us can perfectly obey, and He hasn't demanded that we be perfect. But He warns against "ignoring" His counsel. If we choose to ignore His hatred of immorality, then we should not expect Him to respond to our prayers.

3. *And whatsoever we ask, we receive of Him, because we keep His commandments and do those things that are pleasing in His sight* (I John 3:22).

And now to the focal point of my message - the formula for becoming what God wants us to be.

75

Please examine the following Scriptures thoughtfully! If we meditate on these verses, we can be victorious in our search for clean thoughts and desires. My purpose in writing this book is to present a prescription for victory! Every person needs to understand that *God's purpose* in everything He has said is to help us.

There are hundreds of verses that I have not included. I wanted to give you enough to show God's attention to this subject and yet not so many that you would be kept from carefully considering each verse.

GENESIS

1:1 *In the beginning God created...*

There is enough in these five words to produce a lifetime of clean thoughts. Every person we see is His creation! When I see an attractive lady I have learned to respond with, "Thank You Lord for that beautiful creation!" My praise causes joy to rise in my heart. I would be delighted for the lady to know the thoughts of my heart for they have already been blessed by God.

> 6:5-6 *And God saw that the wickedness of man was great in the earth, and that every IMAGINATION of the THOUGHTS of his heart was only evil continually. And it repented the Lord that He had made man on the earth, and it grieved Him at His heart.*

Evil imaginations and evil thoughts in men's minds caused God to wish He had never created mankind. These verses **alone** are sufficient reasons for us to guard carefully our thoughts.

EXODUS

20:14 *Thou shalt not commit adultery.*

Like any loving parent, God uses His goodness to draw us to repentance. If that fails, then He often administers the corrective action necessary to get our attention.

20:17 ...*Thou shalt not covet thy neighbor's wife...*

This is much stronger than saying, "Thou shalt not *take* thy neighbor's wife." God is saying we are not permitted to *want to have her*. Only a *strong* desire to please God can control what we *want*.

LEVITICUS

In the Old Testament God makes severe judgments against immorality. Most of us would prefer to flee to the God of grace as revealed in the New Testament. But it is important that we refresh our minds as to how God feels about His moral laws. Once we have a clear picture of this, we are much better prepared to understand why He wants our thoughts to be pure.

20:1,7,10 *And the Lord spake unto Moses saying...Sanctify yourselves therefore, and be ye holy: for I am the Lord your God...The man that committeth adultery with another man's wife, even he that committeth adultery with his neighbor's wife, the adulterer and the adulteress shall surely be put to death.*

NUMBERS

One of the children of Israel brought a foreign woman into the Jewish camp and led her to his tent.

> 25:7-8, 10-11 *And when Phinehas...saw it, he rose up from among the congregation, and took a javelin in his hand; And he went after the man of Israel into the tent, and thrust both of them through, the man of Israel, and the woman through her belly. So the plague was stayed from the children of Israel...And the Lord spake unto Moses, saying, Phinehas ...hath turned my wrath away from the children of Israel, while he was zealous for my sake among them that I consumed not the children of Israel in my jealousy.*

This passage gives us a dramatic picture of how God feels when His laws are disobeyed. If Phinehas had not used corrective action, God would have taken many lives. We may often need to take swift, corrective action regarding our thoughts and imaginations. In some Christians' minds, immoral thoughts have been permitted to have free reign. This book is an effort to help combat the tide of immorality that is crashing against the hearts and minds of Christian men and women. Some groups are warning us against x-rated movies and pornography, but I believe we will accomplish much more if we first cleanse our own hearts and then unite to change the world around us.

In my lifetime I have heard many sermons on the need for Christians to become "holy." But the emphasis was nearly always on outward actions. Don't do this or don't do that. Should we spend an entire lifetime trying to avoid doing wrong, while something within us continually *desires* to do wrong? The exciting thing is that the Bible contains the help we need to have desires that *will be* pleasing to God.

DEUTERONOMY

5:29 *O that there were such an HEART in them that they would fear me, and keep all my commandments always, that it might be well with them, and with their children forever.*

God's desire has not changed and His promises are still in force. If we can bring our hearts into harmony with His will, He says everything will go well for us and even for our children. What a blessed promise!

JUDGES

2:14 *And the anger of the Lord was hot against Israel, and He delivered them into the hands of spoilers that spoiled them, and He sold them into the hands of their enemies round about, so that they could not any longer stand before their enemies.*

What caused God's anger toward Israel?

2:12-13 *They followed other gods...*
They forsook the Lord.

Immorality is a "god" that we must be careful never to follow. Israel was God's "chosen people," yet their enemies overcame them when they disobeyed Him.

RUTH

3:11 *...All the city of my people doth know that thou art a virtuous woman.*

An entire book of the Bible, set apart to honor a virtuous woman! What a blessing and what an incentive to all of us. If we want God to bless our homes, our families, our work and our health, we should honor His love and virtue.

I SAMUEL

12:24 Only fear the Lord, and serve Him in truth with all your HEART: for consider how great things He hath done for you.

God's plan of salvation is kind and full of grace. But we can receive the gift of eternal life and still be sadly imperfect. God asks us to consider His goodness and then serve Him with *all our hearts*. We can reject His plea and continue to think whatever thoughts we desire. If we do this, there may be serious consequences. We never know what they might be. It seems to me that often evil forces themselves decide what the consequences will be! This is a painful way to learn - obedience is far easier!

II SAMUEL

11:2-3 And it came to pass in an eveningtide, that David arose from off his bed, and walked upon the roof of the king's house: and from the roof he saw a woman washing herself; and the woman was very beautiful to look upon. And David sent and inquired after the woman...

David looked...and wanted...and so began his tragic downfall. Men, consider this carefully. David probably didn't think he was capable of doing the things he eventually did. The problem, of course, was not that he happened to see Bathsheba, but that he did not control his thoughts.

I KINGS

11:1,4 *But King Solomon loved many strange women...It came to pass, when Solomon was old, that his wives turned away his HEART after other gods...*

If we persist in our desire to have wrong thoughts, our hearts will be turned away from God. It will happen slowly and so subtly that we may not recognize what is happening. Even Solomon, the wisest man who ever lived, didn't realize that his heart was being turned away from God.

I CHRONICLES

16:29 *Give unto the Lord the glory due unto His name: bring an offering, and come before Him: Worship the Lord in the beauty of holiness.*

Two of the most acceptable offerings we can bring to God are clean hearts and minds. These offerings can be brought to Him by anyone - the poorest of men, those in prisons and those confined to their beds. No service to God, no matter how great or well-known, could possibly compare with the service of a heart that reflects the beauty of His holiness. None of us are perfect, but *He knows* when we do our best to let His Spirit control our thoughts. The great tragedy is that many Christian men and women know their thoughts are not right, yet they make no serious effort to change.

81

> 29:1,3,9 *David the king said unto all the congregation...I have set my affection to the house of my God...Then the people rejoiced, for that they offered willingly, because with perfect heart they offered willingly to the Lord...*

When we are fully persuaded that God is making human beings His home, we begin to honor that home as His. We give that honor willingly and joyfully.

EZRA

> 7:23 *Whatsoever is commanded by the God of heaven, let it be diligently done for the house of the God of heaven...*

God has repeatedly emphasized that His house is to be treated with great care. Now God makes His house in the hearts of all who accept His Son as Savior. If we receive the benefits of salvation through Christ, we must accept the responsibilities of caring for God's dwelling place. He has repeatedly told us that the thoughts and desires of our minds must be appropriate for *His dwelling place*.

> 9:6 *...O my God, I am ashamed and blush to lift up my face to thee, my God: for our iniquities are increased over our head and our trespass is grown up unto the heavens.*

The people of Israel saw the men and women of the heathen nations and wanted them. Ezra was ashamed of what he saw. As Christians we should be deeply ashamed of what is going on today. Immorality flourishes.

ESTHER

1:10-12 ...When the heart of the king was merry with wine he commanded ...the chamberlains...To bring Vashti the queen...to shew the people and the princes her beauty: for she was fair to look on. But the queen Vashti refused to come...therefore was the king very wroth, and his anger burned in him.

Men have accepted the idea that if a woman is beautiful in her outward appearance, she can meet their desires and needs. This has proven to be false, but men continue to believe it. The handsome, dashing man can also bring great suffering into a woman's life.

JOB

24:15,18 The eye also of the adulterer waiteth for the twilight saying, No eye shall see me: and disguiseth his face...their portion is cursed in the earth.

What is the "portion" that could come under God's curse? It could be our portion of *anything*! It might be the health of our families or our finances. This *does not* mean that every time we have trouble that God has placed a curse on part of our lives! Too often, God is portrayed only as a God of love. His love is far greater than we will ever realize, but His judgments are also clearly a part of His nature. We need to recognize this.

83

PSALMS

10:1 *Why standest thou afar off, O Lord?*
Why hidest thou thyself in times of trouble?

If our thoughts are unclean, God may seem to be "afar off" when we pray. In times of trouble we may cry for help and it will seem that He doesn't hear us.

10:4 *The wicked...will not seek after God:*
God is not in all his THOUGHTS.

God wants to have a part in all our thoughts.

14:2,3 *The Lord looked down from heaven*
upon the children of men, to see if there were
any that did understand, and seek God. They
are all gone aside, they are all together
become filthy (impure): *there is none that*
doeth good, no, not one.

It must have broken God's heart to say something as strong as this. He is still looking for those who "understand." I, for one, have been slow to learn.

19:14 *Let the words of my mouth and the*
MEDITATION of my heart, be acceptable in
thy sight, O Lord, my strength, and my
redeemer.

Our meditation *is* important if we want His strength to work for us.

23:1 *The Lord is my shepherd; I shall not want.*

Exciting sermons can be preached on this verse but some have placed all the emphasis on "I shall not want." The emphasis being, that if we claim Jesus as our Savior, we will never want for anything. It is then pointed out that we do not need to lack health, wealth, success, popularity or any good thing. I know this kind of teaching is warmly welcomed. Everyone likes to be part of something that promises so much.

The psalmist first said that the Lord *was his Shepherd*. To him that meant that he was following the Lord as a sheep follows the shepherd. As a result, he knew he would never be in need. What most of us want, is to be able to *do* what we want and still *have* what we want. In other words, we want the blessings of following Jesus *without* having to obey Him.

It was common procedure in David's time for a shepherd to discipline a sheep that would not follow. Often that discipline was to break a sheep's leg. Then, when it could not walk, the shepherd would carry it in his arms. By the time the bone mended, the sheep would be so attached to the shepherd, that it would stay close by his side for the rest of its life.

It is harmful to think we can always obtain what we want from God and still do things that He has forbidden. God always chastens those He loves for their own good. He knows that as a sheep needs to be close to the shepherd for protection, we need to stay where our Shepherd can watch over us. Otherwise, we too will be consumed by the wolves.

> 24:3-4 *Who shall ascend into the hill of the Lord? Or who shall stand in his holy place? He that hath clean hands, and a pure heart...*

Any efforts to come into His "holy place" will fail if we do not strive to have a pure heart.

In a very real sense, any Christian can come into God's presence. Our sins do not cause a complete separation. Thank the Lord! But sins of any kind can prevent close fellowship with God and may hinder answers to prayer.

Jesus said He and the Father were always in close communion - not because He was the Son, but because: *I do always those things that please Him* (John 8:29).

Jesus made a distinction between "disciples" and those who were *indeed* His disciples. He said: *If ye continue in my word, then are ye my disciples indeed* (John 8:31). What a blessing it would be if Jesus should ever look at one of us and say, "This is my disciple!"

> 139:23-24 *Search me, O God, and know my heart: try me, and know my THOUGHTS. And see if there be any wicked way in me...*

Now is a good time to repeat this verse as a prayer

PROVERBS

1:10 *My son, if sinners entice thee, consent thou not.*

Members of the opposite sex often "entice" us.

4:14 *Enter not into the path of the wicked, and go not in the way of evil men.*

Evil men say that their way of life is more gratifying and fulfilling than God's way. If we examine their lives, it becomes evident that their personal lives are anything but happy.

5:3-4 *The lips of a strange woman drop as an honeycomb, and her mouth is smoother than oil: But her end is bitter as wormwood, sharp as a two-edged sword.*

Our *flesh* often longs for the things that our *spirits* know will bring trouble. God is warning us that often things that look sweet as honey may prove to be bitter.

6:23-27 *For the commandment is a lamp; and the law is light; and reproofs of instruction are the way of life: To keep thee from the evil woman, from the flattery of the tongue of a strange woman. Lust not after her beauty in thine HEART; neither let her take thee with her eyelids. For by means of a whorish woman a man is brought to a piece of bread: and the adulteress will hunt for the precious life. Can a man take fire in his bosom, and his clothes not be burned?*

How many men have heard the above words read, yet have been "burned?"

Men and women are reluctant to accept the fact that wrong thoughts - all too often - lead to overt acts.

>*6:32-33 But whoso committeth adultery with*
>*a woman lacketh understanding: he that*
>*doeth it destroyeth his own soul. A wound*
>*and dishonor shall he get; and his reproach*
>*shall not be wiped away.*

Our soul is a precious gift from God that can be destroyed. It is sensitive to God's Words, and we can preserve its health by doing those things that He has blessed.

>*12:5 The THOUGHTS of the righteous are*
>*right...*

We have the opportunity to bring our thoughts into harmony with God's will.

>*15:15 ...He that is of a merry heart hath a*
>*continual feast...*

Once we begin the process of permitting God's Word to purify our "hearts" then the heart becomes "merry." Life takes on new joy.

As I removed from my mind the thoughts that were immoral, I noticed a change. Sometimes as I walked along a street I would suddenly feel excited. Somewhere within I felt new joy bubbling up. I frequently wanted to shout, "Oh God, I'm so happy."

>*15:26 The THOUGHTS of the wicked are an*
>*abomination to the Lord...*

Knowing and understanding this is an excellent motivation to have pure thoughts.

>*21:10 The soul of the wicked DESIRETH*
>*evil...*

Notice the emphasis God places on "desires." He wants our desires to be right. This is a high calling.

ECCLESIASTES

2:9-11 *I was great and increased more than all that were before me in Jerusalem...And whatsoever mine eyes desired I kept not from them, I withheld not my heart from any joy...And, behold, all was vanity and vexation of spirit, and there was no profit under the sun.*

What an abundance he must have had!

Someone may say, "If only I could have that woman, (or that man) I would be happy." But achieving such desires often brings vexation to our spirits.

Some may think that as a man or woman gets older the temptation to have wrong things on their minds decreases. Sometimes the reverse is true. As a person gets older he often thinks life is passing him by.

"All is vanity..." Nothing on this earth holds the key to satisfaction. Jesus said, "I am the Way."

Some experiences contribute to a feeling of happiness, but feelings change, perhaps leaving us more unhappy than before. God advises us to seek His will first. Then He will take care of our desires for satisfaction. He has demonstrated this to me so often that I'm gradually learning to believe Him.

SONG OF SOLOMON

8:7 *If a man should offer for love all the wealth of his house, it would be scornfully refused* (MLB).

Inside each of us there is a need for love that can neither be met with material possessions nor sex. I have talked with many men who frequented houses of ill-repute. They often reported a feeling of disgust with themselves when they left the establishment.

Immoral relationships between those who are seeking genuine love, and feel they *do* love one another, invariably lead to resentment, stress and often deep bitterness. When God created our capacity to love, He united it with our obedience to His will. If we ignore His will, the beautiful attribute of love will be changed into baser emotions.

ISAIAH

55:7 *Let the wicked forsake his way, and the unrighteous man his THOUGHTS...for he will abundantly pardon.*

Some have not yet heard that their thoughts could be made clean. I want to help Christians learn the great potential we have in Christ. As we are changed we can help bring a cleansing to our nation.

55:8 *For my THOUGHTS are not your THOUGHTS, neither are your ways my ways, saith the Lord.*

We may not understand why God is so interested in the secret parts of our minds, but He wants *our thoughts* to be in harmony with *His*.

> 59:2, 7 ...*Your sins have hid His face from you...their THOUGHTS are THOUGHTS of iniquity...*

Our thoughts are able to separate us from God. How I wish I had known this years ago!

JEREMIAH

> 4:14 ...*How long shall thy vain THOUGHTS lodge within thee?*

Ask yourself, "How long will I allow bad thoughts to lodge in my heart?" Thoughts "lodge within" as long as we welcome them.

> 6:19 *Hear, O earth: behold, I will bring evil upon this people, even the fruit of their THOUGHTS, because they have not hearkened unto my words...*

God has promised that we will receive the fruits of our thoughts. He keeps His Word.

LAMENTATIONS

> 1:8 *Jerusalem hath grievously sinned; there-fore she is removed: all that honored her despise her, because they have seen her na-kedness...*

When God wants to describe a vile situation, He refers to it as a woman whose clothes have been removed, causing her to stand naked. If a man mentally disrobes a woman, in God's eyes, he is shaming her!

EZEKIEL

8:12 Then said he unto me, Son of man, hast thou seen what the ancients of the house of Israel do in the dark, every man in the chambers of his IMAGERY? For they say, The Lord seeth us not...

If we feel a need to keep our imaginations secret, then we want to keep them "in the dark."

11:5 And the Spirit of the Lord fell upon me, and said unto me, Speak; Thus saith the Lord...I know the things that come into your MIND, every one of them.

Pause...Meditate on God's careful attention to what is on our minds.

16:29-30 Thou hast moreover multiplied thy fornication...How weak is thine HEART, saith the Lord God, seeing thou doest all these things...

In our hearts - where our desires live - dwell the decisions that we will make tomorrow.

22:30 I sought for a man among them, that should make up the hedge, and stand in the gap before me for the land, that I should not destroy it...

There is a great need today for Christians who will "stand in the gap" before God, lest He destroy our land. We can protect our families from destruction by cleansing our thoughts.

33:31 ...*With their mouth they shew much love, but their heart goeth after their covetousness.*

It may be difficult to understand why God is so against covetousness. We may think, I don't intend to *take* something that isn't mine. What harm can it do if I simply *want* it?

There are principles involved that God understands better than we do. For example, Satan *wanted* God's throne and caused great havoc in heaven. Satan *wanted* to rule the earth and used his power to corrupt mankind. Eve *wanted* God's knowledge and disobeyed God.

When man wants something that isn't his, the odds are great that one day he will reach out and *take* it. God has made known His will. *If it isn't yours, don't allow your heart to wish for that which belongs to another.*

DANIEL

When referring to the end times, Daniel wrote:

12:10 *Many shall be purified, and made white...*

God promises that as the end of this world draws near many of His children will be purified. Even as you read this book, the Spirit is calling you to be pure and clean in thought. God promised this, and you and I are privileged to share in the fulfillment of His promise.

HOSEA

*4:12 ...The spirit of whoredoms hath caused
them to err...*

There is a spirit that influences men and women to entertain
bad thoughts. It is a powerful force. Its ultimate aim is to combat
God's Will for His people. Once we come under the influence,
it may be difficult to gain our freedom. Jesus gives each of us the
strength we need to declare our deliverance.

JOEL

*2:27-28,30 ...My people shall never be
ashamed. And it shall come to pass after-
ward, that I will pour out my spirit upon all
flesh...And I will shew wonders in the
heavens and in the earth...*

If we have reason to "be ashamed" of what is in the secret
parts of our minds, we have reason to seek the help of the Holy
Spirit.

Part of the preparation for the last days, with its "signs and
wonders," include God's people being *changed* by His Spirit.

AMOS

5:15 Hate the evil, and love the good...

Unfortunately, some Christians think immoral thoughts and
do not consider them evil. The issue is side-stepped, swept under
the carpet, left to reside in peace.

94

OBADIAH

1:3 The pride of thine heart hath deceived thee...

It is easy to let old habits control our lives. If we are deceived by our *own hearts* it is often difficult for anyone to convince us that we need to change!

JONAH

1:2 Go to Nineveh...and cry against it; for their wickedness is come up before me.

Disobedience comes to God's attention.

NAHUM

1:2,6,9 God is jealous...Who can stand before his indignation?...What do ye IMAGINE against the Lord?

"God is jealous." It is dangerous to misuse what He has created. Throughout Scripture God repeatedly emphasizes misuse of sex as being especially offensive to Him. Through proper use of sex, man participates in the divine act of creation. This experience is so sacred that God demands compliance with His Will. Perhaps this is why He considers homosexuality so repulsive. In the Old Testament He slaughtered every man, woman and child in cities that openly practiced homosexuality. His Word says He gets "furious."

HABAKKUK

2:9 Woe to him that coveteth...

We must *never* covet. His rule is not subject to change.

ZEPHANIAH

2:3 ...Seek righteousness...it may be ye shall
be hid in the day of the Lord's anger.

Scientific wonders make it possible for immorality to spread
world-wide. Side by side march scientific advancements that can
create violent destruction. God may soon allow these forces to
be unleashed. Now, more than at any other time in history, it is
important for us to "seek righteousness."

3:1 Woe to her that is filthy and polluted...

We can decide whether our thoughts are "polluted." If we
act out sexual immorality in our imaginations, we are polluted in
God's eyes.

A little child questions why adults make such a big thing out
of dirty clothes. Christians who do not want to change, may not
understand why *God* makes such a big thing out of immoral
thoughts.

HAGGAI

1:6 Ye have sown much and bring in little; ye
eat, but ye have not enough; ye drink, but ye
are not filled with drink; ye clothe you but
there is none warm; and he that earneth
wages earneth wages to put it into a bag with
holes.

This verse covers a multitude of problems! Working and not
seeming to accomplish anything. Eating and not feeling satisfied.
Drinking but always wanting more. Having clothes but always
feeling there is "nothing to wear." Earning money but seeing it
disappear. What causes these problems? God says: *Consider*
your ways.

MATTHEW

5:8 Blessed are the pure in heart...

Thoughts, desires and imaginations originate in our hearts and therefore represent the quality of purity that is within.

> *6:23 But if thine eye be evil, thy whole body*
> *shall be full of darkness...*

Our eyes reflect the desires of our hearts. If we use our eyes to stimulate evil thoughts, we are placing our whole body in spiritual darkness.

> *22:37-38 ...Thou shalt love the Lord thy God*
> *with all thy heart, and with all thy soul and*
> *with ALL THY MIND. This is the first and*
> *great commandment.*

Please remember the high priority God has given to what happens in our minds.

God is clear and explicit regarding His Will for the human mind. If we entertain adulterous thoughts we do not love Him with all our minds.

> *23:27-28 ...Ye are like unto whited (white-*
> *washed) sepulchres, which indeed appear*
> *beautiful outward, but are within full of dead*
> *men's bones, and of all uncleanness. (Not*
> *morally pure.) Even so ye also outwardly*
> *appear righteous unto men, but within ye are*
> *full of hypocrisy and iniquity (impurity).*

To what lengths are we willing to go to "appear righteous unto men?" Most of us have a strong desire to appear to others as honest, reliable and trustworthy. Our reputation is a valuable asset. But Jesus is saying we should be more concerned with what is within our hearts. If everyone we know could see our every thought, what would they think of us?

MARK

4:19 ...*The lusts of other things...choke the
Word, and it becometh unfruitful.*
If we persist in coveting, our spiritual lives can be choked.

LUKE

12:2 *For there is nothing covered, that shall
not be revealed, neither hid, that shall not be
known.*
The thoughts we now have in secret will one day be known
to all. This is one of God's "promises."

16:15 ...*God knoweth your HEARTS: for
that which is highly esteemed among men is
abomination in the sight of God.*
Our outward appearances can have every characteristic of
goodness, but God looks on the heart.

24:38 *And he (Jesus) said unto them, why are
ye troubled? And why do THOUGHTS arise
in your hearts?*
Thoughts of any kind come from our hearts and Jesus
considers us responsible.

JOHN

3:20 For every one that doeth evil hateth the light, neither cometh to the light, lest his deeds should be reproved.

Those who think immoral thoughts would not want their families or friends to know what they were thinking, lest their "deeds should be reproved."

3:21 But he that doeth truth cometh to the light, that his deeds may be made manifest, that they are wrought in God.

This person would be perfectly at ease if his thoughts were pictured on a screen above his head, for he has already considered that *God* observes what he thinks.

4:23 ...The hour cometh, and now is, when the true worshipper shall worship the Father in spirit and in truth: for the Father seeketh such to worship Him.

To understand this verse we need to remember what Jesus was discussing. He told the woman at the well that she had had five husbands and was now living with another man. This text shows that God wants us to worship Him with a morally uncontaminated spirit.

I believe the Holy Spirit is today renewing the same message.

8:34 Jesus answered them, Verily, verily I say unto you, Whosoever committeth sin is the servant of sin.

If we are bound by the habits of wrong thinking, we lose control of many parts of our lives. Our spiritual life is greatly weakened. Our ability to understand Scripture can be greatly limited. Our relationships with other people can suffer. In other words, we are the "servants of sin."

8:36 *If the Son therefore shall make you free,*
ye shall be free indeed.

If you have bad habits that you cannot break, please understand that you are not living in the victory that God wants. It could be that immoral thoughts are so weakening your mind that you aren't able to exert will-power.

Millions of people are looking for a new way to lose weight. They may have tried every available diet, yet they are continually tormented by their "inability" to control what they eat. When they "control" their intake by under-eating, they become so irritable and grumpy that they aren't fit to live with. Their moral drops so low that they finally decide to go back to eating whatever they want. This is no way to live! I am in no way implying that persons who are overweight have problems with immoral thinking! I *am* saying that Jesus came to give us freedom to control what we think and what we want! This may be a delightful surprise to you. If it is, begin taking charge of your thoughts.

If you are unhappy about *anything*, please believe that it is God's plan for you to be at peace. You don't have to be a super Christian to receive His help, but you do have to be willing to accept His Will. Remember that Jesus said His yoke is easy and His burden is light. It is Satan's yoke that is tough to bear!

14:1 *Let not your heart be troubled...*

Christians often endure great agony because of something others are or are not doing. The Christian tells himself repeatedly that he will not let that person bother him anymore. He means it and intends to be victorious over the situation. Before he knows what is happening, he is back to worrying or being upset. If he examines his thought life, he may see that he has not yet permitted Christ to make him "free indeed."

Consider carefully how exciting it could be to allow Jesus to give you greater control over your thoughts! Many people spend endless hours worrying about one thing or another. They know that their worries are destroying their health and happiness, but they don't have the will-power to stop. I'm sharing with you an exciting truth that can change your life.

We have been conditioned to believe that if a husband leaves his wife, or vice versa, life is then supposed to be miserable for the rejected mate. What Christians often fail to realize is that Jesus can set us free from the heartaches others give us. We may weep for a season, but through Him we can be ushered into peace.

And because of Jesus, even death is swallowed up in victory! We can lose a loved one in death and eventually be victorious! This is real victory! Mary and I learned this not too long ago in the accidental death of our oldest son.

As parents we need to know that it is God's Will for us to release our children to Him. It is not His Will for us to live in continued grief and sorrow when we come into hard places. It is only natural for parents to grieve when their children suffer, but when we release our children to Him, He wants us to believe He is working in their lives for *their good*. We need to remember that God resurrected His own Son from the grave and that He wants us to trust Him to care for *our* children.

A Christian's heart can quickly become "troubled" if he opens his mind to lustful thoughts. That one "trouble" then acts as a magnet to pick up others. Jesus knows that our bodies and minds were not designed by God to carry troubles. If we insist on carrying them, we suffer many things. If we get caught in a cycle of troubles, we always think we are helpless. The truth of the matter is we are *never* helpless. Jesus would not have told us to "never be troubled" if He thought He was giving us an impossible assignment.

> 17:17, 19 *Make them pure and holy through teaching them your words of truth...And I consecrate myself to meet their need for growth in truth and holiness* (TLB).

If we realize what our failures are and spend all our lives feeling guilty, our guilt will *never* help us. If we live in fear because of our sins or failures, our fear will never help us. Jesus is saying that His Words have the strength to change us. We need changing, but our condition isn't hopeless!

Jesus consecrated Himself to meet our need whatever it might be! This is sufficient guarantee to cause each of us to believe He has a solution for our situation.

> 6:26 ...*Verily, verily, I say unto you, Ye seek me, not because ye saw the miracles, but because ye did eat of the loaves, and were filled.*

This means we *are* able to get our priorities mixed up! If we cooperate with the Holy Spirit's efforts to make us "pure in heart," He will take care of other matters. He knows we have material needs, but He wants us to seek Him instead of His miracles.

ACTS

> 8:21-22 ...*Thy heart is not right in the sight of God. Repent therefore of this thy wickedness, and pray God, if perhaps the THOUGHT of thine heart may be forgiven thee.*

We are responsible for whatever comes from our hearts.

ROMANS

1:21 ...*When they knew God, they glorified Him not as God...*

What does the Holy Spirit mean when He says people "knew God" but then did not glorify Him "as God?" He immediately clarifies this. He is referring to those who become disobedient to God in the use of their imaginations! They *become vain in their imaginations, and their foolish heart was darkened.* Verses 24-29 make it clear that those disobedient imaginations include dishonoring the human body (not respecting another person's body as the temple of God).

1:24 *Because men are such fools, God has given them over to do the filthy things their hearts desire* (GN).

It is extremely important that we "desire" the right things!

1:25 ...*They worship and serve what God has created instead of the Creator Himself* (GN).

A strong statement!

2:16 ...*God shall judge the secrets of men...*

If we have anything on our minds that we want to keep secret, those thoughts are scheduled to be judged.

> 6:12-13 *Let not sin therefore reign in your mortal body, that ye should obey it in the lusts thereof. Neither yield ye your members as instruments of unrighteousness...*

If we yield our minds to unclean thoughts, we need to be reminded that God wants that member to be holy. Satan offers delights that are tantalizing. He will stimulate our passions and promise endless pleasures. But the payments he extracts are staggering!

> 6:13 *Do not let any part of your bodies become tools of wickedness, to be used for sinning; but give yourselves completely to God - every part of you...* (TLB).

Each of us decides which rules we will follow.

> 6:19 *...Ye have yielded your members servants to uncleanness....Now yield your members servants to righteousness unto holiness.*

It is easy to yield our minds to uncleanness but then we become the servants of uncleanness.

> 6:22 *But now being made free from sin, and become servants to God, ye have your fruit unto holiness, and the end everlasting life.*

God frees us from the eternal penalty of sin. In return for His gift, He is asking that all the fruits of our lives be holy.

> 8:5-6 *For they that are after the flesh do MIND the things of the flesh; but they that are after the Spirit the things of the Spirit. For to be carnally (sensually) MINDED is death; but to be spiritually MINDED is life and peace.*

The carnal mind always insists that its urges lead to delightful pleasures.

> 8:7 *Because the carnal (sensual) MIND is*
> *enmity against God: for it is not subject to*
> *the law of God...*

Our natural mind does not want to subject itself to the law of God. Some believe that a Christian who abstains from immoral acts is as spiritual as anyone could be. But the Holy Spirit wants to lead us into giving our minds to God. He understands the struggle that goes on in our hearts and He knows how resistant our minds are to God's control.

> 8:13 *For if ye live after the flesh ye shall die:*
> *but if ye through the Spirit do mortify the*
> *deeds of the body ye shall live.*

To "mortify" means to subdue by discipline or self-denial. If you have permitted yourself to become a person with little or no self discipline, study this verse. Spiritual weakness or even spiritual death can result from simply doing what *we want to do*.

> 12:1 *...Present your bodies a living sacrifice,*
> *holy, acceptable unto God, which is your*
> *reasonable service.*

God considers holy minds a reasonable (just and fair) standard for His children.

> 13:9 *...Thou shalt not commit adultery...*

The Old Testament commandment is confirmed as part of the New.

> 13:14 *...Make no provision for the flesh, to*
> *fulfill the lusts thereof.*

If we deliberately look at that which encourages immoral thinking, we are "making provision" for the flesh. If we do this, of course the flesh will enjoy itself.

I CORINTHIANS

3:16-17 Know ye not that ye are the temple of God, and that the Spirit of God dwelleth in you? If any man defile (makes filthy) the temple of God, him shall God destroy; for the temple of God is holy, which temple ye are.

To defile God's temple is a fearful thing! The crafty, carnal mind sometimes reaches this conclusion: "There is no way that I could keep my mind from thinking brief, immoral thoughts. If I *can't* keep myself from doing that, then I am not accountable."

4:5 ...the Lord...will bring to light the hidden things of darkness and will make manifest the counsels of the heart...

God will one day display our secret world of the mind and heart. Will they be X-rated? R-rated? PG-rated? How about G-rated (God approved)!

6:9-10 ...Be not deceived: neither fornicators, nor idolaters, nor adulterers, nor effeminate, nor abusers of themselves with mankind ...shall inherit the kingdom of God.

Immorality in any form keeps us from entering the delightful pleasures of fellowship of God.

6:20 ...Glorify God in your body, and in your spirit, which are God's (RSV).

Since God is Spirit, He is *especially* interested in what is happening within our spirits. If we allow ourselves to have an impure spirit, we are asking God to dwell in the midst of our uncleanness.

A woman could watch an entire football game and not be interested in anything that went on. A man might not be able to understand how she could *possibly* do this. He could give her many reasons why she should show more spirit toward such an "interesting game." But she has no "spirit for football." If you have permitted the Holy Spirit to cleanse your spirit of the desire to think immoral thoughts, another person might not be able to understand how you could have no "spirit" for such things.

> 10:13 *There hath no temptation taken you but such as is common to man: but God is faithful, who will not suffer you to be tempted above that ye are able; but will with the temptation also make a way to escape, that ye may be able to bear it.*

The temptation to think immoral thoughts is common to all men and women, but there is "a way to escape."

II CORINTHIANS
> 4:2 *But (We) have renounced the hidden things of dishonesty...*

It would be dishonest to say we respect others as Christians, if we have hidden adulterous thoughts about them.

> 6:14 *Be ye not unequally yoked together with unbelievers...*

If we should have immoral thoughts about a person who is an unbeliever, this would be union with that unbeliever. The verse goes on to describe such a union as "communion with darkness."

> 7:1 *...Let us cleanse ourselves from all filthiness of the flesh and spirit, perfecting holiness in the fear of God.*

This verse is not directed at spiritual giants. It is to all who "fear God."

> 10:5 *Casting down IMAGINATIONS...and bringing into captivity every THOUGHT to the obedience of Christ.*

God says we *can* control our imaginations and thoughts! This is good news!

> 11:3 *But I fear, lest by any means, as the serpent beguiled Eve through his subtlety, so your MINDS should be corrupted...*

Eve looked at the forbidden fruit and it *looked good.* I'm sure she didn't feel at the time that her mind was being "corrupted." Eve had never before sinned yet she was subject to being deceived by Satan. If you have ever looked at forbidden fruit and wanted it, you were tempted by the same tempter!

GALATIANS

5:16-17 ...Walk in the Spirit, and ye shall not fulfill the lust of the flesh. For the flesh lusteth against the Spirit, and the Spirit against the flesh: and these are contrary the one to the other: so that ye cannot do the things that ye would.

It is extremely important to learn that the Holy Spirit is often directly opposed to what the flesh wants. The flesh can say, "But I don't see why this thing I want is wrong!" This is our wonderful opportunity to say, "I will not do what my flesh wants!"

5:19 Now the works of the flesh are manifest, which are these: adultery, fornication, uncleanness...

This verse gives us a clear picture of what the Bible means when it speaks of "the flesh."

5:24-25 Those who belong to Christ Jesus have put to death their human nature, with all its passions and desires. The Spirit has given us life; He must also control our lives (GN).

As the Spirit controls our minds, He will give us *great joy*. The more He controls, the greater our joy! God created us and He knows what will bring us the greatest pleasure.

There is a war going on. Our flesh demands immoral thinking. Our spirits cry out to be pure in heart. Each of us must decide where the victory will be.

EPHESIANS

2:2-3 *We once conducted ourselves in line with the ways of this world system. We indulged our fleshly desires and carried out the inclinations of our lower nature and our THOUGHTS* (MLB).

If a certain thought is one that God forbids, the mind attempts to find some clever way to excuse itself. It wants to be "indulged."

4:22 *...Put off your old nature which belongs to your former manner of life and is corrupt through deceitful lusts.*

This is something we must do after we have accepted Christ. But we need to be aware that "deceitful lusts" are exactly that - deceitful. They present themselves as perfectly reasonable and logical.

4:23 *Be renewed in the spirit of your minds* (RSV).

A blessed potential, but again it is something *we* must do.

4:24 *...Put on the new man, which...is created in righteousness and true holiness.*

Meditate for a moment on what this "new man" would be like - created *by God* to be righteous and holy. What kind of thoughts would flow through his mind?

5:3,11 *But fornication, and all uncleanness, or covetousness, let it not be once named among you, as becometh saints. Have no fellowship with the unfruitful works of darkness, but rather reprove them.*

Our minds want to enjoy fellowship with uncleanness but our spirits want to reprove.

110

5:12 *For it is a shame even to speak of those things which are done of them in secret.*

Secret thoughts are often worthy of shame.

6:13 ...*Take unto you the whole armour of God, that ye may be able to withstand in the evil day, and having done all, to stand.*

It takes *all* of God's spiritual resources to withstand the temptation toward evil thoughts and desires.

PHILIPPIANS

4:8 *Finally, brethern, whatsoever things are true, whatsoever things are honest ...whatsoever things are pure...whatsoever things are of good report; if there be any virtue, and if there be any praise, THINK on these things.*

If we act on this verse, God sends heavenly hosts to help us. Our thoughts become tools that He can use to bless our own lives and many others.

COLOSSIANS

3:1 *If ye then be risen with Christ, seek those things which are above, where Christ sitteth on the right hand of God.*

What a calling! Willingly do those things, and think those thoughts that would be acceptable in God's presence!

3:2 *Set your affection on things above, not on things on the earth.*

If we pray, "God, change my thinking," we are asking Him to do what He has told us to do.

3:5 *Put to death...evil desires and covetousness* (RSV).

"But how could I possibly stop *wanting* something that I want?"

God's Word can help us accomplish this, but we must meditate on what He has said and then make a decision to change our desires.

I THESSALONIANS

*4:4 God wants you to be holy and pure, and
to keep clear of all sexual sin* (TLB).

If we have things on our minds that are not pure, He is saying, "Keep clear!"

4:7 For God hath not called us unto uncleanness, but unto holiness.

Once we have accepted forgiveness of our sins, we then have a high calling. God's standard is, "Move toward holiness." He is always patient, but He may bring pressure to bear if we are not moving in the right direction.

II THESSALONIANS

*1:11 And so we keep on praying for you that
our God will make you the kind of children
He wants to have - will make you as good as
you wish you could be - rewarding your faith
with His power* (TLB).

God desires to build and strengthen goodness in us. If our minds are infected with unclean desires, He is thwarted in His plans. Since He has given us freedom to choose whatever we will, He accepts our decisions. We have a grand opportunity.

I TIMOTHY

4:12,15 *...Be thou an example of the believers in...purity. Meditate upon these things;
give thyself wholly to them...*

If we, like Timothy, will meditate on God's Word, and give
ourselves to it, we too can become an example "in purity."

II TIMOTHY

2:20-21 *...There are dishes made of gold and
silver as well as some made from wood and
clay. The expensive dishes are used for
guests, and the cheap ones are used in the
kitchen or to put garbage in. If you stay away
from sin you will be like one of these dishes
made of purest gold...so that Christ himself
can use you for His highest purposes* (TLB).

We select the quality of our thoughts and by that select the
quality of our service to God.

To be purified, gold and silver must be placed over fire. The
heat forces the impurities to the surface where they can be
skimmed off. The Word of God is a purifying fire that will bring
to the surface things that have no value.

2:22 *Flee also youthful lusts: but follow
righteousness, faith, charity, peace, with them
that call on the Lord out of a pure heart.*

If we cry to God, "Lord, increase my faith and love and
peace," but permit uncleanliness in our hearts, our prayers may
accomplish little. Understanding this will help us to see why some
of our prayers have gone unanswered.

TITUS

1:15 Unto the pure all things are pure: but unto them that are defiled and unbelieving is nothing pure; but even their MIND and conscience is defiled.

A "pure" mind looks on a member of the opposite sex and has "pure" thoughts. But if our "mind and conscience" have become defiled we think impure thoughts.

1:16 They profess that they know God; but in works they deny Him, being abominable, and disobedient...

It is easy to say, "I know God." But if we are disobedient, we are "denying Him."

PHILEMON

1:6 And I pray that as you share your faith with others it will grip their lives too, as they see the wealth of good things in you... (TLB).

As our minds are cleansed, people will see the "wealth of good things" in us.

Seeds of pure thinking were sown in our hearts when we accepted Jesus. We can cause these seeds to grow and bear much fruit.

HEBREWS

4:12 For the word of God is quick, and powerful...and is a discerner of the THOUGHTS and intents of the heart.

This verse offers to us the solution to the moral and spiritual problems that I have mentioned in this book. God knows our thoughts and has provided His Word to help us. But His Words will not work in us unless we meditate on them and then make personal decisions based on what He tells us.

What would you do if you had the perfect opportunity to commit some immoral act? What you would *like* to do reflects the person you *are* and reflects the "intents" of your heart.

JAMES

1:14 A man's temptation is due to the pull of His own inward desires, which can be enormously attractive. His own desire takes hold of him and that produces sin (Phillips).

I don't ever like to blame myself!

When we are tempted, it seems ever so easy to give in. We need to look into the future and examine what *could happen* if we allow lust to live in our hearts. It is deadly, destructive and powerful.

1:22 But be ye doers of the word, and not hearers only...

Part of being a "doer" of the Word, is striving to cleanse our minds.

4:4 Ye adulterers and adulteresses, know ye not that the friendship of the world is enmity with God? Whosoever therefore will be a friend of the world is the enemy of God.

An "enemy of God?" Not an enviable position!

4:8 ...Purify your hearts, ye doubleminded.

This is having one mind that says, "I want to please God," and another mind that says, "I want to enjoy impure thoughts."

117

I PETER

1:6 ...*Ye are in heaviness through manifold temptations.*

Yielding to the temptation of immoral thinking will bring a sense of heaviness to any person who is seeking to do God's Will. Our conscience is alerting us that something is wrong.

2:11 *Dearly beloved, I beseech you as strangers and pilgrims, abstain from fleshly lusts, which war against the soul.*

Our limited comprehension of spiritual matters prevents us from understanding how destructive lust is.

II PETER

1:5 ...*Giving all diligence, add to your faith virtue...*

All too frequently Christians are led into seeking more faith, but are not taught to seek virtue. Peter is telling us that we must use "all diligence" in this important matter.

2:9 *The Lord knoweth how to deliver the godly out of temptations...*

I have learned that when a man or a woman begin their efforts to have only clean thoughts on their minds, they often feel as if the goal is impossible. The mind may say, "I can never do what you are asking me!" At that point it is a great joy to read God's promise that He knows how to deliver us out of temptations.

118

> 2:19 ...*Whatever overcomes a man, to that*
> *he is enslaved* (RSV).

When another person causes you to enter into lustful thoughts, that person is overcoming you. If a woman does this to a man she is literally overcoming him. He usually has no feeling of being "overcome," and probably would staunchly deny it, but in God's eyes that is what happens. If a man draws a woman into immorality by persuasive words or conduct, he is overcoming her, and she is under his bondage.

> 2:20,22 *For if after they have escaped the*
> *pollutions of the world through the knowl-*
> *edge of the Lord and Savior Jesus Christ,*
> *they are again entangled therein, and*
> *overcome...It is happened unto them*
> *according to the true proverb, the dog is*
> *turned to his own vomit...*

A dog returning to its vomit is a distasteful picture. A Christian whose eyes are "full of adultery" would be equally offensive to God.

> 3:14 ...*Be diligent that ye may be...without*
> *spot, and blameless.*

God is saying to us: *Be pure. Be blameless. Be holy.*

119

I JOHN

2:6 *He that saith he abideth in Him ought himself also so to walk, even as He (Jesus) walked.*

Such a glorious goal - to learn to have thoughts similar to Christ's!

2:16 *For all that is in the world, the lust of the flesh and the lust of the eyes...is not of the Father, but is of the world.*

To lust after something that does not belong to us may seem very natural, but that desire is "not of the Father."

3:3 *...Every man that hath this hope in him purifieth himself, even as He (Christ) is pure.*

This is seemingly an impossible task, but it gives us a vivid picture of what God wants us to do with our minds. For many years I frequently, and I confess, quite piously prayed, "Oh God, please purify me from these bad thoughts." I finally realized that He was saying, "Merlin, you do it!"

3:21 *Beloved, if our heart condemn us not then have we confidence toward God.*

Our heart's ability to tell us that all is not well in our thought life is a valuable gift from God. He is helping us feel what He feels so we can make necessary changes. Then when our hearts are free of guilt we have new confidence. In my own case I recall feeling as if a great load had been lifted from my shoulders. I can easily sympathize with those who carry a burden of guilt. It is both tiring and painful.

3:22 *And whatsoever we ask, we receive of Him, because we keep His commandments and do those things that are pleasing in His sight.*

God's promises of good things can be claimed when we do those things that are pleasing to Him!

II JOHN

1:2 *For the truth's sake, which dwelleth in us, and shall be with us for ever.*

It is this abiding truth, in the hearts of all Christians, that makes us feel guilty when we have wrong thoughts.

III JOHN

1:2 *Beloved, I wish above all things that thou mayest prosper and be in health, even as thy soul prospereth.*

It is good to be ready for our finances and health to prosper proportionately to the moral condition of our minds!

1:11 *Beloved, follow not that which is evil but that which is good...*

The words, "follow not" also mean, "do not imitate." Passion frequently draws us into imitating, in our minds, things that are evil.

REVELATION

3:10 Because you have patiently obeyed Me...I will protect you from the time of Great Tribulation and temptation, which will come upon the world to test everyone alive (TLB).

Involvement in immoral activity is one of the most persistent temptations facing present-day Christians. We are surrounded by every conceivable opportunity to think impure thoughts. Nearly every movie and TV program is, in one way or another, trying to convince us that immorality should not be considered an evil thing. Jesus is forewarning us of what we should expect. He is also promising us great reward if we overcome!

2:7 He that hath an ear, let him hear what the Spirit saith...To him that overcometh:

1. I give to eat of the tree of life (2:7).
2. He shall not be hurt of the second death (2:11).
3. I give to eat of the hidden manna (2:17).
4. I give a new name which no man knoweth saving he that receiveth it (2:17).
5. I give power over the nations (2:26).
6. I give the morning star (2:28).
7. He shall be clothed in white raiment (3:5).
8. I will not blot out his name from the book of life (3:5).
9. I will confess his name before my Father, and before His angels (3:5).
10. Will I make a pillar in the temple of my God (3:12).

11.   I will write upon him the name of my
      God (3:12).
12.   I will write upon him my new name
      (3:12).
13.   Will I grant to sit with me in my
      throne, even as I also overcame, and
      am set down with my Father in His
      throne (3:21).

3:22 *He that hath an ear let him hear what
the Spirit saith...*

19:6-8 *After that I heard what sounded like
the shout of a vast throng, like the boom of
many pounding waves and like the roar of
terrific and mighty thunderpeals, exclaiming, Hallelujah - praise the Lord! For now
the Lord our God the Omnipotent - the All-
Ruler - reigns! Let us rejoice - and shout for
joy - exulting and triumphant! Let us
celebrate and ascribe to Him glory and honor,
for the marriage of the Lamb has come and
His bride has prepared herself. She has been
permitted to dress in fine linen - dazzling and
white, for the fine linen represents the righteousness - the upright, just and godly living
and right standing with God* (AMP).

When we adorn ourselves with pure thoughts we are putting
on bridal garments, preparing for the coming of the bridegroom!

What will you do when you have completed this book? Have I given you sufficient help to cause lasting changes in *What's on Your Mind?*. These questions have been on *my* mind for many months.

Remember the man who loved hot fudge sundaes and had been told he had diabetes? You may have thought, sure, he lost his desire for sundaes but the desire would immediately return if he found there had been a wrong diagnosis. So, his desire really hadn't changed at all - he only replaced it for a time with a stronger desire - to live.

That is the way all our natural desires are. Here is an illustration that explains what happens when we change our desires. Let's climb aboard a rocket and blast off. We go into orbit three hundred fifty miles above the earth. Our rocket is within the gravitational pull of earth but has sufficient speed to stay in its orbit. Picture two possibilities:

1. If the rocket should slow down, it would be drawn back to the earth.
2. If the rocket received a rapid forward thrust it could slip out of the earth's gravitational range and race into space.

Imagine the earth as being your *former* desire for immoral thoughts. You are now out in orbit and are in a sense free. But...you are free *because* of your forward speed. You have decided to follow God's Will and your thinking has entered a new dimension, where you no longer need to be ashamed of your desires.

What influence does your old desire for immoral thoughts have over you? If you "slow down" your orbit, your rocket will be pulled back to your old desires. That's the way life is on planet earth.

What will slow our orbital speed?

1. Getting our attention off the things God has told us about thoughts, desires and imaginations.
2. Deliberately placing ourselves in a position where old desires can reassert themselves.
3. Failing to have regular fellowship with God so His Holy Spirit can hold our attention.

But what about the second alternative where our rocket is thrust into space and leaves the gravitational pull of our immoral desires? I believe this glorious time will come when our spirits slip out of these bodies and race upward to God! At that rapturous moment our impure desires are gone forever! Until then they will be an attraction to us. The Good News is that we can stay in orbit and out of their control. Jesus provided the thrust to set us free.

Here is the plan:

Get into orbit if you aren't already there!

Stay in orbit!

Live where the mind is free of earth's pollution.

A SPECIAL NOTE

Once we are willing to expose our thoughts to everyone, we will be motivated to excellence in *all* our thinking.

God's desire for His children is that even the most secret thoughts of our hearts be blessed by His Spirit. To be blessed by the Spirit of God is the *highest and most rewarding* experience we can have on this earth.

The Power of a Praising Woman

by Hilary Cook

You long for your family, friends and neighbours to find the healing they desperately need, or deliverance from an oppressive situation, or the joy of salvation for the first time. But doesn't it take a special kind of person to see miracles like these? What is the secret of a life filled with faith and power?

Hilary Cook is the first to say she isn't 'special'. She describes herself as a housewife, mother and dentist. But she has learned about the power of praise to release all kinds of miracles into our everyday lives.

Merlin Carothers comments:
'You kindly sent me a copy of The Power of a Praising Woman. *I have thoroughly enjoyed it and have learned new things about praising the Lord. Hilary Cook's dedication to God and her enthusiastic service have inspired me to a new zeal for sharing the Good News with others.'*

K Kingsway Publications